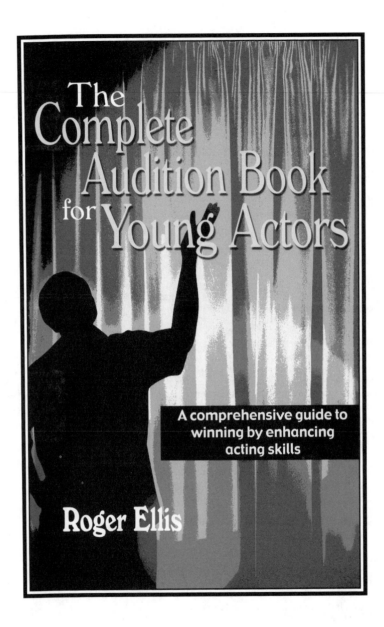

The
Complete
Audition Book
for Young Actors

A comprehensive guide to winning by enhancing acting skills

Roger Ellis

MERIWETHER PUBLISHING LTD.
Colorado Springs, Colorado

Meriwether Publishing Ltd., Publisher
PO Box 7710
Colorado Springs, CO 80933-7710

Editor: Theodore O. Zapel
Cover design: Janice Melvin

Publishers Cataloging-in-Publication
(Provided by Quality Books, Inc.)

Ellis, Roger, 1943 May 18-
    The complete audition book for young actors : a comprehensive guide to winning by enhancing acting skills / Roger Ellis.
    p. cm.
    Includes bibliographical references.
    ISBN 1-56608-088-6

1. Acting--Auditions.

PN2071.A92A886 2001   792'.028
                QBI03-1112

    1   2   3   03   04   05

"I think what makes people come back again and again is that they go to the theatre and are moved, thrilled and excited."

— Cameron Macintosh, producer of
Cats, *Les Miserables*, and others

Contents

Acknowledgments

In addition to the numerous actors, authors, directors, and coaches whose comments appear throughout this text, many individuals generously contributed their encouragement and opinions in one way or another to the original edition of this book and its present revision. I'd like to extend special thanks to Ted Zapel at Meriwether Publishing/Contemporary Drama Service for his willingness to run with every cockeyed idea I come up with, followed by his astute judgment on what will and will not work in the final version. A special vote of thanks is also due to W. Stuart McDowell of the Riverside Shakespeare Company in New York, the late Carlo Mazzone-Clementi of the Dell'Arte School, Jane Brody of Jane Brody Casting in Chicago, the late Michael Leibert of the Berkeley Repertory Theatre, and Robert Goldsby of the Berkeley Stage Company for the advice they provided on helping students break into the professional acting world. A number of my readers for this revised version were extremely gracious in offering their time to read over the manuscript and offer helpful suggestions. These include Ms. Joe Anne Peterson of the Michigan Interscholastic Forensics Association; stage director Rod Terwilliger; actors Michael Page, Demetria Thomas, and Laural Merlington; computer-fiend Stu Halliday at Northwestern University; and playwright/director Max Bush. A number of theatre groups and organizations also were instrumental in giving me access to their staff and studios, some of which include the H.B. Studios in New York, the American Conservatory Theatre of San Francisco, the Joseph Papp Public Theatre/New York Shakespeare Festival, the American Alliance for Theatre in Education (AATE), and the Kennedy Center American Theatre Festival (KCACTF). Numerous other organizations and festival directors were helpful to me in sponsoring my workshops where I could develop and test some of the acting approaches outlined in this text. These include Leonardo Tromp of the International Amateur Theatre Association (AITA/IATA), Dani Lyndersay at the International School of Geneva (Switzerland), Eva Moore of Theatre Canada, the Association for Theatre in Higher Education (ATHE), Barb Elliott of the Community Theatre Association of Michigan (CTAM), and Jim Sohre of the American Association of Community Theatre (Region X — Europe). Over the years, Grand Valley State University in

Michigan has consistently sponsored my research into auditioning and play adjudication. Finally, I also owe a debt I can never entirely repay to the many student, professional, and community actors with whom I've worked over the years in classes, stage productions, workshops, and private coaching.

Introduction

To the Young Actor

If you're looking for a sixty-page, shake-and-bake manual of quickie tips on how to do a good audition, get photos taken, or conduct yourself in an interview then take this book back right now and exchange it for one of those. You paid too much for what you want. There are plenty of those specialized kinds of books on the market written by industry casting directors, professional actors, or teacher/coaches. I've listed the best of these in appendix B of this book, and you can certainly improve your auditioning by reading some of them. You could also have your school or local library obtain an audition videotape for you to watch, or take a workshop somewhere.

In any case, if you want some quick advice, this whole book is not for you. You could find all that nuts-and-bolts stuff here in chapters 5 through 8. This book will do more for you, though. It'll help you develop your auditioning *and* acting skills in a systematic way over time, because it ties your auditioning abilities to what you've already been learning as an actor. Also I've tried to make this book the only one out there that addresses itself specifically to the needs of high school and university students (and their teachers!): how to do good auditions while you're in school and how to make the transition to professional work when you finish. I wanted to make it a really useful text for that.

It's important to bear in mind right from the outset that this is first and foremost an *acting* book, because it aims to help you develop your auditioning ability, not as a special ordeal you have to go through now and then or as some on-again-off-again "technique," but as another kind of acting performance. I know this may sound a bit odd to you, because when it comes to auditioning, most students have their eyes on only one objective: getting cast in a good role for a particular show, or winning that scholarship, or gaining admission to a good school. What else could possibly count? For this reason many students and their teachers regard auditioning as unusual, out of the ordinary, not really "acting," or something of the sort.

Well, let's admit it, there *are* a lot of things about auditions that are very strange and unique. For one thing, an audition is short and fragmented, right? Your presentation will be taken out of the context of the whole show, and because of that your acting often seems phony

3

and unnatural to you. Also, audition performances seem more unprepared and improvisational than the "normal" kind of acting we're used to: you never know what the auditioners are going to have you do after you present something to them that you've prepared. And then there's the competition-angle: you're *really* going to be judged good or bad by those auditors out there, aren't you? Compared with other auditionees, cast or not cast, etc. Auditions are certainly necessary, but they're too short and so competitive that they're not really "theatre."

Well, despite this, you should always, always remember that auditioning is no different than a good, solid acting performance — an *enhancement* of the acting skills that you're learning elsewhere. Too often I see actors make the mistake of treating their audition as something else: something desperate and unreal and exotic. A technical exercise, perhaps, or some kind of self-indulgent advertisement to highlight for a few minutes all their skills and talents for me and other directors. And once the audition is done, then it's over, right? You can put your skills, talents, and "audition technique" away for the next time, right?

But how unreal is that! As though one ever *could* line up one's skills like cans on a supermarket shelf. Now *that* attitude is certainly inauthentic and phony, and I can assure you that despite the pressure and the high stakes of what's happening at an audition, the last thing a director wants to see there is bad, phony acting.

This book builds instead upon your other acting classes. It's based on the premise that good acting — whatever else it may involve — will always require belief in the theatrical situation and commitment to the dramatic relationships. In so doing, the book reinforces the importance of applying what you've learned in the studio to the rigorous demands of stage performance. You'll constantly face this challenge. This text tries to bring it all home to you by first reminding you of where you are in your training and in your acting, and then suggesting how you can use that experience to do a good audition.

I wrote the first edition of this book (1985) for university- and conservatory-level students, and the book was well received nationwide by schools, coaches, URTA committees, and others. But one of the major things I want to achieve with this revised edition is to improve the text by adding more introductory-level acting material, more practical exercises for improving your acting and auditioning skills while you're in school, and more resources and references that young actors need in order to get started on their careers.

You'll find this present edition has benefited not just from the inclusion of this kind of material, but also by the necessary updating that you might expect after nearly two decades. In 1985, for example, the Internet and World Wide Web didn't even exist for us beginning actors; but how can any young actor hope to advance in auditioning and acting today without becoming computer-savvy? All you young actors are surfing the web pretty regularly anyway nowadays; and I hope after reading this book you'll be surprised to learn how much fun and valuable stuff is out there to help you with your career.

Similarly, in 1985 there were few audition texts on the market, almost all of which were for professionals; and hardly any monolog anthologies served young acting students and their teachers. Today, the shelves of bookstores groan with "how to audition" texts and accompanying scene and monolog books — many of which address themselves to specialized fields like commercials, films, industrial productions, voice-overs, and the like. How do you choose? What do you buy? Especially when you're just starting out? I think this revised edition can take some of the guesswork out of that, because in appendix B I review a lot of those books with annotated entries.

Finally, of course, I've revised this current edition for style, and I've included a lot of comments and suggestions offered by my own students and others since the first edition appeared years ago. I don't think there's any substitute for direct experience, so get it into your head right now that this is *not* a theory book. I've used the auditioning approaches here in the workshops and classes I've taught in the U.S. and overseas, with all levels of actors, and I know a lot of it really works; it's really useful. I hope you find the same thing.

To Teachers and Coaches

I think you'll find this book especially useful because it's laid out as a class text. It's not a collection of "pearls of wisdom" thrown together from years of professional experience, but a step-by-step guide for training young actors to audition well. The auditioning handbooks you find on the market these days aren't really set up in this way. My personal god, for example, is Michael Shurtleff from whom I've learned more about acting (and auditioning) than from any other teacher I've had. But his book isn't very helpful for *young* actors: you really need some stage experience to appreciate what he's talking about, and you really need a workshop in his twelve guideposts to put his ideas to use.

You'll also note that there are a *lot* of audition books on the market these days, the best of which I've listed in Appendix B. What almost all of them fail to do, however, is to place auditioning in the context of acting training and to present auditioning methods as an outgrowth of a young actor's school experience. They're very valuable as "how-to" manuals, but this book is a complete class text that will not only give your students auditioning "checklists" and "how-to" techniques (chapters 5 through 9), but also complement other things you're doing in your acting, literature, forensics, oral interpretation, debate, and other classes.

You'll find this book really does "begin at the beginning, proceed through the middle, until it comes to the end, where it stops" (as Lewis Carroll might say). And it permits you to spend as much time on each chapter as you need, depending upon the learning curve of your students in any given year. There are sixty-plus exercises throughout the book that I've developed for my own students over the years, and I'm sure you probably have a few of your own that you want to add to what you find here. The text permits that.

You'll also find the book contains all you need for conducting a good semester-long or year-long acting course in auditioning. There are sample monologs for students to work on, in-class projects to develop, end-of-chapter "review and reflection" sections for self-study or essay/test assignments, and out-of-class assignments where your students can work on their own. I should point out, however, that the book does not serve up *every*thing to the student; he or she will have to get to the library or the bookstore or the video catalog and find material. And this is critically important, too: a young actor who isn't motivated to go after material on his or her own is also likely to be an actor who's unmotivated in general. Not a good thing, either, for auditions or for rehearsals or performances or anything else.

Personally, I use a lot of the "Exploration Exercises" in the text with my own students at the university-level, even though they're also suitable for junior and senior students in secondary schools. This should come as no surprise, I hope, because seasoned actors often return in workshops to many exercises they first encountered years before. As the actor grows and develops, he or she will naturally bring new resources and talents to the exercise and discover new insights as a result. I've also found very often that many university students have never been introduced to these "basic" exercises before, so the activities are necessary first steps even for older students. In any case, I firmly believe that the earlier one is exposed to these exercises, the sooner one's skills will develop.

As you read through this text you'll notice that I draw upon a lot of sources. My own personal experience as an actor and director, interview comments from working professionals, magazine features, auditioning books, workshop leaders, and instructional films are some of these. My purpose in doing this has been twofold: I wanted to offer first-hand, up-to-date, practical information here from people actually "in the trenches," avoiding academic "theory" as well as personal bias as much as possible. Second, I wanted also to pull together the many, many viewpoints on how an actor can audition well, without pretending to offer a single unified approach, in the sense of "one size fits all." Because when it comes to auditioning, there's no one sure-fire way to go about it.

At the risk of discouraging you from adopting this text, I also want to make clear what this book does *not* contain: it does *not* have photos, resumes, lists of agents and agencies, calendars that list national auditions dates, descriptions of schools and conservatories in the U.S. and Canada, nor audition guidelines and tip sheets from national auditions conferences. I chose not to include these things for several reasons. First, most of these items are time sensitive, and your students will quickly learn that the headshot style used this year in New York will not be the headshot style in use eighteen months later in Chicago or L.A. Nor do I want to be responsible five years from now for their decision to overlook an outstanding new graduate training program just because it wasn't listed in my appendix.

Second and more importantly, I think it's vital that students get off the dime and learn to dig this information out for themselves. It's all out there and readily accessible. We need, I think, to do less hand-holding with our graduates if they're going to succeed in this competitive business. We need, I think, to encourage and empower them to locate what information they need on their own, if they're going to be motivated to put it to work for them in advancing their careers. You'll find, therefore, that the text often *points* them in the right direction, but allows them to jump off the dock themselves.

There's an additional reason these materials do not appear in the text — simply stated, there are too many of those "professional aids" out there to include in one book, so I've put them into the appendix instead. The acting marketplace today has become incredibly diverse and specialized, and I've tried to address that fact throughout the text, especially in appendix C where I talk about some of the possibilities and challenges that abound in media acting. Once they graduate from our programs, the industry is going to appeal to our students in many ways that we can't predict, and I think we're going to have to let them find this out for themselves and discover the materials they need in order to follow their own paths.

I believe teachers at all levels need to constantly remind themselves and their students of this fact. Not long ago, for example, two years after one of my prized actresses graduated, she was in Tinseltown feeling mighty fulfilled doing burbly cooing voices for the momma-monster in *Alien III*. Did I want her instead to go to a conservatory, then work a rep circuit for a few years, and then alternate between New York and the coast? Well, go figure. The marketplace seduced her otherwise and now she's burbling all the way to the bank and enjoying her shiny new sports car. The point is that she didn't need a book like this to teach her how to do her demo tape, find an agent, write up her resume, and interview for those kinds of jobs. But I like to believe that I inspired her to do all those things by herself!

So be aware that this text concludes at the point where most college graduates will begin to make their first forays into professional careers: the auditions and interviews for postgraduate professional schools, scholarships, entry-level professional work, and media acting jobs. It's at this point, I think, that students need more than our classes and supportive institutions can provide. They need the practical experience of putting themselves out there, of establishing a network of peers and contacts, and professional workshop training in specific acting skills. This book tells them about these needs and starts them off in the right direction, but ends there. It brings them to the launch pad, sets their controls, and pushes the button. After that, of course, it will be up to them to find their own way, just as we found ours.

Over decades of teaching young actors how to act and audition well, I've learned that developing good audition abilities is a useful skill for students whether or not they choose to enter the acting profession. This belief underlies a lot of my approach in the text, and I hope that many of you share it. Certainly if you work in a liberal arts environment as I do, you probably already know it's true. So much of life is competitive these days, so much depends upon a person's self-confidence and assertiveness and ability to express himself or herself in public contexts, that the experience of auditioning well and presenting oneself positively will serve students well throughout their lives, regardless of their career paths. We have to remind ourselves from time to time, I think, that audition training is not just stage performance training: it also involves a lot of self-discipline, time management, resume writing, guts-ball confidence, tough character building, problem solving, willingness to take big risks, and skill with interviewing.

Hopefully this text will take them there!

Chapter One

The Fundamentals
"Gimme attitude!"

Motivation and Self-Respect

Students who are considering the theatre as a career should bear in mind that they're embarking upon an ancient, respected, and adventurous profession whose ranks have included some of the most illustrious and accomplished human beings who have ever lived and graced society. And while it is certainly true that this field has also included some of the most vain and disappointing scoundrels of every historical age, there is no denying that in the public mind today stage and screen actors are much more highly esteemed for how they move and inspire us than for how they betray themselves — and us — by their often flagrant and tasteless behavior.

I mention this right at the outset, because I think young actors too often forget about their "calling" and instead become obsessed with immediate goals and narrow, practical "job" needs. I know that I was when I took my first steps as an actor. We ask ourselves, "Can I get a job doing this?" Or when it comes to auditioning: "How can I get that part?" "How can I win that scholarship?" or "How can I get accepted into a real theatre company?" At bottom, we're constantly plagued by the nagging question, "How can I beat out all those other people to get the role?" Perhaps a more general way of stating the question might be, "What do I have to do in order to live that life and join the others?"

Put this way, you can see that it's not so much the role or the scholarship or the job that attracts us to this crazy field, it's really the inspiration. The call. The allure of the stage and profession of the actor. Plenty of other "jobs" will get you more money, a cushy life, and possibly even more fame: medicine, banking, pop music, business and finance, TV talk shows, real estate, politics. But none of those carry with them the mystique, the grace, the dignity, the creativity — the "inspiration" — that the acting profession promises.

"Inspiration" is a vague word, I know, and one that even smacks a little of religion. But we don't have to be religious or even pretentious about it. We should simply admit to ourselves that often what leads us to keep doing what we do onstage and on screen —

and what keeps us sticking our necks out at auditions time after time — is some kind of crazy dream that we can call "art" or "inspiration" for lack of something better.

To be sure, it's a risky profession because it's so attractive, so alluring. We all know there are a lot of wannabes in the entertainment and theatre fields largely because of the fame and the glamorized life styles of rich and aimless celebrities. But as I've been trying to explain, theatre should always remain more than just a job or profession for you if you're going to stay motivated. It's a vocation, and like all vocations it's going to demand a lot of dedication, work, and sacrifice.

So keep this in mind as you continue your studies in classes, onstage, in workshops, and at performances. The skills you'll learn and the career you'll enter is an *alternative* to all those other "regular" jobs and professions. It's not necessarily an easier line of work, a form of self-indulgence, or something to do because you're lost and can't think of anything else. And plenty of people make their living in this industry. In fact, next to the communications and aerospace sectors, it's our nation's largest export!

Above all, be proud of what you're doing, and give yourself and your work the respect it deserves. No matter how demeaning the struggle for competing may become — the stressful auditions, the nervous interviews, the constant calls to agents — *never* forget that the tradition of theatre and the field of acting have a long historical track record and what they promise is well worth striving for. Make it one of your personal goals to add something new and important to this great tradition!

The Fun of Competition

Not everyone will make it there, of course, and already you probably know the grim employment statistics in the theatre, film, and TV industries. There are slightly more than 100,000 professional actors in the United States (stage, film, TV), but fewer than half of them earn more money than the national poverty level ($7,500 for a single person). No more than 5,000 to 6,000 of them earn more than your theatre teacher. Your parents, counselors, and drama instructors have probably already discouraged your interest in professional theatre because of that. And professionals in "the biz" want to be sure you never forget what you're up against when you choose this profession:

> ... we find that in a country with more than a million lawyers, 4.5 million mechanics, and nearly 8 million

machine operators, *the number of self-supporting career actors — those who can be said to make their living as actors for at least ten years in a row — is no more than 2,000 to 3,000 people!* This is hardly a profession; it might better be described as a club. [1]

Acting is a field where many are called but few are chosen, because most people who think they want to be actors soon drop out somewhere along the way. Fame draws them, or the glitz of what they take to be "the fast life" of the celebs. Maybe money as well. And when it doesn't pay out after a couple of years, they go on to something else. You're going to need plenty of commitment, persistence, and dedication to compete against them and to stick to it. You're going to have to give it all you've got and compete hard. Let's talk about that.

"Competition" is often regarded as a bad word in our society, and especially in our educational system; so you have to think carefully about this while you're in school. A lot of pedagogy in our K–12 levels and in college is guided by the idea that teachers should be "supportive" of students and their efforts. Many teachers feel that competition creates unnecessary and destructive patterns of superiority and inferiority, marginalizes too many kids, and engenders aggressive or even violent attitudes and behaviors that are damaging and often socially inappropriate. And women are especially at risk because gender stereotypes combine with this teaching approach and mandate that young girls be polite and submissive and avoid seeming assertive and unduly competitive.

While there is something in general to be said for this sort of training and conditioning, the downside of it for theatre students is that it ignores the simple fact that — for men *and* women — everyday life constantly confronts individuals with many situations in which they are going to have to compete and "win" their goals. Or lose out. *And this is absolutely critical to understand and admit in order to act onstage well.*

To begin with, think of relationships — especially dramatic relationships — like games where everyone wants to "win." In a dramatic relationship, the characters compete to achieve their goals. As in everyday life, they all share the long-term goal of "wanting to be happy." Don't you want to be happy? No one wants to be a loser, right? And like you, characters also have medium-range goals. They want to be the guy's only girlfriend or have the fastest car or the biggest wad of money or wear the coolest clothes: something they think will make them happy. Finally, they also have immediate goals: they want to *gain your attention, buy that car, win the lotto,* or *get that Visa card* and head for the mall. Winning these immediate goals gets them closer to their medium-range goals, which gets them closer to their long-range goals.

Now, where does competition and auditioning figure into all this? Simple. In plays — as in life — there are always other characters who want the same things as you do, or at least people ("antagonists") who don't want to give you what you want. You have to compete with them and fight hard to win your goals. You've got to "beat out" the other girls in order to get him to notice you, don't you? You absolutely *must* buy this car and not the one that mom and dad recommend. You've *really* got to buy the winning lotto tickets now before the other guy does. And you *must* look better in expensive designer clothes than the other woman who spent money at the cut-rate store. That's what drama's about, too. You fight to win and get what you want in the scene.

Here's one professional acting coach from southern California who stresses how strongly competition is tied to good acting:

> The stronger you as a character compete with all the other characters to win your goals in a scene, the more engaging the scene becomes. You as an actor and you as the character must always strive and expect to win every scene. When you win, it is important to see and feel that sense of victory — it gives joy to the scene. When you lose, it is also important to feel and acknowledge the frustration. This gives tension to a scene and provides the motivation for the next attempt at achieving victory. Never let the resolution of a goal trail off as if it didn't matter; it does matter, and how strongly you react defines our interest in you as a person and a dramatic character. [2]

As you can see, a lot of us aren't used to behaving this way in everyday life — competing, that is. We may think of ourselves as more easygoing, laid-back, tolerant, cool, whatever. In which case, what I'm suggesting here about "learning to compete" may seem to you offensive, rude, and ill-mannered. But you shouldn't take it that way. See it from another perspective, from the standpoint of communicating. "We are all performers!" one of the greatest actor-coaches in the United States reminds his students. "We all audition, whether for acting jobs or for living and working creatively in daily life. As performers, we need to learn how to feel the energy qualities that go into perceiving, experiencing, and communicating." [3]

So try to avoid allowing "complacent" or overly polite attitudes to infect your acting. Drama is not a win-win situation, it's a win-lose playing field. Acting is conflict, struggle, and trying to win even though in most great dramas people fail to do so. What we pay money to see is their struggle, and "playing it cool" or "behaving nicely" can be even more bland and boring onstage than in everyday life.

Getting used to competition is important not just for those nail-biting moments in the audition hall, it's also vital for pursuing your long-term career goals. As two-time Tony-winner John Cullum recently remarked: "Luck and perseverance. You have to have a kind of a competitive spirit. It's something that you have to keep." [4] You've got to really want a career in this business if it's ever going to happen, and you've got to accept the fact that it's not going to happen unless you beat-out a lot of other people who want the same thing you do. Rosemary Tischler, casting director for Joe Papp's Public Theatre in New York, expressed it this way to me: "The number of actors — the number of people who call themselves actors — in this city and in Los Angeles is so huge. It's the most competitive field in the world, and many people are unprepared and should not be encouraged because they're going to be very pained. They're going to have a lot of unhappiness." [5]

The Need for Constant Training

At this stage of your career, one of the first things you need to remember about learning to audition well is that auditioning is no different than acting — it's merely a heightened, more condensed and concentrated form of acting. In an audition you'll be expected to bring to bear *all* that you've learned in classes and performances when you present yourself to the director. Suddenly, all those years of exposure to plays, acting classes, rehearsals, and audiences becomes very real. You'll be asked to "package" it into a few brief moments to give the director a clear notion of two things: what kind of actor you'll be to work with and how suitable you are for a role in this particular show.

Regarded in this light, you can see that the best advice for developing good audition skills is to keep learning and keep training. Learning to audition is not like learning how to change a flat tire or ride a bike. You have to keep taking classes. Even brilliant actors continue to study and grow throughout their work lives. It's a lifelong journey. Remember, you'll be competing with hundreds and sometimes thousands of other actors in your market who are already making money in the business. So the better training you get, the more confidence you'll have and the better your work will be.

This is something that makes acting different from other professions. For example, once you've earned your accounting or your finance degree or your real estate license you don't have to keep taking classes for years and years, nor do you have the time. You just go out there and earn money, and try to keep "up to date" with changing laws and regulations. Most of what you need to know, you learn "OTJ" (on the job, by doing it). Lots of people don't ever want to see the inside of a classroom again after high school or college. But for an actor, it's different. It's lifelong learning, lifelong growing.

As you continue your theatre studies you'll come to learn how many different types of auditions you'll face to keep working in this business, for all of which you'll need special training. A typical actor in an industry center, for example, will earn income from doing commercials, straight plays, musicals, maybe classics, industrial shows (live and on-camera), voice-overs for radio, films, sitcoms, and other presentations. Each of these forms of paid work require a specific set of audition skills you'll need to land the part — skills that are taught in professional workshops.

This is part of what you're getting into when you decide you want to become an actor. It's part of the commitment and dedication that's going to be required of you. It's what people mean when they use the word "professional" — not "whether you make money or not," or "whether the theatre group hires union people or not," or "whether the shows are big and famous" or not. They mean, how seriously do you take yourself? Are you a dabbler or are you committed to doing the best you can?

Life After Acting

As the final point in this introductory chapter, you also need to think of what else you might be doing if you don't get the roles you audition for. I remember when I first started acting, all I could think of was acting in plays or films or TV shows — that's all I knew, of course. And so rejections were always hard. At first I was being rejected for roles I really wanted to play. Then later I was rejected for summer theatre and other stage companies I really wanted to join.

It was only after performing for a few years that I gradually became interested in other things. Initially it was directing, maybe because I had to work with so many bad directors, or maybe I just liked the "control" that came with the responsibilities. Then it was writing, because then I could guide an entire production — and sometimes even direct it as well (especially in college). Then also producing (putting shows together) where the challenge of organizing all the complexities seemed fascinating to me. Then, of course, it was also teaching and coaching.

Probably you already know about actors who are also singers or painters or musicians. They do plays, they do media work of all kinds (not just commercials), they give readings and one-actor shows. And they often combine several different things. Some actors direct and act. Some actors — the rich and famous ones — also run their own production companies. Many actors also like to write. And as we move further into the twenty-first century, we're going to see less and less of what are called "straight" or "legitimate," word-based, text-based plays being done. "Theatre" is fast turning into mixed media performance where music, movement, light shows, acting, acrobatics, dance, improv, and the visual arts all coalesce. And multi-talented actors are needed for all this work.

This is the direction in which tastes are turning. You can see it happening with Broadway musicals as well as on MTV. You see it in national and international success stories like The Blue Man Group, Cirque du Soleil, the Wooster Group, *The Lion King*, *Riverdance*, and other things. Actors today are really becoming multi-talented, as "theatre" distinguishes itself more and more from other art forms (particularly movies and TV) and at the same time merges with these other arts to explore the frontiers of highly challenging and highly popular "performance art" that take many forms.

All of this means that you don't want to limit yourself down the road to just one form or style of acting, nor just to acting as your only career choice. Performance opportunities abound for the creative individual. I think this is something you want to "keep in the back of your mind" as you audition more and more, and remind yourself that acting is just one part — a big part, perhaps, but still only one part — of your overall creative life.

When I started out acting, people reminded us that even if we didn't make it as actors, there were still plenty of things to do in the industry. And I know from what my students have been doing after graduation that it's still true. Working in a casting agency. Doing all kinds of work in Hollywood for the movies. Directing. Designing. Running arts centers in big cities. Teaching. Writing.

Acting training is the best kind of preparation you can make for a career in the arts, because it places you at the center of all the action. You quickly learn what directors do, what costumers do, what lighting techs do. You get to see how all the parts fit together, what it takes to organize events. And who knows? It may just turn out that somewhere along the line you'll find yourself attracted to something in the field besides acting, and you'll want to run off and study that.

So don't close yourself off to all these related art forms and artistic disciplines while you're in school. Keep yourself open to all the possibilities that present themselves to you in your acting career. What counts is that you do what you really *want* to be doing. Right now, that's probably acting. But things can and will change, and you should be willing to change with them. It's all creative work, so go with the flow. If nothing else, these expanded interests will help you keep your perspective on auditioning when (likely as not) you don't get cast in that role!

We should talk about that, too: getting used to the constant rejections you'll have to endure. The British actor William Redford once remarked that an actor needs "the hide of a walrus and the soul of a fairy." I'm sure you know what that means: growing a thick skin to handle all your bummed-out feelings at getting turned down for the role. How do you do that? By constantly reminding yourself that nothing is ever really "personal" in this business. I know from experience that it always *seems* personal, because after all, you're acting your guts out up there. You're giving it all you've got, and the end result is that someone decides that *you* aren't right for the job. That *you* are lacking something. That someone else is *better than you*.

Well, the fact is, they *aren't* necessarily better than you. What's happening at the audition is that some casting person *thinks* the other person, on that particular day, is presenting the quality that he or she happens to be looking for, and you're not showing that same quality. It has nothing to do with your personal worth as a human being.

I know this is always hard to believe, but I first started to believe it when I began to do a lot of commercials where I met other actors. What I learned at that time was that actors were scoring a role on the average of every twelve or thirteen auditions! Was it luck? Being in the right place at the right time? Accidentally making the director's bells ring for some reason? We all had talent, and we were all good actors with solid resumes, so it was certainly nothing personal.

Let me put it another way. I used to have no trouble selling generators and tractor hitches and other things at my dad's farm machinery store. If a customer came in and checked out a set of tires or some new headlights or something, and left without buying it, then it was the tire or the headlamp they were rejecting, not me. It was nothing personal that I didn't make the sale, right? But when you're auditioning, you really are "selling yourself" in a way; when *that* product is rejected, it can hurt, right? Nevertheless, you still have to believe that it's *never* personal.

Getting used to auditioning means more than just getting used to the stage fright that comes with the actual readings and interviews. I'll talk about that in the following chapters, and discuss what you can do about it. No, getting used to auditioning also means sustaining a healthy attitude about the entire process: remind yourself that acting is only one part of the business, and that a rejection following an audition is never personal. There *is* life after auditioning. There is even life after acting.

The amazing actor and monologist Spalding Gray once joked about feeling like a gerbil on a treadmill every time he went on an audition or an interview. He repeated to himself: "If I get it, I get it; if I don't, I don't. After all, I can still see and walk … As my mother often told me, 'Think of the starving Koreans.'" [6]

Whether or not starving Koreans can help you allay your feelings of depression and rejection, I don't know. In any case, Spalding Gray's point should be clear: never, ever beat yourself up after an audition or a phone call of rejection. Instead, promise yourself a reward! Plan after the audition to go out for dinner with a friend, or take in that special movie you've been waiting to see. And remember — one out of thirteen … one out of thirteen …

[1] Robert Cohen, *Acting Professionally* (Mountain View: Mayfield, 1998), p. 3.

[2] Alex Golson, *Acting Essentials* (New York: McGraw Hill, 2002), p. 41.

[3] Arthur Lessac, *The Use and Training of the Human Voice* (Mountain View: Mayfield, 1997), p. 8.

[4] "Twenty Questions," in *American Theatre*, V. 19 No. 5 (May/June 2002), p. 88.

[5] Interview, 1 March 1982. Ms. Tischler also added the following advice for educators: "I think teachers in the conservatories and in the liberal arts schools should constantly question what they're doing, constantly examine why they're putting people out there for a life of that kind. And unless the student must — unless a student would die if he didn't — act, then he shouldn't act. I face actors, desperate actors, constantly, and I think that educators have a responsibility to these people."

[6] From the videotape version of *Swimming to Cambodia*.

Chapter Two

School Days
"Beam me up, Scotty"

Back Where You Belong

This book is written for students in senior high schools and colleges. *In the United States this is where most actors start their training, so you're in the right place at the right time* in order to begin thinking seriously where all this stage experience might lead you, and how to start learning to audition well in order to succeed at it.

You've probably already thought or heard about some kind of "full time" theatre training, and maybe even considered enrolling in a drama school or conservatory. Outside the U.S. and Canada, in fact, those are the *only* places where you can train for the theatre. (And an audition is part of the entrance requirements!). But in our part of the world we have such an enormous need for actors in our huge entertainment industry that professional drama schools just can't meet the demand. Professional schools exist, of course; there are about twenty to thirty of them in the United States, and they're very prestigious (as well as expensive!).

You don't have to go that route to become a professional actor, however. Most "working actors" in the U.S. don't. And it's important to pause and think about this early in your life, because it won't be long before you're seriously tempted to drop out of school, rush out, and audition for professional work or training.

What you *do* have to accomplish at this point in your life is to see whether or not you're likely to succeed in the performing arts and whether or not you want to. I know a number of people who never "majored" in theatre at a university, but who went into conservatory training after graduating in some other field and were successful as actors. Just as I've seen a large number of drama majors who went into other careers after earning their theatre degrees.

This is one of the most important things you should remember while you're in school, that *you need to take some time to be sure you want to go into the arts field before you commit to it.* You can certainly afford a few years of "looking around" in high school and college in order to help you make up your mind. Your *professional* acting training should start only after you've completed college.

Let me give you two opinions that illustrate this point, and emphasize its importance, so hopefully you won't forget it. First, I remember vividly a conversation I had years ago with Jack Fletcher at the American Conservatory Theatre when I was a young actor starting out:

> Looking back on it, I now say to people who have a kind of juvenile, naïve anxiousness about getting there: 'Look — you're in heaven right now. The profession will wait for you, New York City isn't going anywhere, it will wait for you.' Take your time and study. Students are going to get much more after they've finished the college experience because their vision is going to be much more specific, and their awareness, their desire, their feeling of why they must do it. They're going to be able to articulate their acting career to others and to themselves so much more clearly. And that's everything — rather than getting there and being at a disadvantage: unfocussed and sloppy." [1]

And just to illustrate that times don't really change as much as we often think, this second opinion is more recent. It's from the Hollywood actor, Henry Winkler (remember "The Fonz" from *Happy Days*?):

> Your motor is running, and your impatience is at a peak, and you think, "Oh my god, they're all going out there, they're all getting jobs and there'll be nothing left for me." That concept is actually bogus! There will always be parts to cast, and starting to audition before you're adequately prepared is the biggest mistake an actor can make. [2]

So *be sure* this business is for you, take your time, and avoid the temptation of just rushing into it — if only because *"the biz" can eat you up and spit you out very fast when you start to audition before you're ready.* Anthony Rapp, who got his first big break as the kid in the blockbuster film *Adventures in Babysitting*, then later went on to star in a number of Broadway shows like *Rent*, spoke to my students one afternoon about the kind of commitment they needed to develop during their school years: "The main thing is willingness," he said. "First comes the commitment to risk, the rest follows. You really don't want to go into this business unless you can't not. Some aspects will be disgusting, demeaning, tough, risky, frustrating, disappointing." [3]

Also remember that everything else you're learning in high

school and college — English, history, computer skills, business, science, math, psychology — all that stuff will be important and necessary for you as an actor. You never know what kind of characters you'll be called upon to play, you never know what sorts of skills you'll need to draw upon to help advance your acting career, and you never know what you'll "end up" doing in the entertainment business.

Complacency Is the Kiss of Death

I know school seems boring a lot of the time. You just feel like saying, "Beam me up, Scotty — this is a very boring planet!" People are always discussing this and wondering what to do to make it better, to keep students motivated. Even teachers sometimes find it boring, too. You have to be careful with this, however, because a sense of boredom and cynicism about school can easily infect *everything* you're doing, acting and auditioning included. And boredom can also make you impatient to get out, make you think that you're just "putting up with" stupid stuff until "real life" begins.

It's especially important for acting and auditioning that you learn in school to overcome this sort of boredom by developing a positive attitude towards everything you're learning. How do you accomplish this? Simple: you remind yourself that you don't need anybody or anything "out there" to inspire you and keep you engaged and interested. You don't need to wait on anybody else to tell you how or what to act in a scene or in a monolog when you audition. What choices to make. You can become a self-starter like other successful actors. They've learned how to make their own opportunities and take the initiative — an important skill that will serve you well as you continue with an acting career.

For example, when you're first starting-out you'll really have to be self-disciplined to make it in the business. You'll have to make the rounds of auditions and casting agents' offices and keep at it for years (just like school!). You'll have to keep records of whom you meet and when, follow-up on every lead you get, maintain a day-job to pay the rent, constantly update your materials, attend shows, keep networking, and keep practicing your audition material. After you're rich and famous, of course, you'll have a swarm of agents fighting to "manage" you (and earn ten percent of every job they get you), but at first it's all going to be on your shoulders.

It's also important in school for you to guard against complacent attitudes that can sap your competitive spirit. Do you feel sometimes that your teachers "haven't a clue," that you can get the part "no sweat," that you're "waiting to be discovered," that some class is "completely irrelevant" for you, that you've got plenty of time to "pick that up later?" The professional actor, director, and coach Robert Cohen describes this problem very accurately:

> One must beware of this attitude because it masks itself under seemingly noble forms. Basically it is simple fear. It is also egotism: the belief that one's own talent is so obvious that it need only be seen once to be instantly appreciated and called into demand. It is also romanticism: no Hollywood movie about the birth of a star has ever shown the aspirant plowing through the yellow pages or passing hours in the waiting rooms of an agent's office. The heroine has been discovered by the producer who visits the little summer stock theatre, or has been an understudy who is called on at the last moment to replace the aging star. The fact is that it takes plain work to get work in return, and *you* must go out and do the work because nobody is going to do it for you. [4]

Getting Your Act Together

The first place to start is to *deepen your background while you're in school.* At this point in your life you've likely been exposed to about 12,000 hours of TV programs and commercials, and not much else. The number of hours you've spent attending live plays can probably be measured in the double-digits. Watching films *might* be measured in the triple digits. But what about *reading* plays? Or *watching videos of plays*? Back in the double-digits again, right? And how many theatre books like this have you read? Single-digits? Well, there you are.

The easiest place to begin is with recordings: CDs, audiotapes, videotapes, and DVDs are super ways of developing your skills. Forget the Blockbuster and rental experience for the time being, and concentrate instead on the good old-fashioned free public library. All libraries these days stock CDs, videos, and DVDs just as they do books. Two things will be helpful to you in this regard: audio recordings (not so numerous) and video recordings (much more numerous). Let's start with audio.

You can learn a great deal about voice and speech from audio recordings, because you'll find a lot of famous plays, poetry, and other literary works recorded by professional actors. You probably even heard some of these when you were a kid, because children's stories are an ever-popular (and lucrative) form of professional work. Audio recordings are often overlooked by actors and teachers, perhaps because they seem "old-fashioned." Obviously they were around before video was even born. But need I remind you that folks like Robin Williams, Winona Ryder, Denzel Washington, Bruce Willis, and many, many others do "voice-overs" for animated features, as well as audio recordings of classics?

You will kill two birds with one stone here. Not only are you broadening your cultural base by listening to high quality recorded works of drama and literature, you're also getting ideas on how the actor's voice can and should be used in performance. So when you encounter strange and unfamiliar material at an audition — often more "literary" than the film and TV material you're exposed to daily — it won't seem difficult to you. There are *lots* of technical things to pay attention to: pauses, pacing, pitch (vocal inflections), nonverbal sounds.

Another important area of vocal experience that you can learn about from audio recordings is *dialect* (what some call "accent," which is speaking a language with a special regional pronunciation). Most directors, coaches, and professional actors would agree that you can't get very far on the stage these days without being able to do at least five dialects by the time you hit the job market: Irish, British, American Southern, New York, and standard American or "transatlantic." There are a lot of audio recordings of this sort of stuff out there: contemporary and classical ethnic plays, famous literature, poetry, etc. Recordings from professional voice coaches are also available for learning specific dialects.

The titles of audio recordings that you find won't always have to be plays or classical literature. Popular "books on tape" series (often in CD format) are marketed by many publishers who specialize in contemporary best-selling fiction. Lots of people buy these; it's a huge market. And if you check the credits on the box you'll be surprised to learn how many of your favorite screen actors are recording these works.

All in all, the audio recording is a wonderful resource to start with — probably because it's the most accessible. You don't need a DVD player or TV or anything, just a walkman or a diskman or a small MP3 player. These things are great for trips and those long hours of boredom: cars, airplanes, camping. So remember that you don't just have to pump your ears full of music like everyone else does — pump them full of plays, too! And maybe sometime down the road, you'll be earning that $500 per-hour union scale that actors earn in many regional markets to do these recordings for the publishing companies.

Of course, if you can park yourself and *watch* a screen, then videos and DVDs are the way to go. There are three categories or genres here that you should pick up on: classic plays (most numerous), contemporary plays (less numerous), and "instructional" features.

In the classics department, Shakespeare can be found everywhere, but avoid the omnipresent "BBC Shakespeare" series whenever you can, because a lot of those made-for-TV productions can be really boring. Instead get your hands on recent updates of the Bard like Mel Gibson's and Ethan Hawke's versions of *Hamlet*, Baz Lurman's (and Leonardo di Caprio's) version of *Romeo and Juliet*, or even *Shakespeare in Love*. Two other must-see movies are Kenneth Branagh's *Much Ado About Nothing* and *Henry V*. In fact, grab your boyfriend (or girlfriend) after watching *Henry V* and fool around with the language in the love scene: he absolutely murders the French language trying to woo her, and she's hilarious with her French pronunciation of English!

There are also good versions of some of the Greek plays out there: Aeschylus' *Agamemnon* done by the National Theatre or *The Trojan Women* with Maria Callas. In fact, you can also exploit the *academic* possibilities here. Tell your English teacher you're going to watch the old *Caesar and Cleopatra* by Bernard Shaw or the movie version of *Cyrano de Bergerac*, and write a short paper comparing them with the original plays. He or she will *love* that kind of project, and a grade of A is never hard to take, right?

In addition to the Graeco-Roman stuff, there are also excellent filmed versions of "modern classics." Plays like *A Man for All Seasons* or *The Lion in Winter* are truly heady stuff! Ibsen, Oscar Wilde, and George Bernard Shaw classics are also available. The American repertoire is particularly well represented here, with classics like *Death of a Salesman, Who's Afraid of Virginia Woolf, A Raisin in the Sun, Cat on a Hot Tin Roof, Streetcar Named Desire*, and many others.

Finally, for those with musical inclinations, there's a barge load of VHS and DVD music theatre recordings out there. Everything from operatic classics (Monteverdi, Mozart, Puccini, Verdi, etc.) to the Broadway musical. And of course, this includes the "classic" Broadway stuff like *Camelot* and *A Chorus Line*, right up to the present with *Evita* starring Madonna, and *Chicago* with Renée Zellweger. Hey — take a promenade down memory lane in the musical theatre genre with things like Victor Herbert's *Naughty Marietta* from the '30s or *Singin' in the Rain* from the '50s!

Returning to CDs — the musical deserves your special

attention, because *a lot* of acting work is out there for people who can sing and do musicals. Your audio CDs are especially useful here, because when you come to audition for musicals, you'll be expected to have two or three songs as part of the audition that can show your vocal range. There are many more Broadway shows on CD than there are on video, so you need to keep current musically with show recordings, and keep a list of songs that you hear that you may want to use for an audition someday. If nothing else, the old Hollywood movie musicals will get you hooked on screen entertainment to broaden and deepen your background in countless ways.

The second kind of video recordings to look for are recordings of major plays. Often these have originally been made for cablecast (HBO, Bravo, Showtime, etc.) and then released for home rental to libraries, Blockbuster outlets, etc. In most cases these are not the original playscript, because they've been adapted (usually by the playwright) into screenplays, but they follow the original in many details. Naturally, the big advantage with this genre of plays is that they're all contemporary, so they'll seem far less foreign and stage-ey to you.

They're hard to find, though, because they're usually shelved alongside regular Hollywood "features" in libraries and commercial rental outlets; so they might take you some time to locate. Your drama or English teachers, however, might be able to give you a good starting list of plays that have been successfully adapted to the screen in recent years. And if you're a university student in a drama program, certainly a lot of the faculty will have their favorites to recommend to you. Some of the more famous modern titles to look for in commercial outlets and libraries are *A Soldier's Story, Swimming to Cambodia, Amadeus, Master Harold and the Boys, Dangerous Liaisons, Steel Magnolias, 87 Charing Cross Road, Miss Evers' Boys*, and numerous others.

The Theatre Arts Video Library is probably the most comprehensive source for obtaining play productions on tape, but Insight Media is also an excellent source of recorded modern plays, especially plays by international authors. (Their online catalogs can be found at the web addresses listed in appendix B of this book.)

Your familiarity with these plays will be very valuable to you as an actor, and also when you come to audition. They'll acquaint you with the most *commercially successful* plays that are likely to be done and that you're most likely to encounter. They'll also broaden your sense of "style," so you begin to understand how wide a range of mood and storytelling abilities and performances lies open to you as an actor. Finally, they'll help you to avoid all those "Best Auditions Scenes" and "Best Audition Monologs" books that so many actors use for auditioning — the "kiss of death," believe me! Instead, you'll be able to pick more original and unique material on your own while others are using the all-too-familiar stuff!

The final genre of videos you want to try to get your hands on are the instructional ones — the "how to act" and "how to audition" kinds of things that maybe your drama teacher has already shown you in class. But there are a lot of very useful features available to you as an actor and auditionee.

For example, there are several excellent videos of how to audition well. Yes, believe it or not! And how to find work onstage and on camera. Some of these I've listed in the back of this book in appendix B. Your school or community librarian can locate these and get them free on "interlibrary loan" for you. Just dig around and you'll be surprised by what you find. Finally, don't overlook those videos about actors' working conditions: stuff like *Inside the Actors' Studio, Juilliard,* and other programs recorded and marketed off of PBS, the Bravo! channel, and others.

So you've got your "homework" already done, you've got no tests on the immediate horizon, or you have holiday free time? These are perfect opportunities to do yourself a favor by listening to or watching some tapes, CDs, and DVDs. They'll be immensely entertaining, and they'll do you a world of good. Want some personal advice? Back in the days before CDs, VHS, and DVDs, my professional coaches used to tell us to read at least two complete plays each week. So get started, there's *a lot* out there!

Get Involved in Stage Work

Of course, reading, viewing, and listening to plays isn't going to do it all for you. Remember, you already have 12,000 hours of screen time under your belt, so you also need some hands-on work to develop your skills.

Certainly the main thing you want to do in school is audition for plays. Take a bit of advice about this from the most authoritative audition coach in the modern theatre, Michael Shurtleff: "I think an actor should audition every damn chance he gets. If you're twenty-three and blond and you get a chance to audition for an eighty-year-old, brunette grandmother, go and audition … read for anything where anyone will allow you to read. You need the practice." [5] Never make the mistake of thinking a play or a role "isn't right" for you. What do you know? Can you read the director's mind and know what potential he or she has seen in your audition? And what do you know of a play from the printed page? You must give it a shot, each and every chance you get. You need the experience.

Plays will come in all shapes and sizes for you during these years: those done at your school by faculty, community theatre productions staged by others, student plays and films done by teachers, church plays, summer theatre shows. When you're in high school, you want to be sure your parents know that you're trying out for a show, otherwise you could be placed in an embarrassing situation when you're offered a part and your parents tell you that your grades are more important than constant rehearsals night after night. (A good motivator to keep those grades up!). So while you want to keep your antennae tuned to what's happening around you in order to take advantage of all the different auditioning experiences available, you also want to be realistic about how much time you can commit to doing a play.

Remember, too, that there's a difference between auditioning for a play and accepting a role if it's offered to you. If you were mainly auditioning for the experience of getting out there and competing with others, it's certainly fair to explain that to a director who feels you might be good in the show; you should always mention that on your audition sheet when you turn up for the tryouts. On the other hand, a part that's offered to you may be just too big to accept: it may be something you really hadn't considered, and might take more time than you can afford right now, or maybe some other commitment intervened between the time you auditioned and the time you were notified of the casting. Any of these situations might make it necessary for you to legitimately decline a role that may be offered to you. So auditioning for a show is not the same as committing to do it if you're cast, and the only way to gain audition experience, of course, is to go out and audition.

There are, however, two big no-nos that you must *always* keep in mind. First, you must never, ever, decline a role because you think the part is too small. When you decide that a role "isn't worth it," ninety-nine percent of the time you're dead-wrong. You're just letting your ego do the talking, you're developing a fat head. It's *always* true that there are no small parts, only small actors. At this stage of your training, you'll learn just as much from contributing your talents to a show in a small role as you will from a large one.

The second no-no is more difficult to control. You must *never* cut your classes short in order to perform a role in a show. Classes *always* come first. I think this is more difficult for a young actor, because naturally the thrill of being selected and cast in a play — particularly if it's a big part — can be overwhelmingly exciting. This probably happens more at the university level where there are usually a lot of auditions all year long for a lot of shows. The temptation to become a "theatre junkie" is hard to resist, if only because it's so much more "fun" to do a play than to crack those books and apply yourself to classes.

Only you can create the balance between the number of shows you need to do each year and the amount of work you need to spend on classes — not your director or your other teachers or your friends. And speaking from long personal experience, I've always found the best actors to be the ones with good grades. To get yourself on a "production treadmill" and neglect all the other perspectives that your education can give you is a big mistake. Remember that you're in school to grow in a lot of different directions, to explore your talents and abilities in numerous ways, not just in acting.

Common sense should tell you that an actor can only act what he or she actually *is* — you can only bring to the role what *you* actually possess. And the more you deprive yourself of the knowledge of science, history, literature, and other fields (other subjects), the less you're going to bring to your acting. So keep your grades up, and don't let your auditioning successes get in the way of that. It's all-important for acting.

In addition to stage experience, you should also keep in mind that other competitive forensics activities like debating, speech contests, and oral interpretation activities can be great experiences for you in high school and university. In fact, I was deeply involved in forensics in prep school before I ever even thought of acting. These activities force you to compete, they teach you verbal and physical skills, they acquaint you with a broad range of literature and cultural study, and they generate a lot of self-confidence. Certainly they lack training in teamwork and characterization that dramatic experience also provides, but they tend to "showcase" the presentation of the forensics student in a way that acting does not. So if you're inclined to compete for and participate in some forensics activities, by all means broaden and challenge yourself by doing so.

Learn to Take Criticism (and Never Apologize)

If you haven't yet heard someone tell you, *"You gotta learn to take criticism,"* then you soon will. The phrase sounds awful, I know.

Like you're supposed to listen seriously to some bozo dumping all over your performance and take it to heart? Well, it happens, let's face it. But you do have to start learning about taking criticism while you're in school, because the longer you wait and the older you get, the harder it's going to be. Too often people think "criticism" means "bad comments." That's not what criticism is. Criticism is nothing more nor less than a response that highlights the most significant features of a performance. Considered this way, you can see that criticism can either be positive or negative — or most often something in-between, like mush or vagueness or sentimental raves.

Basically, criticism is *feedback*, and all of us actors crave that. Sure, we all want to be praised and congratulated. *But we also know that we're never perfect.* The quality of our performance is always mixed, though often the criticism we receive is not. Even Tony and Oscar winners know there's a lot of pain that goes unmentioned when the awards are handed out and accepted. So with "feedback" in mind, what you should really look for are comments that are as concrete and helpful as possible for you.

Learning to take criticism means three things: how to seek out valuable comments about your work, how to deal with negative evaluations of your work, and how to apply the positive responses to your work. Let's take them in order.

"Seeking out valuable comments" isn't as stupid as it sounds. Think about the times you've been forced to say something to someone about a performance they've just given: delivering a speech in class, singing a song or playing the piano, or maybe even acting onstage. And you're expected to say something right after they've done it, surrounded by a group of people. You're really reluctant to deliver a lot of superficial, cliché praises or dump on someone to their face, aren't you? And you're sort of caught-up in the moment of excitement following the event, so you kind of want to sound positive instead of bringing everyone down by a cutting remark. And when you're surrounded by everyone else who's just gushing — or dumping — about a performance, you want to go along with the flow, don't you?

So you can see that criticism (in the sense of something concrete and helpful) is not always easy to find. People just don't feel very comfortable saying negative things to your face, and that's as it should be. They're more inclined to "gush" praises instead. It's awfully hard to point out to you a few flaws here and there when you're nervous after a show or an audition, and eager to hear something supportive. It's almost like pulling teeth to get something meaningful and sincere out of people at such times.

For one thing, you should realize that people are naturally enthusiastic and supportive after watching a performance. Either they want to cheer you up, because they sense you're feeling bad and self-conscious about what you did, or they're genuinely impressed and want to gush. That's natural, so you've got to expect a certain amount of gushing — especially after play performances. Remember, most of those people are not performers themselves, and *the last thing they'd ever do* is to get up there and risk themselves the way you did. So, just to publicly perform something — anything — is an amazing feat of courage for most people.

You'll also find that people are impressed by some of the simplest things that you may already take for granted. For example, I'm always amazed after a play performance by the people who come up to me and remark, "How did you ever manage to memorize all those lines?" Well, duhhh! That's what actors do, right? Or how spectators can be genuinely moved and impressed by things that may have seemed phony and mechanical at the time I was doing them onstage. The same is true about auditions. You never know what's going to turn people on, and you just have to let a lot of people "gush" because that's genuinely what they're feeling.

But then, of course, there's the matter of our own self-criticism. We all share the tendency to beat ourselves up after an audition by magnifying each and every little flaw we made or think we made. We can't really see the *whole* performance like a director or an audience can, because we're so totally caught up in giving it, right? So we tend to seize on the most powerful moments of what we've just done — often the most embarrassing or foolish ones — and crucify ourselves, when in fact we may have done a pretty good job overall.

So, learning how to identify good criticism isn't always easy, but it's something we need to seek out. I've always found the best way to get it is to avoid "pumping" people right after a performance; get them a few hours later when things have cooled down a little or maybe the next day. And try to get them alone so they feel a little more comfortable talking honestly in private. Of course, you want to make sure the person you're speaking with is someone who might have something valuable and insightful to say, but even general reactions to a performance of a show or an audition from people who aren't actors can be helpful. Their impressions might contain something useful that you hadn't considered.

Needless to say, the best criticism you can receive is from your drama teachers. They know what you've done in the past, and often they know exactly how hard you've prepared your audition and what you were trying to accomplish. So they can tell you where you succeeded and where you didn't. And they notice details of your performance that others are likely to miss. Tell your director or teacher you'll drop in to talk with him or her at a certain time, because you'd like to hear ideas about what you did, and avoid trying to get instant responses from them right after your performance or when they're around others.

A second way I've found to elicit some good comments, especially from friends who are likely to be favorable anyway, is to say something like, "Well, thanks, but I didn't feel right when I hit the part about … " Or "Well, I was trying something a little different in that section about … How did that come across to you?" Phrases like this relax people and give them an opportunity to agree or disagree with you in more concrete terms. You'll invite more honest responses when people feel you were improvising or exploring something. They don't feel like you're putting them on the spot and just craving praise.

On the downside, though, we all have to learn to take our knocks when we screw it up, and I'm sure you've already screwed up at least one audition somehow, right? I know I have. You blow your lines, or you leave out whole sections of a scene because of nervousness, you mispronounce a word or a name, or you get tongue-tied and stumble over passages that you've rehearsed again and again. It happens.

When you talk with people afterwards as you seek criticism, you shouldn't hesitate to point these things out. After all, we all know where we've blown it. "Yeah, but I really bit the big one in that section about … " Or, "I don't know why I screwed up when I hit that part about … Did I really destroy myself completely?" These kinds of phrases will often loosen people up to speak honestly and more concretely, because you've already admitted that you're aware of the big foul-ups. What they'll want to do is turn your focus around to the more positive aspects of your performance, and that's the conversation you want to have.

Never apologize for mistakes during your audition, because we all know about Murphy's Law: "if anything can possibly go wrong, it will." There's nothing to be done about it, everyone knows that. And no amount of whining and apologizing and breast-beating will make it right. The important thing is to take your knocks, dust yourself off, and keep going. Just like the audition performance itself, *never* apologize and ask to start over; so afterwards, don't start moaning and complaining about how lousy you were. Putting yourself down is just self-indulgent attention-getting, and it makes people uncomfortable. The more important thing is to discover something concrete to make your audition better.

The other aspect of negative criticism you must learn to deal with is handling a lot of disparaging comments from people following your performance. Remember that you really don't want to let these kinds of remarks get to you, they're unimportant. Some people are going to run you down no matter what you do, and you just have to consider the source. Some people knock everything; the put-down — often in the form of constant teasing — is their stock in trade. And it's just their own insecurity and defensiveness talking.

So these kinds of comments you can usually just blow-off and avoid taking seriously. Or else turn them around with a "yeah — but." "Yeah … but I really nailed the emotion all the way through." Or "Yeah … but I've done that a couple times before and it's no big thing." People will quickly get the idea. And don't get drawn into defending yourself against these remarks, because you're not on trial: you're looking for concrete positives that you can use. So remain focused.

Two other special forms of taking criticism, however, are important for you to learn to deal with while you're in training. These are newspaper reviews of stage productions, and formal adjudications of both auditions and play performances.

It's always great to see your name in print, hopefully because of something you succeeded in pulling off, but you shouldn't let such things go to your head. Fame is not the name of the game you're about here. Leave the celebrations and ego-building to the flacks (public relations people whose job it is to pump-up the reputations of their celebrity-clients). Like school athletes or other award winners, what's important is that solid effort gets recognized, but it shouldn't lead to inflated self-opinions or "resting on one's laurels" out of complacency. You always have room to grow and more to learn. And it ain't the cover of *Newsweek* magazine or *The New York Times*, is it?

You should also avoid taking bad comments to heart when they appear in print. I know this is especially hard, because something that's printed carries more punch than something that's just said to you. Also it seems more permanent, and more people are likely to read it. So it hurts. You have to remember that it's only one person's opinion, and I'm sure you've already heard actors declare that they never read reviews — good or bad. And a lot of them don't. So if you get a bad mention in your school newspaper or somewhere else, that's no excuse for walking around with your head in a paper bag. People rarely remember anything they read in newspapers from one day to the next, so there's no reason to dwell on it.

Far more important than reviews, however, are formal "adjudications" of your work. Most frequently these follow play performances at festival competitions, but in the university they also follow auditions. And they take the form of written and oral comments.

An adjudication is a response by a knowledgeable individual or group of individuals (not the audience, God forbid!) to the stage work that's presented. They're set up for two reasons: to determine winners in competitive situations and to provide participants with an objective response to stage work from a skilled, outside observer (i.e., not the play director, friends and classmates, school officials, family, etc.). Adjudications are becoming more and more common these days in schools and professional contexts; occasionally they're even done publicly, with the audience invited to sit-in and listen for all or part of the commentary. They can last from five minutes to about one hour, and in most cases the adjudicator(s) will give written comments following the oral presentation.

Adjudications are extremely valuable for two reasons. An adjudicator isn't a play reviewer or newspaper journalist laboring under a "shoot from the hip" deadline to file a feature story (usually very judgmental); he or she is an experienced, theatre-trained professional whose opinions are more considered, well thought-out, and informed. Second, an adjudicator's main purpose is not to praise or blame actors and productions (although on occasion they'll have to determine winners of a competition or festival). Instead, an adjudicator's purpose is *to respond as one audience member* to what he or she has seen in performance.

In both cases, you're likely to get a well-informed and objective opinion about what happened onstage, so it's important to listen to and remember the adjudicator's comments. Of course, no one can be one-hundred percent objective all of the time, and I've been present at a few misguided adjudications where the person has felt it necessary to re-direct the play to his or her own taste or even to severely criticize designers and student actors for their choices. All of which led me to believe the adjudicator was suffering from chronic indigestion, grinding an axe, or possibly even asleep during much of the performance. But for the most part, his or her "outside opinion" gives you something besides "the home team" to listen to when it comes to taking criticism.

Many of you have already experienced *play* adjudications in high school or in the university, so I don't want to say too much about that here. Instead, I want to remind you that once you're in the university, you'll be able to learn some very special things from adjudications of your *audition* performances. You'll normally present these auditions within two contexts: competition for the "Irene Ryan Acting Scholarship Awards" sponsored by the American College Theatre Festival (ACTF) and competition for admissions and scholarships to postgraduate professional training programs sponsored by the University Resident Theatre Association (URTA). See the following chapter for more complete descriptions of both these special audition situations for university students.

Students who have been singled out as exceptional actors by ACTF adjudicators attending various shows at your school are eligible to compete in the regional ACTF festivals for the Irene Ryan Scholarship. At these regional festivals there will usually be upwards of 500 Irene Ryan "nominees" competing in auditions against each other over a three-day period for only two regional awards. As you may imagine, there is intense competition among actors at both regional and national ACTF festivals.

As an Irene Ryan regional competitor, however, you'll be able to watch the performances of many of the other students competing against you, and you can learn a great deal about auditioning skills from observing these extremely talented young actors. Additionally, all the regional competitors receive group advising following the competition during which students learn the different assessment criteria upon which the judges based their decisions, hear adjudicators' opinions on choosing good material, and discover tips and suggestions that different judges make about the auditioning process.

The workshops, the audition competitions, and the feedback sessions at the ACTF are invaluable, because they familiarize you with exactly the kinds of things people are expecting of you when you come to audition for a role. As one college senior, Carolyn Ratkowski, said to me after competing successfully in unified auditions for the Wisconsin professional theatres: "Going to ACTF was great because it really prepared me for what I had to do in Wisconsin! It was just like the Irene Ryans — except that the people judging me were all producers and casting directors." [6]

URTA auditions are different from the ACTF experience in two ways. First, you don't compete to audition for URTA, your faculty must recommend you. Second, the URTA judges are not ranking you in any "level" of competition; they're considering you for entrance to their professional training schools. The judges are faculty at those institutions. While your audition will tell them a great deal of what they need to know, they'll also require an interview with you in the event your initial "screening" audition went well. At this interview, you can ask the URTA faculty how they felt you did at the audition: Why they called you back to interview? Would they like to see another monolog or hear another audition song? What do you feel you might do to improve your acting or auditioning skills?

Whether or not you receive a callback from one or more schools, or even an invitation to apply, you'll always get a written evaluation sheet from the URTA folks that will give you some idea in writing of what they thought of your performance. Naturally, they're writing "in the heat of the moment" so their comments will be brief; but remember that these are comments from people who are at the highest level of the "training pyramid," so their opinions *matter*. Show them to your drama teacher or coach, and take them to heart.

The Actor's Journal

The last thing I want to draw your attention to while you're in school is the importance of keeping an acting journal. Many artists have found journals invaluable for their work, especially writers and painters. The quick sketch, those flashes that surface momentarily at unforeseen times, those observations of the new and unusual that suddenly strike you, things you feel you really should remember — you'll find many such items valuable to record and return to later, sometimes years in the future.

Broadly speaking, journals will help your acting and auditioning in two ways. They'll reinforce whatever creative impulses you have by forcing you to "highlight" them in the form of writing. And a journal will also keep you focused in an ongoing way about your auditioning work as an actor. A journal is not a "dear diary" sort of book; it should contain only those life experiences that you feel are pertinent to acting. Nor should it describe *everything* that happens to you in the theatre (you'd quickly tire of this!). Instead, you must keep it selective and well-focused so that it stays useful to you as an auditioner.

In addition to these broad purposes, there's another valuable skill you'll learn from journal-writing: how to put yourself down on paper. As you probably already know, an actor's resume is one powerful calling card, because it's the only thing that's going to "represent" you once your audition is finished and you've left the stage. By starting in school to develop a journal — which should always contain a current resume of your experience — you'll have no problem once you get to college of working up a good professional resume of your experience and speaking confidently about it in an interview situation for professional training schools, jobs, and scholarship awards.

A lot of what I've been describing in this chapter can and should be part of your acting journal: what you've learned from watching, reading, and listening to plays and films and CDs; your personal critiques of your acting and auditioning skills; your blow-by-blow record of getting used to competition and the various competitive situations you've tried to explore; comments from adjudicators and others about your stage work.

Some of these things you need to jot down *immediately* so you don't simply push the "delete" button out of laziness or defensiveness or denial. For example, write self-critiques of your performances following every audition, or jot down those adjudicator's comments during the talkback session. Other impressions you'll want to record in a more leisurely fashion, in between those times you're actually onstage: that particular scene you noticed which might be good for an audition sometime or the different attitudes you noticed among your fellow auditionees waiting in the corridor outside the theatre.

But it all gets recorded there somehow, and the actual journal itself should be a handy thing — something that stows easily in the purse or bookbag. Doubtless you'll fill more than one as you go through school, and you'll find other useful things to record in it than just the stuff I've indicated here. A professional actor does *a lot* of record-keeping as he or she starts out in the business, everything from which agent or casting director you interviewed with yesterday afternoon to what your lunch cost you. Starting early in your career, therefore, to make friends with a journal or notebook eventually helps you to develop some *very* practical skills.

I think it's very easy to "let things slide" with your acting as you go through school, in the sense that you tend to lose some of your focus on training and developing your abilities in a structured, effective way. Maybe that's because acting is different from other kinds of skills. If you fail to keep up your dance exercises, if you neglect your gymnastic routines for a few weeks, if you slack-off on your daily piano practice, then you're going to notice your mistake very quickly. But with acting, a person can go for weeks and months really doing nothing that feeds his or her art. And still that person can feel that he or she's an actor when they certainly aren't.

And you know, to a lot of people it seems like the art of acting isn't really an art at all. At its best it seems so "natural" that many people think it's just "playing oneself." And who needs to work at that? A ballerina, a gymnast, a concert pianist — well, *that* we can understand takes practice. Hours at the barre, hours at the keyboard, each and every day if you're going to get good at it. But an actor? Just have the guts to get out there and do it, that's all it takes, right? Just be casual about your training? No sweat? It'll happen?

You want to be careful to guard against this attitude, and this is where journal-writing can help. It tends to give you a sense of purpose and it prods you to keep building on your life experiences, to keep growing as an actor. I know that a lot of what I've been suggesting in this chapter has probably placed your "boring" school work into a new context for you. Hopefully, though, my words have fired your imagination to undertake some new activities and make your acting and auditioning much better. So put all of that into your journal.

But I also know that this chapter has probably made you wonder about how far you really want to take this "acting" business, now that you see there might be a whole lot more to it than you considered at first. Well, you're probably not alone. Alan Ruck, a successful screen actor (*Spin City, Ferris Bueller's Day Off, Star Trek: Generations*) who trained for years on the live stage in Chicago and New York, remarked to me:

> Sure, I meet these people all the time and they ask me, "How do I become an actor? How do I get started?" And I say, "Well, you gotta get some experience. You have to start acting in the theatre, maybe your local community theatre." And I can see their eyes glaze over, like they're not really thinking about "acting." They're just thinking of being in TV shows or being a famous movie star or something. But not about learning how to act. [7]

Was there ever an actor who never wondered if he or she was going to "make it big?" Probably not. But on the other hand, fame shouldn't be the primary motivator. The greatest and most influential acting teacher of our time was the Russian director and actor Konstantin Stanislavski. And when you feel like calling Scotty to "beam you up" from your school, remember what Stanik said about learning to apply oneself in disciplined training in the classroom and studio:

> In every branch of art there are first hundreds of people who wish to study it. Many come in response to the bait of "learning creatively," but having realized how much of their time they have to devote to it; how difficult it is ... the majority of those who come to study the art of acting will leave the studio. Many of those who stay behind will also very soon leave, for the temptation to earn money by slipshod work is very great. [8]

You could do a lot worse than take this advice. Think about it, the choice is yours. And it all begins in school.

Exploration #1: Beginning the Journal

Take the plunge and direct your first journal entry toward the whole subject of auditioning by writing a short commentary on your major impressions after reading this chapter. What topics or themes or subjects stand out in your mind now that you've finished reading? Why? Because they surprised you? Offended you? Sounded right to you? Don't try to "structure" your commentary like an essay for English class, but write it instead as you think it and feel it — honestly and spontaneously. These aren't words carved in stone and deathless prose, "consequently intended for publication" (as the young Cicely states in Oscar Wilde's *The Importance of Being Earnest*). They're your first stab at self-reflection on the art of acting and learning to audition well.

Exploration #2: The Sincerity Contest

Stand in a large circle with the class group, everyone facing toward the center. Even though many in your group may know each other (or perhaps not), begin this exercise with everyone introducing themselves to the group in the following manner: as each person's turn comes up, he or she steps forward, says his or her full name only, and follows that statement with a small gesture or movement that seems to the student best expresses his or her present feelings towards the group. Elaborate movements aren't necessary, and in fact should probably be avoided in favor of simple gestures, shrugs, etc. The class as a whole then repeats the name and the gesture, and the turn passes to the next student. The class should concentrate on noting each person's manner of speaking and gesturing, and at the end "vote" anonymously (using slips of paper) on which student seemed to speak and gesture in the most honest and sincere manner. Without mentioning any names or singling-out individuals, the group should then discuss the degree of "stage fright" that affected everyone during this exercise, and how "complacency" or "coolness" might be used as a defense against nervousness. Is role-playing also a form of defensiveness? Is it necessary, however? Does unwillingness to compete tend to "dampen" one's performance or one's communication skills? Following the discussion, at least five minutes should be given over to journal-writing.

Exploration #3: The Growth of Commitment

Describe in your journal one or two projects that demanded some important kind of personal commitment from you: a regular job, some assignment with your church group, some sort of athletic team responsibility, or joining the cast of a play production. Having done all that, can you say at what point your "commitment" to follow-through with that task ever really became "concrete" for you? Or does commitment sort of grow on you over time? Write about this a little. Ask yourself about your commitment to studying theatre and learning the art of acting — you must have some commitment to that or you wouldn't be taking the trouble to read this book, right? So, what does "commitment" mean in terms of the theatre, in terms of learning about acting and auditioning? Write a little about this, too. Keep an eye on this over time as you study acting and auditioning, and see if or how that commitment grows or diminishes.

Review and Reflection

1. **What are the main reasons for seriously applying yourself to finishing high school and college before "launching yourself" on a professional acting career?**

   - Colleges and universities are where most actors in the United States start their training.

   - You need to take some time while you're still in school to be sure you want to go into the arts field before you commit to it.

   - "The biz" can eat you up and spit you out *very* fast when you start to audition before you're ready.

- You must learn while you're still in school to overcome boredom and to develop self-discipline.
- You must start to learn while you're still in school to fight complacent attitudes.

2. What kinds of things should you be doing in order to make the most of your high school and university theatre experience?

- Deepen your background by listening to CDs, audiotapes, videotapes, and DVDs.
- Audition for plays.
- Participate when you can in other competitive forensics activities like debating, speech contests, and oral interpretation activities.
- Learn to take criticism.
- Keep an acting journal.

3. What kind of CDs, audiotapes, videotapes, and DVDs will deepen your background while you're in school?

- You can learn a great deal about voice and speech from audio recordings, because you'll find a lot of famous plays, poetry, and other literary works recorded by professional actors.
- Shakespeare can be found everywhere.
- There are also good versions of some of the Greek plays out there.
- In addition, there are also good, recent remakes of modern classics.
- For those with musical inclinations, there are VHS and DVD music theatre recordings out there.
- Look also for recordings of major contemporary plays.
- Get your hands on instructional media — the "how to act" kinds of things.

4. How exactly can you learn to take criticism while in high school and college?

- Seek out valuable comments about your work from friends, teachers, and directors.
- Pay attention to formal adjudications of your work at play performances and festival competitions.
- Audition and compete in college for the Irene Ryan Scholarship.
- Audition and compete in college for URTA nominations.

5. What kinds of entries should you make in your acting journal?

- What you've learned from watching, reading, and listening to plays, audiotapes, DVDs, films, and CDs.

- Your personal critiques of your acting and auditioning skills.
- Your blow-by-blow record of getting used to competition and the various competitive situations you've tried to explore.
- Comments from adjudicators and others about your stage work.

[1] Interview, 3 May 1981.
[2] "Inside with Henry Winkler," *Audition Today*, v. 2, no. 1 (April/May 2001), p. 14.
[3] Interview, 31 January 2001.
[4] Cohen, op.cit., pp.43–44.
[5] *Audition* (New York: Walker, 1978), p. 19.
[6] Interview, 27 February 2003.
[7] In conversation with the author, 11 October 2002.
[8] *On the Art of the Stage* tr. David Magarshack (New York: Hill & Wang, 1961), pp. 161–162.

Chapter Three

The Auditions Context
"O brave new world!"

One of the greatest U.S. presidents of the twentieth-century, Franklin Delano Roosevelt, once declared, "The only thing we have to fear is fear itself." Truer words about auditioning were never spoken! The apprehension that grips a young actor contemplating a big role in a show, a scholarship, or a summer theatre audition can go far toward undermining that student's self-confidence and successful performance.

In order to help build your self-confidence, this chapter presents an overview of the different auditions that you can seek out and explore during your high school and university years. I've found with my own university students that understanding the full range and context of what it means "to audition" helps them feel more positive about auditioning. And I can recall when I was a young college actor, seeking jobs and auditions outside my university "home," there was precious little information available to me about "big time" auditions — and this made the situation even more terrifying to me.

Perhaps this chapter, then, can go a long way to allaying your fears about "exposing yourself" in different audition situations. And who knows? Maybe this chapter will also alert you to some audition possibilities at your school or elsewhere that you never even considered. Like Miranda declares in Shakespeare's *The Tempest* when she sees other humans for the first time: "O brave new world that hath such people in't!"

Let's take a look at that "brave new world" of audition situations and see what it has to offer.

The High School Auditions Context

If you're reading this book, it's likely that you've already been through some play auditions at your high school, so I don't need to say too much about that here. The flyers get posted, the teachers announce tryouts in their classes, you show up, give your name, and then you read a bunch of stuff from a script. Auditions aren't "prepared," they're always "cold" or "semi-cold" readings from the script being cast, usually combined with improvisations. If it's a musical, the band or music director is also there to listen to you sing a little bit and see whether or not you can carry a tune and what your vocal range is.

But there are a couple of things going on at high school play auditions that a serious acting student needs to pay attention to, regardless of how routine and familiar it all seems. **Number one: your drama directors are probably going out of their way to make the whole activity seem unthreatening.** Of course, everyone knows that the juicy roles, the big parts, are the ones to shoot for, and probably a lot of the more-talented students are quietly sizing each other up in order to see if you're going to get the role instead.

That kind of competition is natural, but the tryouts are still very unthreatening, because everyone also knows that practically everyone who tries out will be cast in the school play. And if they're not assigned a role onstage, they'll be assigned to do something backstage. This is very unusual, so be careful about getting complacent and losing the edge you need to compete strongly. Remember, this is the only time in your life when you'll try out for a play and be guaranteed *something* in the production!

Another thing to be careful of — in high school and in college — is the fact that you'll know the drama director from other contexts like classes or previous productions. This, too, can lead to complacency, encouraging you to think: "I don't really *have* to work hard at tryouts to show him or her what I can do — she already knows that, and besides, she likes me." Wrongthink!

Bear in mind that when your drama *teacher* dons another hat and becomes the drama *director*, he or she is not necessarily going to "play favorites" when it comes to casting. After all, the director doesn't want to come off as an idiot to others, and especially to the audience, just because some "teacher's pet" was put into a role that could have been performed much better by someone — even a newcomer — with talent. Take this advice from a professional director and actor:

> I suppose I'm least patient with students who saunter into an audition ill prepared, mistaking their teacher for their friend and not realizing the teacher has become director and that friendship has nothing to do with the casting of a play. These students (the most talented are frequently the greatest offenders) are teaching themselves very bad work habits. Their teachers are doing them a grievous injury by permitting such poor professional behavior. [1]

Or take this advice from an acting coach at Chicago's Goodman Theatre who regularly auditions high school graduates: "There's a self-centeredness there that has got to go away. That's the trouble with being a high school star. Everything has come too easy." [2]

So beware the sense of *complacency* that always creeps into the high school audition situation. Go back and read chapters one and two if you have forgotten what I've been saying about complacency. Always strive to do your personal best, no matter what the audition context. Always give it your very best shot. And after the casting is over, be sure to ask the stage director (and the vocal director) how well you presented yourself in the audition and to give you some tips. All of this information goes into your auditions journal as I explained in the last chapter.

Your familiarity with teacher-directors, though, also has a flip side to it. Just as one can become too complacent presuming that the director will already know what you can do, one can also be cynical and negative about one's poor past performance. If you messed-up somehow in the last show or in classes, if you never get your assignments in on time, or you're always late or cutting class or rehearsals, you may well need a one-on-one talk with the director:

> How you performed *in rehearsals* in the last play you were in will have an enormous bearing on what part you do or do not receive in the play you are auditioning for. If you came on time, worked hard, took direction, learned your lines on time, were not too disruptive, helped other people, treated the backstage people well — all this will have as much to do with your getting a part in a play, than your audition or your talent. If you know you did not perform well in rehearsals last time, and you really want to be in the new play, talk to the director prior to rehearsals and explain that you know you didn't perform well, and that you will do better this time. That confession will help greatly; so will the talk. [3]

The other component of a high school audition, improvisations, also bears some mention here. While casting at all levels — university, community theatre, scholarships, professional — is always likely to test your improv skills in some way, the high school improv is almost always required. And too often we'll find students going for the "big effects" in improvs: the big laugh, the extreme dramatic emotions, "mugging" (playing exaggerated reactions to the camera or "the house"). All of which is phony, of course — a fear reaction or the result of self-consciousness or unseriousness.

No matter what kind of "improvs" you've been used to (and especially if all you know about improvisation is the work of standup comedians), you should always avoid "blowing them off." On the contrary, take them seriously as acting opportunities, as acting experiments, because this is what they are for the director. Play them honestly, listen to and observe your fellow players (this will always stimulate more original and interesting responses in you and suggest excellent lines of action to play), and especially *work with* the others in the improv, no matter how silly it may seem. An improv is not an opportunity for you to grandstand and horse around.

In addition to trying-out for plays, you can learn vital auditioning skills in high school by participating in festivals for the Thespian Association and the Interscholastic Speech Association (assuming that your school is a member of one of these national groups or both of them). I'm not talking about play festivals, where you do forty-five-minute cuttings for district, regional, and state competition. I'm talking about the annual spring (sometimes mid-winter) state conferences where students present auditions for awards and where faculty from state universities and colleges are often in attendance.

A couple of things that happen here are very important. Number one, you'll receive very good experience and criticism at these events, and number two, you may also win awards recognitions and even scholarship offers (if you're a senior) from colleges that are attending and observing. In fact, most of the time the college faculty will be at these events for two reasons: they're recruiting for their schools and they're also serving as judges for the acting performances.

You should press your drama teachers about these annual events and encourage them to participate if your school isn't already doing so. And certainly, you should look to enter yourself as a contestant. This will give you the first major opportunity outside of your school to learn the ropes about an audition situation and to prove yourself in competition with other talented actors in your age and experience range from the district and around the state. You will always receive feedback from the judges regarding your performances, because the judges rate each competitor on a graded form.

Additionally, these conferences will help you prepare your professional paperwork (if you're a graduating senior) by listing all the auditionee/competitors in a notebook that's handed out to the attending colleges. Each auditionee will have his or her own page, with a color photo attached, listing experience, background, training, address, etc. (much like a professional resume). The intention here is twofold: it gives students their first taste of putting themselves down on paper (which is what "real" actors do all of the time), and it gives the judges/recruiters a handy file for contacting talented students. Your drama teacher will help you to fill out the form and submit all the information for getting listed in the handbook.

Your auditions at these events will be just like any audition at a "real" theatre. You'll be able to choose monologs, two-character scenes, musical theatre songs, and often some special category such as "mime." The time length for each of these pieces and their order of presentation may vary from state to state, depending where you live.

Obviously the important thing here is that it'll likely give you your first shot at preparing an audition with some real stakes attached: state awards for excellence and/or college scholarship offers. Of course, not all your favorite colleges will be represented at these events, so the auditions and resumes you create for the Thespian or Forensics conference may also be very useful to you if you choose to apply to other universities. And let's not forget, too, the *socializing* that goes on at these events where you meet new faces and begin networking in a theatre group larger than your own school!

The final audition opportunity you'll encounter in your high school will come in your senior year when you apply to different schools in order to enter their drama programs. All professional conservatory-type schools will require this. And many universities will not only have entrance auditions but also scholarship auditions as part of this entrance process. Preparing to audition and compete for entrance and financial support will force you to put into practice all you've learned in high school dramatics and will bring you into close contact with one or more of your teachers who will need to coach and recommend you for whatever program you're applying to.

This may sound a bit puzzling to you, because in high school, you'll normally follow a general type of curriculum in order to graduate, one which permits you to enroll in any course you choose so long as you fulfill the core requirements for graduation. You can also sign up for any one of a number of activities you wish: band, theatre, debate, computer club, etc. You should understand, however, that universities are very different. They do have "core requirements" that all students must complete, but they also have "major requirements" that all students must fulfill. To "major" in college means that each student must take a concentrated number of courses in a given field such as business, history, foreign language — or theatre. And many colleges also require you to be a drama major if you want to be in plays.

As a high school senior applying to a university, you'll be encouraged to declare this major field of study, but schools will ordinarily accept you as an "undeclared" student if you haven't yet decided upon a major concentration. Before you can graduate, however, you will be required to choose a major, and if you choose to major in theatre, then you may run up against separate auditions for entering the drama program.

This is referred to in college as a "secondary admission" process, and it's very common for popular fields like business, medicine, film and television, teaching — and theatre. It's sort of like collegiate sports: anyone can play "intramurals" in college, but you've got to try out and compete to earn a seat on the varsity bench. And you know how many of those players are on athletic scholarships, don't you?

What's really at stake here? Well, first of all, the ability to graduate with a theatre degree. This is important because post-graduate professional theatre training is normally linked to successful completion of an undergraduate degree in theatre. Second, you can't hope to win a drama scholarship at the university without auditioning and competing for it, and without being a "major" in drama. Finally, as I mentioned above, you might not be able to participate in college plays at all unless you're a drama major.

So don't cherish any illusions in high school that things are going to continue rosily for you as an actor in college — don't get complacent! Once out of high school you're going to have to earn your way in the profession and it gets more demanding and more selective the further you advance! See appendix D for more details about college entrance and scholarship auditions.

What You Can Expect in Community Theatre Auditions

Auditioning for community theatre productions is an option for students of all ages, regardless of your educational level. I'm certain most of you reading this book already have some experience at your local community theatre, if only because parents frequently try to get kids involved in plays and similar cultural experiences at an early age.

The single most important advantage for you in getting involved with a community theatre show is that the experience will allow you to "test" yourself against actors who are not "automatically" cast at your school by directors who already

know them. Thus, you're more likely to learn your true strengths and weaknesses as a performer than you might within a "favored" casting process in your school by directors who have worked with you before as your teachers and advisors.

Additionally, you may be able to make important contacts for your future performance work by doing community theatre. College and university theatre people are often involved in community theatre, and you'll have the chance to work with actors having a wider range of experience than can be found on high school or college campuses. In addition, university faculty in many major cities have set up important experimental theatres in the community which permit them (and you!) to do more difficult work than they could otherwise undertake on campus — theatres which often make the transition from amateur to professional status in just a few years. [4]

Finally, keep in mind that you may also be able to make money for your acting and related stage work in community theatres. These stages sometimes compensate actors from $15 – $30 per performance[5]; you can also earn money by making yourself available as crew for road shows that occasionally play the community. All in all, community theatre tryouts can seem more like a "real world" auditioning experience, so they're more fun because they're more challenging!

When you first arrive at the audition you'll be asked to fill out an audition form and you should do so professionally. The information required is pretty straightforward, but it's important because the way the entries appear will have a lot to do with the way the directors regard you when it comes your turn to read. So get set beforehand thinking of what and how you're going to list your experience. Be clear about what you list there, and be proud of it — don't hold back. That stuff is important for new directors to see, especially with younger actors and newcomers.

After you complete and turn-in the form, you may or may not be given something "to look over" before you're called on (see Chapter Eight on "cold readings"). In any case, you'll likely have a chance to ***sit around and observe other auditionees reading scenes, so you can learn what's going on.*** Be sure you observe the readings closely; you'll be surprised what you'll learn about good and bad auditioning skills.

While you're waiting, you'll also have a chance to ***consider carefully all the performances scheduled for the play, to make sure you can make those commitments in case you're cast.*** This is important to note, because unlike high school and university productions, community theatre shows often run longer and perform during weeknights and on matinee dates. Their production schedules can often be very different from what you've been accustomed to at your school. Be certain you can make all of these dates — as well as nightly technical and dress rehearsals the week before the show opens — if you land a role.

Normally there will be two sets of readings here: general auditions and callbacks. The purpose of the callback is for directors to look more closely at certain people after the initial screening. This may mean having them read new material once the director has an idea of which role they might be good for, having them read material they were given to prepare overnight following the general tryouts, in order to see what they do with it on their own, having them read with other actors in combinations to see how people look together onstage in the possible roles, or putting the "finalists" through improvisations or movement exercises of some kind to learn more about their acting skills.

This is important for high school students to bear in mind, because unlike your high school auditions, casting decisions in community theatres will rarely be made after the general tryouts. Directors in community theatres and elsewhere take more time to consider the actors and assign the roles. So *at your general audition, you're not trying out for a part — you're auditioning for a callback.* The only exception occurs when an actor might be the only *obvious* choice for a specialized role, in which case he or she may be cast after the general readings and not necessarily called back.

How does this affect your general audition? It means that you should feel more open during your general audition, more willing to "take risks" with your reading in order to show directors your *overall* talent. Unlike the high school audition (and some professional auditions such as commercials) where directors are often looking for specific character "types," your general audition should provide a good overall glimpse of your skills that will earn you a second go-round.

So keep this in mind at the first community theatre readings. If the director asks you to read for what seems to you to be a totally unsuitable part, relax and read for it. Understand that he or she may be challenging you with difficult textual problems, or testing your emotional or movement skills, or seeing how you relate to other actors onstage. Realize, too, that in community theatres and elsewhere you'll never be cast in roles that are opposite your gender or way outside your age range, as frequently happens in high schools and occasionally in college. There will likely be plenty of older actors to fill those parts. (Hooray! No more parents, grandfolks, and old man or woman roles!)

Another important aspect about community theatre auditions to keep in mind is that *the directors may want to interview you a bit or have you do some improvisations for awhile in order to get to know you a little better.* Remember that if they've never worked with you before, they don't know you from Adam or Eve. Can they depend on your being there for rehearsals? Making all performances? Memorizing your lines? Paying attention? Working well with adults onstage? Taking directions cooperatively? A lot of young people who are otherwise very good in their high school shows can't do these things in a community theatre setting. So part of your community theatre presentation may include an "interview" conversation, and you should be ready to communicate your skills in these areas in an upbeat manner.

One final word needs to be said about high school students trying out for community theatre productions. Don't undermine your self-confidence by feeling at the auditions that you're the low man or woman on the totem pole just because you're young and in high school. Remind yourself that there are plenty of plays with characters that are your age, and actors like you are needed to fill those roles. It's as simple as that. For the same reasons that a director will avoid casting a teenager in the role of a fifty-year-old, the director is not likely to cast a twenty-something or thirty-something or even forty-something in the role of a teenager.

You've got a good chance to land the part, so go for it with your best shot! And one added bonus for high school students doing community theatre shows — the plays can often be much more challenging for you than the kinds of shows your high school normally presents!

What You Can Expect in College and University Auditions

An increasing number of universities now require an acting audition for entrance into their theatre programs or continuance in the program, and many already have audition requirements for drama department scholarships. Normally, you arrange for these auditions in the fall of your senior year of high school when you apply to the university. Then the theatre department will audition you in the winter, so that your notification of acceptance to the university (which is normally sent by April) can also contain information on the financial aid you're eligible to receive.

Some universities will also have auditions for their continuing majors (sophomores, juniors, seniors) every year in order for these students to renew their existing scholarships, qualify for new scholarships, or maintain their status as majors in the program. You should understand that in four-year schools where there is a strong emphasis on academic and performing excellence, you will be "reviewed" annually in order to determine whether or not you're making appropriate progress. In schools offering the B.F.A. degree (a pre-professional program that concentrates your courses in the art form, leading to the Bachelor of Fine Arts degree), students will absolutely be reviewed each year. B.F.A. music students, for example, must present a "spring recital" that is attended by all the faculty. B.F.A. acting students will present an audition or scene for the faculty. But even if you're not enrolled in a B.F.A. program, annual auditions may be required in some schools.

Every university will have different requirements for these kinds of auditions, but all schools will also require you to participate in their stage productions, which are different auditions altogether, and which I describe below. For scholarship, entrance, and B.F.A. auditions, you need to contact the specific program you plan to apply for and read-up on what's required. And in preparing these auditions, you should follow the procedures in this book outlined in chapters 5, 6, and 7 for working within those school guidelines (length of pieces, kinds of material to select, etc.).

With regard to play auditions, university students new to the college campus often feel themselves "swamped" by the number of auditions and performance opportunities that are available to them. In fact, one of the strongest challenges you face in college is learning to budget your time wisely, because most students who flunk out of school do so in the first two to three semesters. This happens because they become sidetracked by the many extra-curricular activities that present themselves — like getting involved in plays — and inexperienced students often shove their academic studies to the back burner in order to grab as much "college life" as they can right off the bat. So be careful, because frequent auditions for student plays, faculty shows, and TV/film productions abound on many campuses, and you'll likely have a lot of opportunities to choose from.

A second feature of university theatre that may surprise you is that many drama departments only permit drama majors to act in their shows. As I mentioned in the earlier section on high school auditioning, a "major" is a student who has officially "declared" theatre arts as his or her major field of study, and all universities require you to choose a major field in which you'll concentrate your coursework. This may obviously limit your choice of auditions if you aren't signed up for the performing arts program, and may force you to reconsider whether or not you want to pursue theatre in college on a serious basis.

Students committed to studying theatre are sometimes given preference in casting, because they've often had the acting classes that strengthen their skills. Similarly, students who are acting or performance majors are also given preference in college casting, because faculty directors have a real obligation to support them as they prepare for theatre careers. And it stands to reason that a faculty director — whose contract is partially determined by the success or failure of his or her productions — will give preference to students on the basis of their class work in acting or from their performances in other shows. Why? Simple: these students are a dependable, known quantity as far as the director is concerned. Graduating seniors may also be given preference in casting — especially if they're promising actors — because they need that "extra boost" at the end of school to propel them into the demanding environment of postgraduate training.

As you can see, it helps to understand what's at stake in the university audition when the directors make their casting decisions. This is something you won't have encountered before in high school or community theatre auditions, because those institutions are not primarily *theatre training* institutions. So keep this context in mind when you audition for a university show, and don't become cynical about it. Remember, this "system" will also work in your favor as you continue your acting studies.

The actual process of the university audition — sign-in, general tryouts, callbacks, cold readings — will pretty much resemble what you've been used to in high school or in community theatre. But there are other casting twists that can occur in a university situation that you should be ready for.

Twist number one: *you may be required to prepare and memorize a one- or two-minute monolog beforehand (and/or a song for a musical) and present it at the general tryouts.* This sort of "prepared audition" is a very common requirement that accomplishes two things. It tends to weed out lazy people "wandering in off the street" who are undisciplined and lackadaisical about working on a play. Who wants them in a play anyway? Do you want to act with those kinds of students? The requirement also helps directors to see some of your real strengths before they put you under the stress of a "cold" (unprepared) reading or anything else they may wish to have you do.

Twist number two: *the general auditions may be "closed" to everyone who is not auditioning onstage.* This means that all the auditionees will remain in a waiting area while others actors are called-in for the readings. Many directors feel they can elicit better presentations from actors without an "audience" of other competitors in the room. Additionally, a lot of actors waiting around in the same room for their turn to read often become noisy and distracting. In this situation, after you turn in your registration form, you wait with everyone else to be called-in.

Twist number three: *the auditions may be casting for a new play in its premiere production.* This is always an exciting situation to encounter, because the director has few preconceived notions about how the roles should be played. He or she will be hearing the play for the first time, and hence will be very dependent upon what the actors show him at tryouts. This is where you can really shine by "taking risks," interpreting the script in a bold, original, and creative fashion.

Twist number four: *the director doing the casting may be a guest artist from another theatre.* This means that he or she will know *absolutely nothing* about you except what you show during the readings. What a marvelous opportunity to compete just on the basis of talent! So if you're a freshman, this means that upper-classmen will have no advantage over the "new faces" — earning the role will rely heavily on audition talent alone! And if you've already been in the program for a few years, this means that the guest director will have no preconceived notions about your abilities — "type casting" may be reduced to a minimum in this situation.

Twist number five: *you may encounter "pick-up" and "unified" auditions for the first time.* A pick-up audition occurs when a director suddenly needs to add actors or replace an actor for some reason. It will usually be a speedy audition, very concentrated and focused, because the role must be filled immediately and the new actor will have to work very specifically and quickly. He or she must fit into a partially-formed cast and a production that has already been blocked and rehearsed to some extent.

The unified audition (becoming increasingly popular at larger schools) is one in which several plays are cast at the same tryouts. All the directors are present at the general auditions, and usually they "divide up" the auditionees after the general readings. Actors are then given different callbacks for each of the shows, depending upon which directors feel they can use them. Finally, the directors get together and "duke it out" to see which students will play the assigned parts. When the cast lists are posted, the student actors know all the roles they'll be playing during the coming season — a great help in learning to budget your time and "pace yourself" by planning for months ahead!

What You Can Expect in ACTF and URTA Auditions

University students who are planning on acting careers absolutely must take advantage of two unique auditioning opportunities: one that is available throughout their college career (ACTF), and a second that is only available during their senior year (URTA).

The Kennedy Center American College Theatre Festival (ACTF) occurs annually as a series of regional competitions and festivals across the United States, culminating in a national festival in May at the Kennedy Center for the Arts in Washington, D.C. It is the largest and oldest amateur theatre festival in the world, involving more than ten thousand individuals each year. ACTF *competitions* provide opportunities for students to win awards and recognition for all types of theatre work, especially acting. ACTF *festivals* provide opportunities for everyone, whether or not they're competing for awards, to immensely broaden their theatre appreciation by attending play productions from around their region, participating in many kinds of workshops, observing the acting competitions and exhibitions, and networking with their peers.

Of primary interest to acting students are the ACTF auditions for Irene Ryan acting awards, which include scholarship prizes. Two winners of these awards are selected from each region during the year, and these finalists then compete in Washington for two national awards. Students become eligible for the "Irene Ryans" at their schools when their stage productions are "adjudicated" (observed and responded to) by visiting ACTF adjudicators. An adjudicator will normally nominate at least one student as an outstanding actor in the production, and the stage director may nominate another — although three or four nominees for a production are not unusual.

Nominees from the different colleges are then eligible to participate in the regional Irene Ryan competitions, where they present an audition with 500–600 other competitors. As you might imagine, the competition is fierce at these regionals, because only two winners will be selected. Almost two dozen of these regional winners then compete in Washington as finalists for the highly prestigious Irene Ryan acting awards. Finalists are generally regarded very highly by acting conservatories across the nation, and winners of the Irene Ryans are commonly regarded as the finest and most promising collegiate actors in the United States.

Some college students continue to earn Irene Ryan nominations year after year while they're in productions, and you can do this also. This gives you a chance to build your auditioning skills with each festival experience. Even if they're never selected as regional winners, many advance to the level of regional semi-finalists — which is also very prestigious, considering the fact that there are 500 to 600 students competing! And a number of university students who are not Irene Ryan nominees at all attend the regional festivals anyway to join in the fun and experience of high-powered university theatre.

As you can gather, the ACTF festivals are the equivalent of those "annual conventions" you hear so much about in all professions. People spend a lot of money and take the time to attend these events each year not just to schmooze with old friends and meet new ones, but also to learn about new developments, recognize the "super-achievers" in their field, and generally keep abreast of what's happening in their professions. And if you're a serious theatre student, you too should plan to attend at least one ACTF festival before you graduate. I guarantee that you won't be disappointed.

The rules governing auditions at the Irene Ryans are very specific, affecting the length of your selections, how to introduce yourself, how to present your music (if you choose to also do a singing audition), application deadlines, and such matters. Additionally, you will have to secure written permission for your audition pieces from the copyright-holders, and be prepared with copies of your professional-quality resume and photograph (should you be selected as a regional semi-finalist). Needless to say, these requirements closely reflect the way in which actors customarily present themselves at auditions in the professional theatre, so the Irene Ryans are an excellent preparation for "getting your feet wet" for a serious acting career.

To learn more about the Irene Ryans, you should ask your drama professor and visit their website listed in appendix B.

While ACTF programs are open to all university students and cover a broad range of theatre studies, the activities of the University Resident Theatre Association (URTA) are much more selective, and they focus narrowly upon career placement for actors, directors, designers, and arts managers. ACTF presents festivals with outstanding productions, workshops, competitions, and awards; URTA presents only competitions and interviews for placement at the finest advanced acting training programs in the country.

The University Resident Theatre Association was initially set up to provide a "clearinghouse" for college seniors desiring advanced, professional-level training at graduate schools and acting conservatories. The word "association" refers to the group of about thirty training schools nationwide, almost all of which have professional acting companies attached to their training programs. You've probably heard the names of a lot of these schools and theatres before now: the Cincinnati Playhouse in the Park, Alabama Shakespeare Festival, Missouri Repertory Theatre, University of California Irvine, etc.

These outstanding acting training schools have teams of faculty who tour the country each winter and spring in regional URTA auditions at various major cities. Their job is to screen potential students for their schools, and nationwide they watch over 1,200 auditions of recent college graduates who are hoping to pursue professional acting careers at their institutions. Candidates must "pass" screening auditions and then final auditions before gaining interviews; the annual auditions are held in New York, Chicago, and (as of this date) San Francisco.

Students selected through the URTA process are eligible to attend the schools who are interested in them with paid graduate assistantships and fellowships. Although the URTA auditions are only an *indirect* avenue to professional employment as an actor, they are *the primary* avenue for receiving the necessary postgraduate training at schools that will equip you for professional work. The vast majority of undergraduates will absolutely require postgraduate training in order to compete effectively for stage roles. Just as doctors and attorneys and stockbrokers need advanced training in their fields before they can practice (medical school, law school, business school), future actors and designers and directors also need postgraduate training.

Although the URTA organization has now expanded to include a number of additional services for employers of union artists, alumni of theatre conservatories, and others, it is still primarily the major avenue for acting students seeking the required training for careers in theatre, film, and television. Put simply, candidates for advanced training can audition at an URTA regional audition for twenty to thirty schools all at the same time, instead of auditioning singly for schools all over the country. Following the audition, representatives of the URTA schools "call back" for interviews those students whose auditions they found "promising" and encourage them to apply to their programs for the coming year.

But URTA auditions are also very selective. In the first place, you must be nominated by a faculty member at your school in order to attend the URTA regional auditions, and there are only a limited number of audition slots available. Faculty are expected to pick and choose from among their best graduating actors in order to decide on the few URTA nominees they send forward from your school. And will you be one of these "chosen few?"

It may come as a shock to some of you to learn that university faculty are under no obligation to recommend every student for advanced work just because he or she has been enrolled as a major in the drama program, taken all the required courses, and received good grades. Unlike high school, that is, there is no need to "pass on" underperforming or average/mediocre drama students. Such students are certainly entitled to graduate with a drama degree, but that degree in no way implies that he or she is likely to succeed professionally in the field.

Additionally, URTA "judges" are very strict in their criticism and selection procedures. Only a few of the very best student-actors receive callbacks at the regional competition, and even fewer students receive offers of acceptance there to the programs they wish to enter. In short, if you find yourself "unacceptable" at any level of the URTA competition, you'll have *no* chance of entering an URTA school, and you'll know that your present skill level is below that of your peers around the nation. Thus, you'll have to take your chances "hitting the streets" in a major city somewhere, taking workshops and classes, and trusting your luck at whatever auditions you can attend or arrange for. Conversely, if you receive *any* callback and offer from an URTA school, you'll know you've at least got enough *talent* to aim for a professional career as an actor. The URTAs, therefore, are an excellent benchmark of success for young actors, and you should strive to be nominated by your faculty as you enter your senior year of college.

What You Can Expect in Auditions for Regional Theatre

By far the most exciting audition and performance experience that you can gain while in high school or college is committing your vacation time to working with professional theatres: summer Shakespeare companies, regional professional theatres, dinner theatres, "summer stock," resort theatres, etc. Or you can "get your foot in the door" at local dinner or regional theatres near your home during the regular academic year when you have the time. This isn't as forbidding as it sounds, and the auditioning challenge is well worth the effort, because the learning value of this sort of experience is incalculable.

What is "regional theatre" exactly? You've probably heard the term before. Well, to begin with it isn't "exactly" any one kind of theatre. As one audition coach describes it:

> Regional theatre is a general term, and not entirely specific. Generally, one uses it to include the spectrum of nonprofit theater companies, sometimes called "resident companies," throughout the country (including the nonprofit theatre companies in New York City) plus commercial dinner theatres and stock companies out of New York ... The nonprofit (or "not-for-profit") sector is of the greatest current importance, and has experienced a meteoric growth in the past generation. [6]

For one thing, you may astound yourself by actually getting paid (or at least be "taken care of") while you act — a shot in the arm for your self-confidence.[7] And second, you'll profit from living and working with people who come from different backgrounds and experience levels. Summer companies and resident (year-round) companies run the gamut from all-amateur (non-union but skilled, experienced, and paid) actors to "semi-professional" (a handful of union actors in a theatre with some level or "tier" of union contract), or fully professional companies.

Depending on the company's non-union or union status (which means how many union actors it must hire, and what the pay scales will be), you can be hired as an actor, actor-technician, apprentice, or intern. Realistically, however, you should expect to be paid little or nothing when you first start out. But in all cases you'll soak up an immense amount of practical know-how from rubbing shoulders with performers more seasoned than yourself.

Finding such professional work, however, is difficult, because there are plenty of actors already out there who have a lot more experience and skills than you do. These theatres certainly know how to find such actors, and their skills are readily identifiable by comparison with yours. Also, a very important difference between auditioning for professional theatres — at any level — and auditioning at your school is that professional theatres are under no obligation to give you an audition. Unlike your school, you haven't paid tuition that entitles you to be seen by the stage directors nor have you been enrolled in a drama program that may have earned you the right to audition.

On the other hand, don't conclude that someone with relatively little experience hasn't a chance. Hundreds of young students are hired every year by summer companies to play major, minor, and walk-on roles required in their shows. And most of these companies don't require that you have professional experience. In fact, some professional theatres have arrangements with the acting union whereby non-union performers can earn their union status ("Equity card") after a few seasons of summer work — a great help for young actors planning to start careers after their university training.

Summer theatre companies hire younger actors for a variety of positions. Probably the most common is that of "actor-technician," which means that you'll also have to do some technical or box office/administrative work in addition to acting. Or you may find that the theatre has several companies for which it's hiring: the major acting company (where you could act in one or more shows, for part or all of a season), a children's theatre company, a promotional show company (malls, special events performances), and so on. Resident professional companies may grant you an audition in order to "keep you on file," because they often need local non-professionals to play walk-ons or minor parts without having to provide accommodations (as they must for visiting professionals) and pay them.

There's a good chance, therefore, that your audition can pay off with an offer to do *something*, and you should try to plug into any of these operations if you can. Scott McMorrow, an actor-playwright who took years to establish himself in the business, puts it this way: "Get experience. University-level experience is great, but more professional theatre companies are looking for work beyond college. This could mean working at low pay/no pay companies, community theatres, and summer stock. A wide variety of this type of experience shows that you can work in different environments." [8]

There are two stages of auditioning to go through in order to land this kind of summer work. The first is setting yourself up for the audition. This is the point at which you must begin to take yourself seriously as a professional performer. You'll usually be required to submit three things in advance: an application form or letter (including a reference or two), a resume, and a photo.

The application is important, because you'll have to secure references from teachers or directors with whom you've worked, and because it will be used to contact you about when and where auditions will be held. Be sure your application is filled out neatly and completely, that your address and phone number(s) are accurately and clearly listed, and that the form is returned with its accompanying documents on time.

Be businesslike and efficient when doing all the necessary paperwork: cover letters, applications, resumes, etc. (see chapter ten). Avoid wordiness and B.S. Recall when you were applying to colleges: choosing which to apply to, getting the paperwork done, keeping records of whom you wrote to and when. Landing work in summer theatres is no different, although normally you will have to submit a resume and photo in advance

Pay special importance to researching the groups for whom you're auditioning and to the professional appearance of your resume and photo. You want to be able to speak intelligently and ask appropriate questions of their staff at the interviews, and appear as dependable and organized as possible on paper, even though you may not have much stage experience. Try to survey all the groups in your area, note the different kinds of plays they produce, check on the financial and housing arrangements they advertise, see where they're located, estimate how much money you'll need to live on, see when their seasons run, etc. Then send your application letters to the ones you like. [9]

This first stage of the auditions process for summer work is extremely important for you, and is one major reason why I strongly recommend summer work for student actors. You'll be surprised, once you've assembled the package and made all the arrangements, how clearly you're able to perceive yourself as a potential actor, and how unthreatening the whole process really is when you proceed in a step-by-step fashion like this. The tryouts may also be at some distance from your school, so there may be some physical and financial effort needed to enter the competition. All of this will improve your self-confidence and strengthen your motivation for doing more and better work onstage!

This is the point at which you'll begin to take yourself seriously as an actor. Once you've accomplished the large amount of busywork involved with setting yourself up for auditions, the world of professional theatre will lose much of its dreaded mystery for you. You'll be able to make progress with your work and your ambitions with greater ease.

The second stage of summer auditions, of course, involves preparing and presenting your audition. *The procedures and purposes for summer theatre auditions are different in two respects from those of educational or community theatre. First, summer theatres are not looking for raw potential, they seek people with specific entertainment skills. Second, you're auditioning in order to be called back; you're not trying out for a part.*

These considerations will affect many areas of your audition. For example, *many directors recommend that you avoid quiet, or "psychologically internalized" scenes and monologs and choose instead those with energy and upbeat liveliness when picking pieces for the general audition.* This can help make your audition stand out from the crowd and may also convince potential employers that you have the ability to project your acting off the stage into an audience often made up of vacationers hungry for diverting entertainment.

You should also be prepared to "tailor" your audition for the kind of group you're auditioning for. A Shakespeare company will want you to present something very different from a dinner theatre organization, and a group that produces a lot of musicals will want to see you doing something very different than a company that specializes in young people's entertainment. [10]

If summer theatre directors like your general audition (and this may very well also include eight to sixteen bars of a song), they'll call you back and interview you. This is where they'll ask you to do a few more monologs in order to see your range or give you something to read from the play they're casting. You should be prepared with other monologs to do just this, and show them what other skills you may possess.[11] The interview is your invitation to speak personally with the auditioners in order to give them a sense of what kind of person you are to work with, how well you may fit into their company, and how much financial support you require. For your part, the interview is a chance for you to learn about the producing group and get a feel for the kind of "management" and artistic staff you may be working for.

Thus, your first audition at summer theatre tryouts should be specific enough to "put you in the ballpark" for the types of shows being cast, as well as general enough to communicate a sense of energy, enthusiasm, and talent. All this will help you to earn a callback. This is very important to remember. "I don't know any actor who's gotten a job from a monolog," Cathy Goedert from Chicago's old St. Nicholas Theatre once remarked to me. She felt that monologs were most useful when they helped to separate talented actors from the crowd: "The more you can show me in two minutes of who you are, the more I can get a sort of instinctive feeling about whether I'd like to spend three weeks working intensively with you, whether we're going to 'click.' And the more you can make me laugh, the better chance you've got of coming back to read for a part." [12]

Sometimes you may be performing at "combined" or "unified" auditions where casting people from several theatres are watching you. This is a difficult and challenging situation, because each of these groups may be looking for different skills, and you won't be able to streamline your monologs for any one group. In this situation you need a couple of vividly staged, contrasting pieces for the general auditions that develop quickly from the outset in order to catch the auditors' attention and also to suggest that you could do more if called back. Show the auditors what you can do with zip, professionalism, and feeling, and you'll greatly increase your chance of winning a callback.

The one exception to this advice for summer theatre auditions is auditioning for a summer company that produces the classics. These theatres, too, are looking for liveliness, energy, and enthusiasm in the general audition but they're also seeking the serious acting skills that enable actors to play challenging and difficult roles from the classical repertoire. Of course, their audition requirements will stipulate the kind of classical material you should prepare for them, in addition to anything else they may require (children's plays, musicals, etc.).

A final piece of advice for you if you decide to seek paid summer work concerns your motivation. *If you audition for a summer theatre company, you should have made up your mind about your commitment to pursue an acting career and be prepared to speak about this during the interview.* Usually summer theatre producers and directors have a lot of people from whom to cast, and a person who's serious about his or her acting work is generally a "safer bet" than one who's merely "testing the water." Remember that summer theatre directors are under intense pressure to get a *marketable* show up in a very short amount of time — something that is never done in community or educational theatre. Such people seek hard workers, dependable actors, and committed artists who are also dedicated to that same goal.

So, let these producers know that you mean business when you apply, audition, and interview, because they mean business also. *Money* is their business, and the possibility of paid work raises the audition stakes exponentially. Be committed to showing up on time, working hard, and delivering the goods they need for a strong production, and you'll increase your chances of getting cast.[13] Also, be sure to send a postcard to the casting people following your audition, a couple of weeks later. This reminds them you're serious about working with them, and it may "jog their memory" a bit while final casting decisions are being made. And remember this to allay your fears: they can only say "no," right? The only thing you have to lose is a job you already don't have, right?

Exploration #4: The ACTF

Divide your class up into two-person teams, each of which investigates the website for the Kennedy Center American College Theatre Festival (ACTF). Each team should go to the section explaining the Irene Ryan acting awards, and note twenty plays approved for scene- and monolog-cuttings for Irene Ryan competitors, which do not need agents' permission to perform. Team members should then visit your school or local library collections to see which of the twenty plays are contained there. If some or all of the plays are not in your libraries, be sure to ask your librarian how you could obtain a copy, how much it would cost you, and how long it would take. You should also make a quick search of commercial booksellers' websites such as Meriwether Publishing Ltd., Amazon, Samuel French, Dramatists Play Service, or Barnes and Noble in order to see if the plays are available there and their cost. Each team could also change their lists by searching out more play titles (maximum of twenty) in order to locate as many as possible that are available locally. Teams then bring their lists of twenty back to the whole class and present the results of their exploration. The team tracking down the largest number of plays that are free and locally available is the winner. Second place should go to the team finding any combination of locally-available and commercially-purchasable scripts.

Exploration #5: Audition Tips and Requirements

Divide your class group into three teams, each of which investigates one of the following websites: The Kennedy Center American College Theatre Festival, the University Resident Theatre Association, and the Actors Equity Association. Each team member should list what he or she regards as the most important audition advice given by each organization, as well as important background information about each organization that has not been mentioned in this chapter. The team then prepares a ten-minute report for the entire class that explains the following:

a. What is the nature of the organization? Its stated mission? Its history? Its perceived importance? Who participates in its activities, and what is the range of these activities? What services does it offer actors?

b. What does this organization recommend as far as auditioning is concerned? What are the requirements (if any)? What sort of "tips" does it provide? Does it refer actors to any "additional sources" for further information? If so, what are they?

c. What sort of costs are incurred by individuals wishing to participate in the activities of this organization? What are the benefits (as far as you can determine)?

Exploration #6: Battle of the Schools

Divide your group into three teams, each of which locates a recent copy of *American Theatre* magazine (not necessarily the same edition). Each group should identify what seem to be two large universities with good reputations advertising their M.F.A. acting training programs. Members of the group should contact the schools by phone or through their Internet websites, requesting an application and information on the program and its entrance requirements. Once your team has these materials, decide which of the schools seems better and why, and then prepare a five-minute report to present to the class, attempting to convince them that the school your team has chosen is the most promising. After each team has made its presentation, debate and discussion should begin among the teams, challenging each other's assertions or defending one's own. The following points should be considered in your team's analysis of the different schools (and your thoughts after completing this exploration should be recorded in your journal).

a. Are all these programs seeking the same kind of student in terms of age, interest, background, etc.?

b. What sort of written requirements (essays, etc.) might be required of an acting student before being accepted? Does a written essay seem appropriate for a student who is interested in performing?

c. Are "guest artists" a part of this program? What about visiting teachers from the professional theatre?

d. How selective do you think this program is, judging from the entrance requirements? Is there an audition required? What type of audition is the school looking for?

e. What are the major "selling points" each program seeks to highlight by its program description? Which one do you think would be of most interest to you?

Exploration #7: Interviewing a Casting Director

Contact a local community, summer theatre, or resident professional stage director in your area and set up a time to meet and interview him or her for thirty to sixty minutes in order to discuss auditioning skills for young actors in your age range. Prepare at least seven questions before you go that you can ask this person, being as concrete and specific as possible in focusing your questions. But also be ready to ask "follow up" questions after receiving some answers during the interview that seem interesting to pursue further, even though you may not have anticipated them among your original seven questions. Be sure to bring a tape recorder with you so you won't forget anything. Then note the following things in your journal:

a. What seemed to be the *major* skills this director is looking for when he or she auditions young actors?
b. What sort of advice can this person offer to young actors like yourself who want to become professional actors or improve their auditioning skills?
c. What were your feelings during the interview — emotionally or intellectually or physically — while in the presence of this person?
d. How well do you think you "carried-off" the interview?

Exploration #8: Unified Professional Auditions

Divide your class into three to four teams, each of which selects one of the groups listed in appendix B under the title, "Major Unified Auditions Centers in the U.S.A." Each of these centers operates a casting service for different types of theatres with various numbers of theatres participating in the casting, and each has different requirements such as fees, audition pieces to select, deadlines, supporting materials to send along, audition locations, etc. Each team contacts the audition center they've chosen, then divides up the information obtained from the center in order to present a report to the entire class describing the type of audition service offered to actors, the requirements, the size, etc. Each team should also write-up this summary of their center and distribute copies of it to everyone in the class, so that at the end of this exploration the entire class has a complete picture of what these professional auditions are like and what they offer.

Exploration #9: Verbal Resume

Write a 250-word prose statement of your theatre experience — one paragraph. Depending upon your experience, highlight your stage roles, your classes and training, your career goals, shows you've been involved in, your major learning experiences, etc. Then practice delivering this "verbal resume" out loud so you can speak it confidently, smoothly, and above all naturally — just like lines from a play! When you have your statement down to sixty seconds, try it out for your drama class and see what they think! Are there things you omitted that they think you should mention? Was it well-memorized so that you could look them in the eye as you spoke and communicate sincerity? Did you sound and look happy and upbeat about your self-description? You can keep practicing this verbal resume at different times throughout your career, because more and more you'll find yourself relying on it when people ask you who you are and what you've done!

Review and Reflection

1. **What are the two major pitfalls to avoid when auditioning in high school?**
   - That you're guaranteed a part no matter how poorly or how well you audition.
   - That the stage director likes you and already knows what you can do, so you can be complacent about getting cast.
2. **What are the major auditioning opportunities for you in high school?**
   - Auditions for stage productions.
   - Participation in yearly festivals for the Thespian Association and the Interscholastic Speech Association.
   - Senior year auditions for college drama programs and drama scholarships.
3. **What are the major features of community theatre auditions that are important for students in high school and college to bear in mind?**
   - The experience will allow you to "test" yourself against other actors who are not "automatically" cast at your school by directors who already know everyone.
   - You may be able to make important contacts for your future performance work by doing community theatre.
   - You may also be able to make money for your acting and related stage work in community theatres.

4. What should you do differently at community theatre auditions than you do at your school auditions?

- Fill out an audition form carefully so your stage experience reads well.
- Observe other auditionees reading scenes, so you can learn what's going on.
- Consider carefully all the performances scheduled for the play to be sure you can make those commitments if you're cast.
- At your general audition, don't try out for a part — try out for a callback.
- Be prepared for the directors to interview you or have you do some improvisations in order to get to know you a little better.

5. What special considerations apply to college and university auditions that may not be found in high schools or community theatres?

- Some universities will have annual auditions for their continuing drama students in order for them to maintain their status in the program.
- Many drama departments only permit drama majors to act in their shows.
- You may be required to prepare and memorize a one- or two-minute monolog beforehand (and/or a song for a musical) and present it at the general tryouts.
- The general auditions may be "closed" to everyone who is not auditioning onstage.
- The auditions may be casting for a new play in its premiere production.
- The director doing the casting may be a guest artist from another theatre.
- You may encounter "pick-up" and "unified" auditions for the first time.
- You'll find the opportunity to compete regionally and nationally for scholarships and graduate training through the Irene Ryan Competition and URTA auditions.

6. What are the major kinds of professional theatres where you could audition and perhaps find summer work while still in school?

- Dinner theatres.
- Resort theatres.
- Theme park entertainments (Disney, Great America, etc.).
- Regional professional theatres.
- Summer festivals.

7. **What important considerations must you keep in mind when preparing for professional summer theatre auditions?**
   - Summer theatres are not looking for raw potential; they seek people with specific entertainment skills.
   - Your resume and photographs should seem as "professional" as possible, even if you haven't much experience to list.
   - You're auditioning in order to be called back; you're not trying out for a part.
   - You should be prepared to "tailor" your audition for the kind of group you're auditioning for.
   - Avoid quiet or "psychologically internalized" scenes and monologs and choose instead those with energy and upbeat liveliness when picking pieces for the general audition.
   - You may be performing at "combined" or "unified" auditions where casting people from several theatres are watching you.
   - You should research the background of the group(s) you're auditioning for in order to speak intelligently and ask appropriate questions about them at the interview.
   - You should be certain about your commitment to pursuing an acting career, and be prepared to speak about this during the interview.

[1] Professional actor and director Tom Markus, in his book *The Professional Actor* (New York: Drama Book Specialists, 1979), p. 34.

[2] "The Goodman School's Dramatic Resurgence," *Chicago Tribune Magazine*, 23 March 1980, p. 35.

[3] High school director and playwright Max Bush, interview with the author, 6 December 2002.

[4] In the San Francisco Bay Area, for example, where I first began my training, some now famous professional theatres began as outgrowths of college drama programs: the Actors Workshop, the Berkeley Repertory Theatre, the Marin and California Shakespeare Festivals, the Magic Theatre, the Berkeley Stage Company, and others.

[5] Strictly speaking, community theatres belonging to the national organization American Association of Community Theatres are not in any way supposed to "compensate" their actors (in keeping with their status as "amateur" or "arts advocate" theatres), although they do compensate their technical, design, artistic, and administrative staff. However, many of these stages do pay actors on a sort of "honorarium" basis, recognizing the costs in time and travel that participants incur in order to act in shows.

[6] Cohen, op.cit., p. 57.

[7] Starting salaries and pay arrangements for summer theatre work vary widely across the nation and from theatre to theatre. They range from simple food and housing arrangements, or college internship tuition credits, or $50–$150 weekly at the low end, to full housing and meals plus hundreds of dollars weekly for playing more demanding roles. Generally, meager pay scales are always negotiable with summer theatres, and they depend upon the size of role in which you're cast and the number of actors the theatre has to support. In no case, however, will you "get rich," and in most cases you'll lose a lot more money doing summer theatre than you're able to earn in a regular "day-job." Summer theatre work is more like an investment in your career, although even a small amount of compensation helps to make it more than just worthwhile.

[8] Internet conversation with the author, 18 April 2002.

[9] Information about summer theatres in your area can be found in several ways. Asking your teachers or community theatre directors can give you a helpful start. Watching the bulletin boards in your university or community theatres during the winter will turn up posters advertising summer companies. An Internet search for your state theatre association will turn up listings of summer theatre producers in your region. The directories found in appendix B can also be valuable.

[10] Remember it is always inadvisable to prepare a scene for summer theatre work from a play that will actually be done by the group you're auditioning for, except when these producers ask you to do so for a callback. You narrow your chances of being cast, because directors may already have cast the larger roles, or else they'll tend to see you in only one part and ignore your potential for other, less important roles.

[11] The famous actress and teacher Uta Hagen recommends that actors have at least thirty pieces ready to go for any occasion, and this is fairly standard among professional working actors. (Chicago acting workshop, 12 February 1982). More realistically, however, you should come to the casting call armed with five monologs. The "basic tools" that all actors should have with them ready to go at all times include: classical comedy and classical tragedy, modern dramatic and modern comic, and a specialty piece that highlights something unique about you.

[12] ATA Region III conference, Chicago, 27 September, 1980, author's notes.

[13] This treatment of professional theatre opportunities is only intended as a thumbnail sketch, "a preview of coming attractions" for you to keep in mind as you progress through your school years. If, however, you're seriously committed right now to auditioning for professional work off-campus, you should read the extensive treatment of this field provided for young actors by Robert Cohen in his book, *Acting Professionally*, op. cit., pp. 53–72. I advise all my students not to try breaking into the field without touching base with Cohen's book, widely regarded as the "Bible" for starting a professional acting career.

Chapter Four

Background Skills
"Cut to the chase!"

You now have an overall understanding of the role that your high school and university education plays in your acting career, and you're also familiar now with what to expect at the various types of auditions you're likely to encounter during your school years. At this point, let's "cut to the chase" and single-out those audition-related skills (your "chops" as actors call them) that you'll need to develop during your educational career — especially those skills that your theatre training program won't automatically develop for you.

Getting the Self-Image Straight

Throughout your acting career, you'll constantly be considering and re-evaluating something very important about your casting ability: "your type." In everyday life, of course, we resist "stereotyping" or "profiling" people, because this implies reducing a complex personality to a few broad strokes in order to make the person easier to deal with. To do this to someone in real life seems insensitive and unfair, and often it leads us into making wrongheaded decisions about people. And we *certainly* resent when it's done to us. But of course we do it all the time, don't we? It's a natural tendency of human nature even though we avoid doing so whenever possible.

In auditioning, however, understanding your type in relation to dramatic characters is a critically important and absolutely necessary skill if you're going to land roles effectively. To "understand type" means to know yourself — your own strengths and weaknesses — and it also means to know what kind of character you're playing, what makes him or her tick.

In high school, for example, you're sometimes called on to play characters far beyond the range of your own age or life experiences; if you've ever had to do this, you know how phony it feels and how difficult it is for spectators to believe in what you're doing and saying. When you get to college, however, the likelihood of this happening is greatly reduced. And when you venture into community or professional theatres, it will almost never happen.

As you increase in experience and skill, you'll find yourself being cast more and more "closer to type." Only when actors become well established, or in productions that have unusual staging, will actors be able to "play against their type" and land roles that ordinarily they wouldn't be considered for.[1] So for the young actor, the question becomes: "What *is* my type? How do directors see me? What kinds of dramatic characters am I good at playing, and what should I audition for?"

As you can see, *"knowing your type" implies two things. It means doing some honest self-appraisal to recognize qualities you already possess that you can use in order to build the character. It also means the ability to analyze a dramatic character from an actor's standpoint and recognize what universal (type) features the part requires.*

Thinking in these terms helps you to distinguish between yourself and the character, to "see" the character as distinct from yourself. If you can do this, then you'll have a clearer sense of how to "get there" and play the role effectively, and you'll certainly have a clearer idea of how to audition for the role in the first place! Take this piece of advice from Elizabeth Wong, playwright, screenwriter, and Hollywood director: "Be realistic. If you look young, use audition pieces that allow you to capitalize on your youth. Use audition pieces appropriate to your style and type. Don't try to show your versatility and don't come in with an audition piece for a forty-year-old woman if you look eighteen years old. It's a waste of my time." [2]

Throughout your school years, therefore, you should be paying attention to this notion of "type" and constantly asking yourself what your own type is. Like it or not, we can all be typed to some degree, and a lot of dramatic characters — even in the classics — are based on types. In fact, this is a handy place to start your thinking about "types," by looking at the ones that appear in plays, films, and TV shows, both historical and contemporary.

You've probably already heard a lot of character types referred to in your theatre studies. Some are centuries-old and well-known such as the "seductive courtesan," the "oily villain," the "braggart soldier," the "pedantic scholar," the "old fool," the "handsome leading man," the "clown," the "young ingénue," and so forth. Today's stage and screen media have produced an even greater abundance of types: the "bimbo," the "company spokesperson," the "stud puppy," the "bad guy," the "news anchor," the "action hero," the "housewife," the "sex queen," the "good cop," the "tough cop," the "Mr. Clean cop," the "young cop," and so on.

Forget whether or not such people actually exist in real life, and forget whether or not you "really are" a certain type; leave those questions to the shrinks and philosophers. Your concern is with the *dramatic presence* of types and how they work. They exist onstage, in films, and on TV. People *watch* them, audiences *recognize* them, writers *create* them. Your job is to play them. What must you do in order to do so?

The main dramatic types that you'll be suited to playing at this stage in your career will be the following: young leading man, young leading woman, ingénue, young lover, fool or clown, the "other" man or woman (either good or bad). Notice that I'm not talking of parts you want to play, but those you actually *could* play, based upon those God-given gifts (mainly emotional age and appearance) that you possess at this point in your life.

In determining your own type and the types of characters you play best, recognize that these are going to change over time as you grow and develop as a person and as more features of your personality come to be expressed. So you've got to stay on top of this notion of type and constantly re-examine your range. As one young Chicago-based actress remarked to me (when she turned thirty): "Ninety-five percent of young women think of themselves as ingénues, and believe they're going to play ingénues the rest of their lives. That ain't what's happening! Heck! I can't play an ingénue any more, and I probably won't even grow into my face until I'm at least thirty-five!" [3]

Another huge influence on you will be the range of plays, films, and TV shows to which you're exposed. We learn "to see ourselves as others see us" by our viewing habits, because we automatically compare ourselves with the characters in those media fictions.

So in the exercises that follow, be prepared to spend more than a couple of hours on each exploration and then simply shelving it. Plan instead to return to these exercises on an ongoing basis in order to refresh your self-image, your sense of who you are and what you can do best. And a word of caution here: resist the temptation to psychoanalyze yourself as you move through the following explorations, because theatre ain't therapy, it's communication. Leave therapy to the therapists, and keep your eye fixed on portraying characters. This way you'll begin to learn how to use yourself more effectively in playing a role.

Exploration #10: Adventures in the Boobtube, Part One

In the left margin of your journal, write the names of four or five characters in your age range (and your same gender) from TV sitcoms that you enjoy watching and that you think you could "play" if given half a chance! Watch a current episode or two of that sitcom and quickly scribble-down a single "one-liner" from that character during the course of the episode that strikes you as especially effective, expressive of that character's "personality," or funny or well-timed (a "typical" remark). Now practice that one-liner yourself, combined with a simple physical action (not necessarily the same one from the show) that takes no longer than sixty seconds to perform. Your physical action should contain a beginning-middle-end, such as walking onstage/sitting down/delivering the line; or sweeping the floor/looking up/hitting the line/continuing to sweep. Be sure that you perform the physical action "in character" the same way that you speak the line "in character." If you're successful, the class should be able to guess the identity of the character just from the physical and vocal "type" you were able to create! Then in your journal, note the degree of success you had with your classmates and how easy or difficult it was to accomplish this. Do you think you could "play the role" for a full twenty-two minutes plus commercials? For an entire season? How might that change your "real personality"?

Exploration #11: Adventures in the Boobtube, Part Two

In the left margin of your journal, write down four or five characters in your age range (and your same gender) from TV commercials that you think you could "play" if given half a chance! Study these commercials, and quickly scribble-down a single "one-liner" from that character during the commercial (if the character speaks) that strikes you as especially descriptive of him or her (a "typical" remark). If the character doesn't speak, note the physical action, pose, or gesture (usually demonstrating the product) that he or she performs which really types him or her, and invent a line that the character might speak. Now practice that one-liner and/or physical action/gesture/pose yourself, using the actual product from the commercial. (It helps to choose "simple" products like food, beverages, cosmetics, etc., that are easily obtained for this exercise.) And find some clothes, too, similar to the character's costume on the TV. Bring it into class and perform it, being sure that it lasts at least sixty seconds (you might have to invent a few actions or an entrance/exit to meet this time requirement). If you're successful, the class should be able to identify the character and the product even before you demonstrate it. Group discussion should follow on "character types" and how damaging or useful they are. And your journal should record your impressions of this exploration following the presentation.

Exploration #12: The Outside Eye

Select four people in your life: one a parent or other family member, one a close friend, one a boyfriend/girlfriend or "authority figure" of some kind, and one a near-stranger whom you've recently encountered. Now write one or two sentences in your journal about each in which you try to "typecast" that person, as though you were describing him or her briefly and quickly to a stranger. Then write a second couple of short sentences from each, describing how that person probably regards you — whether or not he or she really sees you as a type. In fact, you may want to phrase these sentences in the actual words that person might really use to describe you in a nutshell! This second part of the exploration will be much more difficult to write than the first, and you must be brutally honest with it: try very hard to "see yourself as others see you" and to write in their own words! Don't worry, that person will never actually read what you've written, so you don't have to "censor" your thoughts (or theirs!) by being polite or diplomatic. Just write it the way that person probably actually would say it to himself or herself if one were being honest.

Exploration #13: Frankenstein

You know the story of Frankenstein — the guy assembled by the mad scientist out of body parts stolen from corpses? Like Frankenstein was a collection of a dozen people? Well, in this exploration you're going to become such a Frankenstein by asking about a dozen people to "type" you in a sentence or two, and you're going to write these impressions in your journal and learn how others tend to regard you. *That* will be Frankenstein: a picture of you drawn from a dozen other people. (This is an exercise you should do at least every year or every time your circle of friends and acquaintances changes in some significant way.) But of course, people are never going to be honest about saying these things to your face, so you have to devise an *anonymous* way for them to do so. This is where the fun comes in! For example, have them all use one of the school computers to write out their type-casting descriptions, and then you won't know which of them word-processed which. Or have them write out their sentences and give them to an outside person to type-up for you. Again, anonymity can be preserved. And be sure these dozen people (or more if you want!) are a range of individuals: friends, enemies, teachers, coaches, family, strangers, etc. I guarantee these pages of your journal will be an eye-opener for you, but remember not to take *all* the comments seriously. Some of them (like from "enemies") are bound to be biased. And as we all know, nobody really understands us, do they?

Exploration #14: Life Studies for Type

You've probably heard the term "life studies" that artists use for their work. In acting, these are observations and imitations of people, animals, and objects discovered in the student's environment. The great Russian acting teacher Stanislavski advised life study exercises frequently, urging his actors to imitate the speech patterns, physical traits, gestures, etc. of people they could observe and study in real-life situations. "Take your models from life," was one of his most famous sayings. In this exploration, practice your understanding of types by going to some public place where you can find a number of strangers from different walks of life. Bus stations, airports, malls, and parks are always good for this kind of work. After observing passersby (discretely) for about a half an hour, select four strangers who seem very different from each other and observe them especially closely for awhile. This might even require that you follow them around unobtrusively for a bit as you observe them. (Be careful about stalking!) Then write a short paragraph about each that tries to "type" them in some kind of nutshell form. Perhaps you can imagine yourself "giving a police report" of a criminal you happened to observe or "telling your friends about the weirdo" you ran into. Your type-description might also include snatches of conversation involving the subject that you were able to overhear or descriptions of some unique aspect of "body language" you observed — anything that helps to define that person as a type. Then bring your journal to class and report what you've turned up. Remember: truth is stranger than fiction!

In order to place this discussion of "types" into a final perspective, you have to remember at all times that the character you play onstage is never a character, it's *you*. In fact, in my acting classes and workshops I rigorously avoid coaching students as "you" or as "the character." I address them at all times by their character-names, because the actor *is* the character.

Actors don't create some "character" who is separate and apart and different from themselves; *they become the characters they play by using themselves in the role.* And this is where your understanding of character types becomes extremely valuable. Once you begin to recognize essential traits in the playwright's character that you must bring to life, you'll be better able to infuse them with your own personality, energy, passion, and life. And in an audition situation — particularly with "cold readings" — you'll be able to seize upon these dominant character traits very quickly and play them boldly.

Acting, you see, is one of the few professions in which your *professional* advancement and success are going to be directly related to your *psychological* growth as a human being. As the famous Israeli movement coach, Moshe Feldenkrais, points out:

> The majority of people in each generation stop growing with sexual maturity when they are considered to be adult and feel themselves adult. Most learning achieved after that involves essentially what is important socially, and personal evolution and growth are mostly accidental or a fluke … Only artistically-inclined people, be they cobblers, musicians, painters, sculptors, actors, dancers, and some scientists continue to grow personally as well as professionally and socially … by dint of the art. [4]

All the arts function in this way, because every art object — a painting, a piano sonata, or a player's performance in a role — is in some crucial way an expression of the artist's own sensibilities. It's gotta be! It doesn't work any other way! A performer "filters" his or her experience of the play and the character by the way he or she sees it. This implies personal values and judgment in selection, emphasis, and communication to the audience. Thus, your unique personality is your sounding-board, *your instrument is yourself* — body, mind, emotions. The playwright wrote it, but you render it. Your "art" can only be as good as "your instrument" can make it.

Students don't often think of acting in this personal way. Our admiration of a film or stage performance may disguise itself as due to the writer's skill, the makeup and scenic artists' wizardry, the technical abilities of the director or editor, or even the actor's voice, body language, physical skills, or appearance. Or else we may confuse the actor with the character he or she is playing and just blow it off: "Well, she's type cast, of course. Easy enough for her to do." But if you stop to think about it for a moment, you have to admit that underneath all these features of live performance there's something much more fundamental working on our judgment: admiration and appreciation of a human being's ability to successfully create such a strong illusion for us.

We are fascinated by the double-natured phenomenon onstage of the performer as a person and, at the same time, as a dramatic character. And this is why you must learn to analyze yourself in order to feel relaxed and natural exhibiting yourself before the critical eyes of spectators. ***You must feel comfortable using yourself and thus being vulnerable in auditions.*** Just as you criticize other actors and read them into the roles they play, so too the auditioners will try to read between the lines of your audition in order to learn things about you as a person. This is what brings "characters" to life, this is what we want to see, and you must be unafraid to use yourself in order to do it.

What this means in terms of auditioning is that each time you read for a role, you've got to be aware that your first reaction will probably be a defensive one. You'll often seek to throw-up "a character" instead of yourself. This is a common pitfall even for professionals who often attempt to use a character as a mask behind which to hide and disguise themselves. (Ever hear of someone "playing a role?") It's important for you to begin early in your career to avoid this bad habit by realizing that *you can play only yourself!*

It is this *combined* self — you *in* the role — that the auditors want to see! It is this "naked you" that makes live stage acting so thrilling: to be actually in front of that process as it's happening is almost like witnessing a holy or spiritual moment! The celebrated actor Eric Bogosian once remarked about this process that "my work is about my taste or style as an artist. It is a function of the way I see things, and so it's about the way I choose to act ... **What I make is unique to who I am."** [5]

This is never easy to do, but it's absolutely essential for good acting and dynamite auditioning. As one professional coach in southern California complains: "The fear that what you feel and express onstage will be taken personally, and yourself held responsible for it, stops most actors. They hide behind the lines and the character, and if it gets hot, they cop out by saying, 'That isn't me. That's the character!' There is only you. There is no character. The character is you." [6] The same fear stops a lot of ordinary people, too, believe me! They'd rather have their guts ripped out than ever get onstage or in front of a camera, because then people might see them as they really are! They're afraid to "use" themselves.

Jane Brody, a Chicago casting agent and Shurtleff-method teacher, constantly reminds students of how successful film actors are at using themselves: "Those aren't 'characters' you see on the screen," she remarked to me. "They're people, actors who use and reveal themselves. It's Robert Duvall and Gene Hackmann and Al Pacino and not a 'character'." [7] *From the writer's and audience's standpoint* when watching the film, the actors are characters; *from the actors' standpoint,* they are never "characters" but always themselves or parts of themselves.

A final warning about "playing characters" from one of our foremost modern directors, Charles Marowitz: "When people denounce a performer for 'playing himself,' what they are really condemning is his basic shallowness and lack of personal resources … The crime is not acting oneself, but not having enough of oneself to act." [8] Take this lesson to heart: learn what your strengths are as an actor, what character types you are best at playing, and don't be afraid to *use* those personal traits and strengths when you present your audition. The casting directors don't want a cardboard cutout that anyone can play: they want a unique portrayal that only you can play!

Exploration #15: Your Favorite Movie Actors

Divide a page of your journal into three columns. Select four screen actors you admire and enjoy seeing, and list them in the left column. In the second column, list all the films you can call to mind in which those actors played. Then in the third column, using the film titles as a guide, try to identify in a sentence or two the special qualities those actors brought to their screen roles that made the characters seem "alive" and most interesting. What seemed to be the dominant "drives" or "types" of characters that those actors were able to capture? Note also below the columns whether or not you found this exploration easy or difficult to accomplish? Can you "type" a complex character effectively? Do you think that an actor's ability to grasp the "type" of character is really any help in building up an effective portrayal? What would happen, for example, if an actor made the decision to play a different "type" for this character? Could the character "work" when played "against type"? What does this mean exactly? Sharing your "thumbnail sketches" of famous actors with the class is bound to generate a lively discussion!

Exploration #16: Role-Playing and Role-Playing

Select any of the monologs contained anywhere in this book for practice and class exercises, and memorize the first ten to fifteen seconds of the opening, attempting to deliver the words as sincerely and expressively as possible, given what you believe to be the character's situation. For purposes of this exploration, reduce all your physical stage movements (blocking) to a minimum, concentrating instead on the sincerity of the statement, your belief in the dramatic situation, and the character's mood while speaking. If possible, observe yourself in a full-length mirror while doing this in order to keep it physically simple and uncluttered. Once this has been well memorized, rehearsed, and set — physically and vocally — prepare an introductory statement for yourself to add to it, as follows: "Hello! I'm Jane Brown. Today I'd like to present to you a selection from John Doe's play, *Here Is the Name of the Play*." Now connect your introductory statement to the monolog you've just rehearsed, *trying to represent your true personality as sincerely as possible, in contrast to the dramatic character you're about to enact.* Practice this with a simple entrance where you come before the class or actually onstage, introduce yourself and your piece to the group, and then turn your back to the group for one or two beats before beginning the "character monolog." Did you succeed? Did the class "see" two different "characters" onstage? Note in your journal whether this was difficult or easy to accomplish. Did the exercise make you feel that your real name and purpose actually sounded somewhat phony? Or did "the character" become phony? Maybe *neither* was phony? Did you truly feel you were giving the class "the real you" or "the important you" before the character monolog? Did the two blur? Were they both sincere?

Getting the Voice in Shape

In speaking with theatre people across the country while gathering material for this book, the single piece of advice I heard most frequently was that *auditionees need to understand and fully play each and every word in their monolog or scene.* There is absolutely no substitute in this business for the ability to become skilled with literary analysis. You *must* understand and feel what you're saying, and you absolutely *must* get started on this while in school. Unlike many other professions you could choose, you certainly won't be able to mumble your way through an acting career.

Remind yourself that our society has conditioned you to use an extremely narrow range of your vocal and verbal resources. In fact, most people get along just fine in life with a pathetic vocabulary of less than 5,000 words! But a successful actor in stage and screen needs about 100,000. The impact of TV and film has certainly contributed much to the dumbing-down of society and impoverishing everyone's speaking abilities. Electronically controlled audio tracks, hypervisual emphases, blurted thoughts, pedestrian hack-writing — remind yourself that this is what you were raised on and what you must overcome if you're going to succeed as an actor.

In fact, there are a lot of influences in modern society — advertising, radio, talk shows, comics, news programs, Internet chatrooms, cartoons — that induce us to speak in half-sentences and clichés and to rely on language that is no more complicated than that needed to order lunch at McDonald's. But people don't come to the theatre or watch films to hear that sort of drivel; they can turn on their radio or their tube for free when they want to park their brains and relax. Remember that stage and screen actors must command a wide range of literary styles, both classical and contemporary, in order to make sense of what they're saying and to express the inner motivations and drives of often very complicated characters.

Don't fall into the trap of assuming that only boring teachers and school kids engage in literary analysis. And don't be so naïve as to assume that the dialog in plays and films like *Lord of the Rings, Hamlet, Interview with a Vampire, Art*, and others can be approached in the same way as an episode from *Days of Our Lives* or *Sex in the City*. Language takes a lot of practice and a good actor can take a phrase — from Shakespeare or *Titanic* or George Bernard Shaw — and wrap a half-dozen meanings around it in the snap of a finger until he or she gives the casting director what's wanted. That takes skill and training, and you've got to be "word-friendly" in order to do it.

There are three places to concentrate your attention while in school in order to develop good speaking habits and become word-friendly: broadening your exposure to information drawn from many different fields of human experience, paying attention to the structure and mechanics of language and sound in English, music, and foreign language classes, and general background reading in fiction and literature. Let's take a look at how you can use each and make the best use of your time during school years.

Many people in professional theatre and in film have pointed out to me *the value to an actor of a liberal arts background in science, history, psychology, and other fields.* When you get to college, of course, you'll actually be required to take approximately a third of your courses in disciplines outside your major field in order to become "well rounded" (conversant with many different fields of human understanding). So don't think for a moment that after completing the general range of subjects in high school, you can blow-off all of that forever: math, science, social studies, English, arts, history, and all the rest.

In fact, if you stop and think for a moment of the range of characters in about a dozen of your favorite films, I'm sure you'll turn up a good number of them that required fairly specialized knowledge by the actor of that character's occupation, background, working environment, frame of mind, speech pattern, etc. I'm speaking of people like lawyers and doctors and computer scientists and psychiatrists and lab technicians and others (some of the most frequently-seen characters in films and TV). How can you ever expect to play *any* of these roles without some basic understanding of where those people come from — their education, knowledge, and training?

Can you see what I'm getting at here? If an actor is to constantly portray characters different from herself or himself, then she or he has got to have some "handle" for entering into that character's life and personality. And at an audition, you can do that quickly by keying-into a character's language. Liberal arts courses and a broad educational background come in very handy for making that leap of the imagination. Try the following exploration and see what you turn up.

Exploration #17: Tube Life

Check the current issue of *TV Guide* magazine and note the top ten shows currently running, then tune in to three of them and watch an episode from each. In the left margin of a journal page, write down as fast as you can the names of the speaking characters, principals as well as minor ones. Then beside each name note that character's occupation, background, or special identifying characteristics. After the show, fill-in the page with guesses about how much technical information each of those different actors had to speak or how much background prep or "life study" the actor might have done to portray his or her role effectively. Some characters, of course, require no *specialized* background training in order to portray them: extras on the street, students, bimbos, thugs, postmen, delivery boys, taxi drivers. Others, however, do require that the actor have some familiarity with official reports, medical procedures, legal terminology, and even the "thought processes" of people like detectives (who must understand forensic science), psychologists (who must be comfortable with speaking about jargon-laden definitions and pathological conditions), and computer technicians (who are constantly trying to explain the arcane things they do to people they regard as computer-illiterates). Bring *your* list and its important conclusions into class and compare it with those of the other students, asking yourselves the question: if someone handed me a page of dialog for that character and gave me five minutes to look it over before presenting my audition with it, would I be able to pull it off? Would I stand a chance of sounding natural, relaxed, and at home in this character's TV environment?

Exploration #18: Screen Life

Follow the same procedure as in the exploration above, except that the subject this time will be three of the top ten films currently playing. Avoid "stacking the deck" here by choosing three very similar films; instead, pick three films in different styles, countries, or historical periods. And don't "cheat" by selecting a currently running film that's an adaptation of a stage play, classic or otherwise. We all know that classic stage roles require a lot more background research and preparation than contemporary ones. Keep all your selections contemporary. And avoid watching these on your boob tube with DVD or VCR — see them larger than life in a theatrical screening. Once again, I'm sure you'll turn up at least a dozen actors who stand out by their abilities to portray characters who are far removed from the actor's own life and circumstances. And ask yourself what "background study" or "inside information" the actor might have used to help him or her with the role. In fact, you might also uncover actors whom you think did a poor job with the role because of the lack of such preparation. For example, did an actor absolutely fail to convince you of her social status, because she didn't seem to know how to wear the unusual costumes — skimpy or elaborate — of the character she was portraying? Or when he opened his mouth, did the actor sound like he was in a Burger King commercial or sitcom instead of a person from a very different social class or occupational background? When you compare your conclusions this time with others in your class, you're probably going to encounter a wider range of opinions than in the previous exploration simply because films, for the most part, seek out more original characters than TV, which relies more heavily on contemporary social stereotypes.

The second area upon which you need to concentrate while in school is — Oooh! Aauugh! — language study, literature, and music. Yes, that's right, English and singing classes. But also foreign language study. For example, if you can diagram sentences and understand the syntax of your monolog — its complicated arrangement of principal and subordinate clauses, modifiers, parenthetical remarks, etc. — then you're way ahead of the game. You'll know how to handle both good writing and bad when it comes to auditions, and you'll be able to grasp those mechanics quickly.

For one thing, *you need to become skilled with speaking dialog in order to do a good audition*. Directors are quick in judging your ability to handle spoken language, because it's not something that you can fake. You must show the casting director that you can speak with confidence, whether you're called upon to read the witty plays of Oscar Wilde from the 1890s or "fill in between the lines" of a thinly-written soap opera. As one actor-director remarked to me: "After all, you've only got yourself and the word up there at an audition. You've got to tear that monolog apart word-for-word and make friends with each and every idea, identify with the images and the emotions — what Stanislavski called 'the diction' — fall in love with those words and make sense of them." [9]

A second thing that English language study can help you with (perhaps in combination with classes in oral interpretation and forensics) is proper pronunciation. I don't just mean whether or not people can understand you. You must certainly be understandable or you wouldn't have lived this long, right? I'm talking about *proper* pronunciation that's free of regional dialects, personal habits (like slurring of consonants, dropping word-endings, nasal tones, mumbling, monotone speech, etc.) — all those things that, like coral polyps gradually building up reefs in the ocean, have come to color your speech patterns in order to produce someone who talks differently from the rest of us.

Why is this important? Well, for one thing, it's distracting. When we watch TV or attend a play, we want to listen to what you're saying — not wonder where you got that funny pronunciation. And you really need to think seriously about this, because it's hard for you to be objective about the way you talk. Your present speech habits seem "natural" to you, so what's the big deal? Well, here's a suggestion from Louis Felder, a thirty-year veteran Hollywood actor in commercials, films, TV, and theatre (and who also directs productions for the American Academy of Dramatic Arts in L.A.):

> ... the most important ingredient for a successful career in theatre (and film and TV) is the ability to speak. Most students cannot speak Standard American speech ... I was talking to a casting director the other day and she said, looking out at a room of gorgeous models: "They're all beautiful, but they all grunt." I could go on for hours (and pages), but tell your students to work with a tape recorder, listen to yourself, develop your ear, let your voice reflect what you are thinking about. Most students will not do this, because they hate the sound of their own voice. I ask if they check their reflection in the mirror before they go onstage and they all say yes. But when I ask if they checked the reflection of their voice (tape) they say no. Voice, speech, hearing, it is essential. And, if an actor can speak, he will be a standout today, believe me. [10]

Next on the list of your studies should be foreign languages. Why foreign language, you may ask? Well, duuuhh! Do we live in a culturally diverse society, or what? How many Hispanics or eastern Europeans or others have you seen on TV and in films recently? Those roles are out there, and they certainly abound in plays. More importantly, if you can get your brains and tongue around one or more languages besides English, *you'll be much better equipped to handle dialects!* Foreign language skills are a sensational form of intellectual and vocal calisthenics.

Go back to the explorations above and re-do your list of characters with different TV shows and films in order to turn up actors who had to express themselves in street jive, regional dialects (southern, New York, southwest American, etc.), speech impediments, foreign accents, etc. in order to build their characterizations. Do you think those speaking abilities came naturally to the actors? Or were they cast for their ethnic or regional backgrounds? Forget that — they were probably cast because of their talent first and foremost and also because their resumes listed several dialects under "special talents" and the casting director checked them out before they were cast.

In the case of feature films, actors will often have to immerse themselves in the culture and the dialect before shooting begins or hire a vocal coach. Just read-up on what people like Jack Nicholson, Katherine Turner, Nicolas Cage, Al Pacino, Julia Roberts, Noah Wylie, and others do in order to portray some of their most famous roles. You'd be surprised! And all of this vocal work will come so much more easily to you later on if you've trained your brain while in school to handle the different sounds, pitch patterns, pronunciations, pauses, and other features that characterize our own and foreign languages.

This isn't the easiest recommendation to follow, I know, because English and foreign language courses require a lot of brain work. By the time you graduate from college, you ought to have a mastery of at least four principal dialects in order to audition well: British, Cockney, Brooklyn, and American Southern. It's hard, I know, but the payoff here is huge, because an ability to handle many different kinds of "language" will be one of the strongest features that set you off from your competitors when it comes to an audition.

So knuckle-down in your English Lit classes and challenge yourself to get on top of every piece of writing that comes your way. When the stage manager hands you a script to look over at the auditions, you're not going to tell her, "Sorry, this is too hard to read. Gimmee something more up my alley."

The following exploration is probably the single most important self-training exercise that you can practice every day in order to audition well!

Exploration #19: Reading Aloud

For at least twenty minutes each day of your life, go someplace where you can be alone without anyone hearing or distracting you, and read aloud. You can and should do this indoors and out. You can and should choose everything possible to read that you can lay your hands on: cookbooks, newspapers, textbooks, the stock reports, the telephone book, fairy tales, *War and Peace*, computer manuals, product assembly instructions, Hamlet, cereal boxes, the Bible, this audition book, etc. This should be material that you've never seen before. As you grow more skilled with this exploration, you can concentrate just on different types of dramatic material (comedies, tragedies, melodramas, classical, contemporary, etc.). Practice holding the pages in one hand and reading aloud with expressiveness, energy, and animation. You need to pay special attention to several things while doing this. First, you need to *learn to read smoothly, fluently, and without hesitation.* Struggle to get your tongue around difficult and unfamiliar words, and look up jargon and technical language in a dictionary with pronunciation until you can master the text like a pro. Once you've gotten on top of that, try to *look up from the page as you read,* by training your eye to scan ahead a few words or phrases, and by moving your thumb down the page as you read in order to keep your place. Also learn to hold your script away from your face and somewhat to the side. These techniques will enable you to establish eye contact with your acting partner when auditioning. Third, you also need to *move and gesture as you read* so you don't become a talking head at auditions. Finally, *memorize the first and last lines* as you become more skilled, a technique that will greatly help the impression you make at cold reading auditions. Do this exploration religiously every single day and I guarantee that your auditioning will show an immediate improvement, especially as you apply yourself to other reading-related courses in English, foreign language and literature, and the liberal arts.

To reiterate, reading aloud is one of the best training exercises you can do to improve your audition technique while in school. You can do it on your own, and your teachers should also include this sort of practice in all your theatre classes. *Related to the need to read well at auditions is the ability to memorize.* Naturally, actors know how to do this when performing a play, but being able to memorize quickly in an audition situation will help you in theatre, film, TV, radio — just about any acting medium you eventually go into. Here's a piece of advice from William Paul Steele who has acted in many stage productions, as well as hundreds of films and videos. He's talking especially about the importance of memorization skills even for actors in technical media:

How do you get to Carnegie Hall? Practice, practice, practice. In *Stay Home and Star* I urged aspiring actors to practice reading aloud. It's probably the single most important preparatory activity in which you can engage ... Finally, you'll need to practice *memorization* so that you can accomplish this chore as efficiently as possible. Even with such technological advances as teleprompters and earprompters, the call for memorization is still great, particularly in dramatic situations. Most directors prefer not to use prompters of any kind for dramatic pieces, rightly believing that a memorized performance will be better — stronger, more natural, and more convincing. [11]

Need I belabor the point of how important it is to *enroll in singing courses whenever you have room in your academic schedule? Or to join choral singing groups (if you have a good voice and enjoy singing a lot)?* This is the next thing on your "must study" list.

The point of voice lessons is not to make a professional singer out of you (although your music teachers may want to do that!). If you're heading into musical theatre, of course, you'll need a lot of singing training. But the point of music training for every actor is to train your voice and keep it in shape. If you already have a good voice and like to sing, then you're miles ahead. It really doesn't matter what sort of a choral group you want to join at your high school or university: gospel, glee club, jazz, bel canto, hip-hop, opera, pop, madrigal, sacred. No matter. Just be sure to keep developing your voice on a regular basis, and build up your sight reading skills.

Voice classes, on the other hand, are also important, particularly if you're not a born singer. One-on-one coaching can be invaluable for the student who's not quite right in pitch, who needs to start learning sight-reading techniques and proper breathing. Here's an instance to keep in mind: the human voice is capable of reaching at least three octaves in range, but we rarely use even one octave in daily conversation. So train your voice in pitch, inflection, enunciation, volume, and control, because it ain't gonna matter how much you know about the script if you speak like a chump! And the earlier you begin voice training, the better.

The third and final area upon which you need to concentrate while in school is possibly the most enjoyable of all: reading historical novels. Yes, I said novels! And I don't mean renting the DVD version of *Out of Africa* or *War and Peace* or *Pride and Prejudice* as a substitute for reading the book. I mean the actual book, because a film adaptation is always a "reduction" of the book and will fail to acquaint you with the important dimension of language. As I mentioned in the previous chapter, "background videos" (especially from earlier historical periods) are valuable, too, but you'll find far more novels available than media adaptations.

The importance of reading novels can hardly be overestimated for the actor. First, a novel will supply you with *background research into other lives and times* that can be enormously helpful when preparing a role. The novelist has done all that research work on places, manners, fashion, and social conventions for you! Second, a good novelist can *pique your imagination with words* — just what you want to do with your audience! Third, novels are *strongly story-oriented*, and an actor is nothing if he or she is not a storyteller! Finally, historical novels — especially those written by past authors — are another valuable avenue for engaging language in a very different form than what you've been used to.

Of course, I'm sure that your studies in English (and possibly also in foreign languages and literature) will introduce you to novel-reading. Unless your teachers are hopelessly enamored of the modern as opposed to the classics, you'll likely get a good dose of writers like Dickens, Austen, Thackeray, Melville, Conrad, Hawthorne, Twain, Hemingway, and others. Don't miss out on the fun of spending time with the greatest (and often the most popular!) authors the world has ever known.

Take novels on trips or to bed or on the bus with you, and stuff them in your backpack. Let these books quicken your mind and fire your imagination, escaping the humdrum and the everyday and journeying instead to places you've never encountered before. *A lot* of what you'll be doing as an actor will take place in former historical periods and in societies and social relationships you may never have dreamed of. Let the world's best novelists introduce you to those things. Remember, too, at an audition you're not going to have the time to research the play's background! So be sure that you're doing all you can in your spare time to bring that background with you by reading widely and voraciously whenever you get the chance.

Getting the Body in Shape

From the earliest times in the western world and also in the Far East (places where we have records of the performing arts in human societies), actors have always been skilled in expressive movement.

In a very real sense they were always "actor-dancers." Today, we've lost a lot of this sense of the actor, because the spoken word, since the sixteenth century, has come to dominate our western stages. Thankfully, however, recent research and performance styles have realigned themselves in the West and the East to restore the tradition of the actor's physical expressiveness in the modern theatre, and the pendulum has begun to swing back again.

As you continue your education in high school, and for the most part also in college, you should be careful to avoid making a psychological separation between your voice and your body. Although each of these skill areas tends to be taught "mechanically" in separate classes, there is a fundamental unity to them that you should never ignore. Of course, temporarily isolating the voice or the actor's movement skills for training purposes can and does produce valuable results in educational settings. Like a well-designed watch whose pieces may be disassembled for cleaning or repair, however, those two skill areas must eventually be put back together and function as a whole for the actor.

I suppose that young actors in high school and college tend to ignore voice and body training either because they're lazy or because their educational programs fail to include them. At most, you're going to have some sort of physical education requirement in high school, but that's about it. And a lot of young people believe that dance is for girls or fairies or that mime is for weirdo groupies (especially in high school). So there are definitely social attitudes you've got to ignore when it comes to training your voice and body.

But the need for early training in vocal-physical expressiveness is certainly great. As a university teacher, I spend most of my time "peeling away" from my students bad vocal and movement habits that have been allowed to develop for years and years, before the basic work of "re-training" could begin. And when it comes to directing plays that call for a lot of acting skills — musical theatre (acting/singing/dancing), Shakespeare (acting/singing/dancing/combatives), Greek drama (acting/choral chant/dancing) — I'm hard-pressed to find students with the vocal-physical skills that are up to the task.

Theatre has an expression called the "triple threat": actors who can play scenes, dance, and sing (without looking like they're killing themselves onstage). "You really have to be a triple-threat performer to get anywhere these days," remarked Kirk Frederick, San Francisco producer/director of Cameo Productions. "Try not to allow your students to get too artsy-fartsy about the kind of acting they do in college or they'll find themselves very limited when they get out and start looking for work." [12] And speaking for many, many directors of "straight" plays I know (myself included), I have to gag myself at auditions every time I find myself looking at yet another actor who's no more than a talking head: no movement, no gestures, no body energy, no physical characterization skills at all. Believe me, the expressive actor rules, the others drool.

Let's look closely at the kinds of physical training you should look to acquire for yourself, on campus or off. *There are three general areas: physical conditioning, dance, and specialty physical courses/workshops in areas like mime, martial arts, combatives, and circus.*

Physical conditioning means simply staying in shape. *You need regular, vigorous exercise, serious attention to weight control, and muscle toning.* Probably the best all-around activities for accomplishing these goals are swimming or running. Becoming a "regular" at your school gym is also very useful because of the variety in workouts that a gym can provide: running, free weights, weight machines, bicycles, rowing machines, and stair machines. Of course, two other advantages that gyms provide are trainers and the ability to isolate certain muscle groups for intensive work. Avoid becoming involved in your school athletic teams because of their time-consuming activity schedules.

Most young actors have little idea of how much energy it takes to do a show, perhaps because acting onstage seems so lifelike and natural (from the audience's standpoint). But if you've ever done a musical production you know how physically exhausting some kinds of productions can really be; if you've ever done a major role in a straight (non-musical) play where you've had to be onstage a lot of the time, then you know how much energy it takes to sustain your concentration and vocal abilities. Nervousness, tension, and concentration required in doing any kind of play requires a lot of energy, and the best way to be ready for that is to keep yourself in good physical condition.

Auditions are especially demanding in terms of the energy they require. You have a lot of stage fright and nervous tension at work in an audition situation. Also you normally have a lot of waiting around for your few minutes of stage time, so it's a situation that can sap the energy you came with. When you're called upon to read, you'd better have some energy reserves on tap in order to give the audition everything you've got. I'm sure you know what I mean when I remind you that it's hard to be creative and "hot" in a monolog or scene if you're strung out and feeling dumpy to begin with. Your body is an energy machine — the only one you've got. So keep it tuned and keep it full; the energy must be ready on tap when you call for it.

Two final reminders about staying healthy: when you become run down and strung out, your body is vulnerable to sickness and disease. Keep fit, avoid controlled substances and late-night partying, and take care of yourself. And if you are ill, never use that as an excuse to cut classes or rehearsals. Come to class and rehearsal anyway, in order to observe, to stay connected with the group, and to keep up as much as you can with the work.

Second, *your physical condition is a reflection of your artistic condition.* If people regard you as fat and slovenly, slow-moving and dumpy or if they perceive you as gaunt, anorexic, and strung out, then you'll have a very difficult time overcoming those first impressions at an audition. In short, you'll be type-casting yourself for fat and dumpy or starving and strung-out roles. And those ain't the exciting roles we want to see onstage or anywhere else.

Dance is the second area of training you need to nail-down in your school years. Like training your voice, starting early to train your body movements will definitely give you an edge in all walks of life and especially in acting. Men are especially challenged in this area, because parents don't normally send elementary school boys to dance classes like they send little girls. So, gentlemen: get out there and make up for lost time! If your high school doesn't offer dance classes, then take them at your local community theatre or dance schools. In college, dance teachers normally welcome all the young men they see in their dance classes, so you'll have little trouble there.

The purpose of dance classes is not to make a professional dancer of you; it's to develop your kinesthetic abilities (sense of movement and physical expressiveness) as an actor. And it really doesn't matter what form of dance you choose to study, although traditionally the best form of dance training has been classical ballet. The regular, disciplined practice with body movement in a dance class will enliven all your physical parts to express and communicate, will stimulate your imagination, will greatly help to keep your body fit and in shape, and may also actually teach you dance skills that are essential for performing certain kinds of roles.

You can develop a lot of sheer physical confidence by taking dance classes. When casting a play I notice a lot of actors distracted as they audition, because they're overcome by the stage fright of being "judged" by a director while reading from a script. They stand frozen in place, or they shift nervously from one foot to another. Their gestures are either nonexistent, limp, or twitchy and scattered — unformed — as they read. And their facial expressiveness is either deadpan or fearfully self-conscious. Regular dance practice will help you overcome all these weaknesses by making you more confident and "at home" in your body while others are appraising you.

A second important audition skill you can learn from dance training is the ability to coordinate all of your body parts and focus your acting. Dance training will help make a lot of your movements intuitive and effective: how to walk across a stage, how to turn and face the audience, how to stand together with someone, how to gesture with more of your body than simply a hand here or a smile there or leaning your torso now and then. On the contrary, you want to animate the ideas and the action you're portraying in the scene physically as well as vocally; dance training will teach you how to physicalize these meanings instinctively. Here's a pearl of wisdom from the great dance/theatre artist Martha Graham: "Through all times, the acquiring of technique has been for one purpose — so to train the body as to make possible any demand made on it by that inner self which has the vision of what needs to be said." [13]

Finally, *dance training can teach you an enormous amount of physical characterization ability.* Too often young actors think of simply building a character psychologically ("What is my motivation?"), without giving any thought to that character's physical and vocal life — without making vocal-physical choices at the audition or in rehearsals. *How does* this character move? *What is* the level of her body energy? *How would* he stand or sit or walk at this moment? *What sort* of body rhythm do her movements display? *What kind* of gestures does he make? *How does* she express her nervousness or fear or bullying or need in this scene?

Dance training introduces you to such things as the physical expression of emotions, the precision of communicating with a gesture, the muscle tone and energy required for executing simple or complex physical actions. And all of these qualities help to define "the character." To be able to quickly seize upon and execute some of these at an audition gives you an enormous edge in being selected for a part, because the director will be able to see you as an actor creating a role rather than as a talking head.

The final area of movement training you should seek out during your school years is work in specific movement skill areas: mime, combatives, circus and clowning, and martial arts. In fact, once you get to college many of these courses or even short-term workshops will be available on campus. Classes and workshops in these areas help you to continue with your general movement training (physical self-confidence, coordination, balance, body fitness) as well as to teach you specific performance-related skills.

Mime is enormously important for an actor, because so much of what you'll be doing onstage is nonverbal! *Combatives* teach you how to slap and get slapped, how to fall down, how to wrestle and struggle, or work with period weapons like daggers, swords, pistols and the like. *Circus and clowning* introduce you to physical comedy, scenario-building and improvisation, mask characterization, and skills like juggling, balancing, acrobatics, tumbling, etc. *Martial arts* will teach you concentration and psychological centering, physical coordination, breathing techniques, physical conditioning, discipline, and self-confidence.

These final explorations aim to help you better appreciate the importance of vocal-physical characterization in your acting and sharpen your awareness of how to physically enliven your auditions. They can be done on your own or as part of a class project with each student reading or performing his or her own work. Be sure to write-up a self-critique in your journal following each of your presentations that not only describes what happened during your performance but also records your personal discoveries along the way to that performance!

Exploration #20: Tube Moves

Turn on two of your favorite TV shows and watch at least three or four half-hour episodes. Be sure these are different genres (comedy, melodrama, soap, detective, etc.) and that you watch the whole show. You should turn the sound off entirely so you can only watch the actors' movements: arm and hand gestures, postures, speed and rhythm, facial expressiveness, timing, etc. This will be very frustrating for awhile, because you'll be constantly tempted to turn the sound back on and follow along with the story, but don't do it! Keep your journal handy and record the following. First, **see how much of the story you were able to understand** just from observing the actors' body language. Second, **note any "special" physical skills** that any of the actors had to do during the episode (fall, fight, physical stunts, dance, etc.). Third, **identify which actors seemed the most physically "alive"** because of their body energy, facial expressiveness, etc. Fourth, **identify which actors seemed the most physically "dead"** because they lacked much expressiveness in their body energy, facial expressiveness, etc. Fifth, **what unusual physical characterizations did you observe?** Did a minor character or even an "extra" suddenly pop-out as a vivid character because of his or her movement? Did the principals seem the most alive or actually the most "dead"? Was there a surprising amount of physical skill needed in this episode than what you had previously thought?

Exploration #21: Screen Moves

This exploration allows you to indulge yourself: visit a movie theatre or else rent a video or DVD of a feature film that you really enjoy, currently running or an oldie. As you watch it (again?) note in your journal the number of times the actors were called upon to perform movement sequences *without dialog*. If it's a film you've seen before, you'll be surprised how much of the actors' nonverbal skills went right over your head — you just never recognized and appreciated them until you actually *looked* for them as part of this exploration! And how expressive they were! How much they contributed to the actor's characterization! But also note in your journal how demanding these physical sequences were: some nonverbal physical actions are routine, of course, and practically any competent actor could perform them. It's the others you want to think about: the longer actions, the actions where a series of complicated ideas are communicated, the actions involving special kinds of movement (occupational, for example). And don't overlook the obvious nonverbal actions. How about love scenes?!? Sleeping or waking up scenes? Eating and drinking scenes? How difficult do you think it would be to perform those? And perform them again and again with absolute conviction and naturalness and spontaneity until the director was satisfied with "the take?" Can you imagine adding any of these to an audition, or does it seem to you that auditions should be "all talk?"

Exploration #22: Life Studies for Movement

This is a basic but very common mime exercise that can be enormously helpful in introducing you to the possible movement qualities you can develop in your audition. Earlier in this chapter you may have completed exploration #14 entitled "Life Studies for Type," which guided you toward zeroing in upon a stranger's personality type, but this exploration requires that you zero in on a stranger's *movement* style. Once again, you need to position yourself in a public place, select a human subject who seems very different from you, and observe him or her closely until you can pinpoint distinct features of the way he or she moves — movement qualities that tend to make him or her "distinct" as a person. These could be the pace of movements, the kinds of gestures, his or her posture, physical mannerisms, particularities of age, occupation, or gender, etc. It isn't necessary to find a subject who's walking (although in most cases that's a preferable activity and easy to get on top of). Even a subject who is sitting or who is standing stationary while performing an action can be a valuable subject **so long as he or she is moving differently than you would.** Your goal here is to **physically imitate this person for sixty seconds.** You can choose either to imitate the action just as you observe it ("a slice of life") or to devise an imaginary situation with a beginning-middle-end in which the subject would be physically moving. Once you get the hang of it, seizing-upon the physical type of a "character" will be much easier to accomplish and an invaluable asset to you in auditioning! [14]

Exploration #23: Ripping Your Tongue Out

Pick one of the monologs contained in this book and memorize it. Rehearse it as dramatically as possible for presentation to the class, including movements, vocal expressiveness, etc. Once you have it finally prepared, and are confident that you're performing all the ideas and emotions contained in the piece to the best of your ability, **try to perform it without words!** Try to communicate all the ideas and emotions contained in the piece through body language alone. You may certainly exaggerate your movements and "act out" your thoughts and feelings in any way you choose in this nonverbal performance (roll on the floor, stomp your feet, clap your hands, jump around, etc.), but you must not revert to any type of sign language like a charades game in order to get your point across. Then, once you've explored all the movement possibilities for communicating the sense and action of the piece, you should try to speak the original words in "gobbledygook" language: nonsense sounds that capture the rhythm, inflections, and emphases of the original. Rehearse the piece exploring combinations of both nonverbal movements as well as gobbledygook in order to communicate the original monolog as effectively as you can. Then bring it to class and see from the responses you receive how well you've succeeded!

Review and Reflection

1. What major acting areas should you especially look to develop during your school years that will help you audition well?

- You should understand your type and how that can help you create dramatic characters.
- You should cultivate a liberal arts background in science, history, psychology, and other fields.
- You should develop a strong appreciation of language study, literature, and music.
- You should take every opportunity to develop and train your voice.
- You should take every opportunity to develop and train your physical instrument.

2. What are the three ways to develop good speaking habits and become word-friendly while you're in school?

- Broaden your exposure to information drawn from many different fields of human experience.
- Pay attention to the structure and mechanics of language and sound in English, music, and foreign language classes.
- Spend time in general background reading in fiction and literature.

3. Just what speaking abilities do you need to develop in school in order to do good auditions?

- You need to become skilled with speaking dialog.
- You need to develop proper pronunciation.
- You need to become competent with dialects.
- You need to be able to read fluently and expressively off the page.
- You need to have sharp memorization skills.

4. What are the three areas of your physical development upon which you need to concentrate while in school in order to develop strong auditioning skills?

- Staying in good physical condition through a program of regular exercise.
- Developing confidence and expressiveness through dance classes.
- Taking advantage of opportunities to learn specific movement skills like mime, combatives, circus and clowning, and martial arts.

[1] Nowadays many people in theatre, film, and television recognize "type" casting as an important social as well as artistic problem, and as a result the notion of "nontraditional casting" has become widespread. Nontraditional casting refers to the effort that directors now make to cast certain kinds of actors in roles that formerly they would not be considered for. As an example, actors with disabilities or actors-of-color now play more roles where ethnicity, race, or physical handicaps are not important considerations. Gender, too, has been affected by this, with women cast in roles that traditionally might have gone to male actors. Indeed, entire plays have been re-staged by innovative directors who intentionally reverse the gender roles in order to "score points" about gender-based relationships and social power structures.

[2] Internet conversation with the author, 27 February 2002.

[3] Demetria Thomas, Interview, 18 January 2003.

[4] *The Elusive Obvious, or Basic Feldenkrais* (Cupertino: Meta, 1981), pp. xi–xii. The Feldenkrais system is an intensive body-mind training approach that is taught all over the world. It is one of the most important movement training methods for actors and is used on an ongoing basis in most acting-training conservatories in the U.S.

[5] "Cutting Loose," *American Theatre*, 19 No. 4 (April 2002), p. 60. Bogosian's discussion of this creative process at work when creating his character monologs is one of the most articulate expressions of this aspect of acting theory. Cf. his remarks about "using oneself" on pp. 16–19.

[6] Eric Morris and Joan Hotchkis, *No Acting Please* (Los Angeles: Whitehouse/Spelling, 1979), p. 68.

[7] Interview, 11 February 1982.

[8] *The Method as Means* (London: Jenkins, 1961), p. 42.

[9] Robert Goldsby, the Berkeley Repertory Theatre, interview with the author, 1 February 1982.

[10] Internet conversation with the author, 25 February 2002.

[11] *Acting in Industrials* (Portsmouth: Heinemann, 1994), pp. 26–28.

[12] Interview, 29 December, 1981.

[13] Quoted in Selma Jean Cohen, *Dance as a Theatre Art* (New York: Dodd, Mead, 1975), p. 139.

[14] I was once privileged to witness the famous mime Bobby Shields get slugged to the pavement in San Francisco by an indignant passerby who caught Shields mimicking his walk and body language. Before he became commercially successful, Shields used to entertain lunch-hour crowds in Union Square by doing improvisational routines and life studies, passing the hat around afterwards.

Chapter Five
Selecting Material
"Words, words, words"

Always remember that your audition pieces are you. They represent the package you wish to sell to the casting people, the fundamental "property" in the transaction. What the auditors conclude about you will be based heavily upon the image your material conveys, and your choice of that material reflects how you see yourself. Remember this and think about it. It means that in selecting audition pieces for prepared auditions you must be sure that the impression they create of you is the one you wish to create and one the director will want to see.

Suitability and Appropriateness
The most important criterion of a good audition piece is that it shows you at your best, that it is suitable and appropriate for the kind of person you are. In some of the previous chapter's explorations you began to take an inventory of your personal and professional traits as a human being. You learned to keep an eye out for the strengths and weaknesses in your acting and began to discover some of their sources as you analyzed your stage experience and personal history. This activity is valuable when choosing material for tryouts, because you must be objective about your assets and feel confident about foregrounding them. In short, you must choose audition material that plays to your strengths. In order to begin learning how to do this, let's take a moment to consider some of the most common mistakes that young actors make when it comes to selecting their audition pieces. Of course, directors all have their own particular bugbears; but in gathering material for this book, I encountered three common "no-nos" from just about everyone I interviewed.

Many young actors make the mistake of selecting pieces that are not suited to their abilities nor good for the kind of play being cast. Perhaps it was a film or play performance that excited them; or maybe they studied a play in drama class during which students and the teacher read some scenes and did some fun improvisations. Or perhaps they were once in a production where someone played the part and turned the audience on. None of these reasons is important (although it's always good to be on familiar speaking terms with dramatic literature!).

In fact, a number of coaches pointed out to me that students often will pick material from a play in which they were once cast, and this can be a big mistake. While your experience with the play may have been moving and exciting, nonetheless the staging and interpretation that's appropriate for a play is not usually suitable for an audition, and it may even restrict you from discovering new approaches and interpretations of the material. You should keep in mind, therefore, that *an audition is its own performance with a different purpose than "re-creating" the play or the role again;* it's not an opportunity or an invitation to rely on past successes that may once have satisfied a general theatre audience.

A more serious and widespread problem these days is the large number of students who represent themselves with potty-humor: in seeking to be original, they pick sexually crude monologs or pieces filled with vulgar language, which are always the kiss of death at an audition. No one cares about your sex potential up there, and there's no point in using cliché, adolescent four-letter words when there are so many *good* scripts available. You only reveal your ignorance of good writing and always embarrass the auditors.

It's amazing how many silly people actually believe that the way to get noticed in an audition is to be as bizarre as the clowns they see mugging on music videos and late night improvs! Most directors will tell you this. Here's one of my favorite pearls of wisdom from Molly Thon, artistic director of Toronto's Beggarly Theatre:

> Never choose a piece in order to outrage or shock. Some actors believe this is the way to be remembered, to distinguish them from thirty other actors that are being seen that day. I had an actor once do a striptease in the course of his monolog right down to his boxers, and all I could think about was, "When and where is this going to end?" When am I going to have to say, "Thank you, that's enough." If your audition is well chosen and well performed, the director will remember you. [1]

You're not at a tryout to bring another show back to life onstage, nor to show how much you love and appreciate *Pippin* or *Hamlet*, nor how daring you can be in front of an audience. What's important is only whether or not you can handle *this* piece; does your audition material give you a chance to reveal who you are and what you can do? If your audition selection doesn't reveal your best talents, the director can't possibly know what you can do and if it's beyond your abilities you'll probably cause embarrassment instead of scoring a favorable impression.

Perhaps the most common trap of all for young students is to choose audition pieces from one of the many popular monolog and scene books currently on the market. Under no circumstances should you ever do this, because any director is bound to have seen at least a half-dozen other actors doing the same audition selection that you'll want to present. As soon as those books are on the shelves lazy and unimaginative actors are buying them and desperately memorizing the same monologs or scenes; then they run them by all of us poor, miserable directors who must sit through the same piece again and again and again, year after year. These books are valuable for general background reading and excellent class or studio resources. But they should never, ever be used for competitive auditions.

As I explained in chapter 2, you should be doing a lot of background reading and viewing throughout your school years. When you need audition material, draw on that background to find scenes and monologs that are more original and seldom seen. Or pull material from novels and other non-dramatic sources that play well for an audition. Or edit together passages from several scenes to make a complete and seamless monolog. Only lazy actors will use those scene and monolog books for competitive auditions, and believe me there are a lot of lazy actors out there. Don't be one of them. It's the kiss of death.

So the essential features of a good audition piece are its suitability and appropriateness, both for you as a person and for the play being cast. And there are six tests that you can apply as a guide. *First you must search out at least a half-dozen scenes and monologs to start with,* because it's impossible to locate just one or two pieces that display all your abilities. Professor John Louis Dezseran, acting coach at the University of Minnesota, recommends that beginning students establish for themselves "the same standards ... that you might expect to find in a professional situation. Try using as a model the requirements for the University Resident Theatre Association auditions ... one of these pieces should be from classical literature (drama written before 1800). The total audition should not last more than five minutes." [2]

The two or three pieces you perform, however, should be drawn from a repertoire of others that you've also prepared. Some actors recommend having at least five prepared, others as many as twenty or thirty. There are several reasons for this. Preparing numerous recital pieces permits you to constantly adjust them to your developing abilities; a repertoire enables you to select different pieces for different types of plays being cast (you won't ever be doing only one audition a year, you know); and if the auditors tell you they want to hear something more or something different (as frequently happens at callbacks), you're ready to deliver the goods.

Second, the selection must conform to your physical type, your vocal range, and your age. The auditors should be able to "see" you in the role, any audience should be able to believe that at least you "look the part." This means you should avoid pieces in dialect (unless the auditions specifically require it), and stay away from poetic drama (including Shakespeare) if you have no training or experience with verse. And stay within your age range. You'll find this advice contained in all audition books and you should always follow it. [3] The ages of characters and occasionally their physical and personal features can be found in a play's cast list, stage directions at the character's first entrance (in many of the scene and monolog anthologies listed in appendix A), or simply by asking your instructors.

The third test of a good monolog is to be sure that your piece is strongly dramatic so that the material itself contains excitement. What is "dramatic" in a scene? Well, this can mean many things to different people. However, good dramatic material possesses some kind of character development or "discoveries" the character makes, one or more climactic points, a strong and clear conflict (either internal/psychological or external), a good range or "palette" of emotions, and enough turning points or shifts in direction to permit the ideas to develop and change with variety and interest. Sydney Walker, auditions coach at San Francisco's American Conservatory Theatre, gave these suggestions to his students:

> You have to develop it, structure it, orchestrate it. It must have a beginning, a middle, and an end. Don't, under any circumstances, let the character be at the end ... where he was at the start. In an audition, honesty and truthfulness just aren't enough. The piece must have strength and variety, and it's got to go somewhere. When you're auditioning, you have only a few minutes to show them what you can do, to reveal that you have a whole spectrum of brilliant colors on your palette and not just one nice little pastel. [4]

Avoid attempting to knock yourself out and "wow" the director by selecting razzle-dazzle material. Directors know more dazzle than you, so don't try to surprise them. In the short space of an audition you lack the time to justify and motivate extreme emotional states, and you don't want your audition to look forced or silly. Remember, too, that some scenes might permit you to "pull out the stops" only because they come from plays that have a couple of hours lead-in time beforehand. So try to remain within your own emotional and imaginative range. As one director advises: "George in *Our Town* and Nick in *Virginia Woolf* are both boy-next-door types, but the two present as much variety as is needed in a typical audition." [5]

The final thing to consider with the "dramatic" quality of your material is that it should develop quickly: it should have strong conflict right from the beginning. This is crucial for an audition because, like it or not, you have the auditioners' undivided attention only for the first fifteen seconds or so. In other words, you want to avoid choosing material that has a long "dramatic build" where you kind of "drift into" the dramatic situation for a few lines, and instead select something that requires you to engage a relationship powerfully right from the outset. You want material that has strong "given circumstances" at the top of the scene, something that *propels* you into the starting moments.

The fourth test of a good audition selection is that it should be out of the ordinary. This can mean several things. For example, if you're trying out for a particular play, never choose a scene from that as your general audition because you'll be competing against the director's own interpretation of the role. Except in a rare case or two, I've never cast anyone who has done this because I feel that a person's preconceived ideas of the part — from wherever or whoever the interpretation came — would be too difficult to change in a short rehearsal period. Select a part that is *similar* to the role being cast. In fact, you'll find on many general audition notices that auditionees are actually prohibited from using selections from the play under consideration. Only when theatres stipulate material from the play being cast should you prepare a monolog or scene from that particular script.

A second consideration regarding "out of the ordinary" pieces is that many directors who watch hundreds of auditions each year advise actors to avoid shop-worn selections, no matter how famous or powerful or "favorite" they may be. This includes, for example, those sexy new anthologies I mentioned earlier. They're published every year along the lines of "the best of Broadway" or something similar. But classics, too, can also be shop worn outside of high school and collegiate tryouts — and even within the educational theatre. For example, one of my personal visions of hell involves my having to sit through yet another Juliet at general auditions declaring, "Gallop apace, ye fiery footed steeds!" or humpbacked Richard grousing about, "Now is the winter of our discontent ... " So check with your teachers or coach about hackneyed material.

One note of caution here for foolish students who may be tempted to select audition pieces written by themselves or their friends or some unknown author: you're never going to be able to overcome bad material, so why cut yourself off at the legs before you even start? By this I mean that you can rely on the work of major, established writers to sell itself in a way that something by a lesser-known writer cannot. So *an established, recognized playwright will always be a safer bet than an unknown.* As professional actor and coach William Anton declares: "Dull is dull no matter how brilliantly performed." [6]

Some actors try to adapt material for auditions from non-dramatic works such as novels, poems, and short stories in hopes of producing something original to present. A lot of coaches recommend this, because it allows actors to be creative with their editing and selection skills, and it can often result in a highly original selection. This can be risky business with young actors, however, and I usually discourage students from doing it. You see, material that isn't specifically written for actors often lacks the dramatic qualities necessary to pitch the situation and the emotions and the struggle actively across the footlights into a live audience at an audition. Narrative prose, for example, is often flabbily discursive onstage, and poetry often becomes too solipsistic and interiorized in the actor's mouth. Besides, I remind actors, there are plenty of good scripts out there written for the stage: use those, bank on those.

No agreed-upon rule exists concerning "originality" for a tryout piece. While one director will recommend that you stick to theatrical selections, others will often perk up when a student presents an adapted piece, because it suggests intelligence and creativity. Still others will recommend something totally off-the-wall, either to score an unforgettable impression or to simply have on hand when the occasion warrants.[7] Remember that no one can actually pick pieces for you (and never let anyone do so). They may only recommend. You are the one who must decide and then live with your selections; you must feel confident that they are the best ones to represent you.

The dramatic potential of a scene or monolog is usually easier to spot than its potential as a vehicle for your particular talents. This comes only from rehearsing and experimenting with the piece. Only when you've analyzed the emotional range of a character, for instance Helen Keller in *The Miracle Worker* or Father Rivard in *The Runner Stumbles*, and tried to play the selection for awhile will you be able to learn if you can feel comfortable with the portrayal, handling its demands without performing a cliché.

"Feeling comfortable" with your selections can be extremely important for you when you finally get to present your pieces on that "long-awaited" audition day, because it'll make you a lot more confident. One of my students, Tamira Henry, who received only a mediocre response the first year that she competed at regional URTA auditions, raked-in a fistful of interviews as an URTA finalist the second year she went up. "It was my pieces, definitely," she reported to me. "I really felt good about them this year, really felt solid. Like my moons and my planets were all in line or something. But in my interviews they all told me how much they really liked my selections." [8] Whether or not astrology will work for you, I don't know, but the importance of relying upon good, solid material comes through loud and clear.

The fifth criterion for choosing audition selections is that the total package is tidy, covering the range of your talents. By "tidiness" I mean self-contained and complete in itself. As a director I want to see people act when they audition, I want to see an audition performance **designed to present the actor in only a few, well-focused minutes**. For example, the piece should require no elaborate explanation before beginning. My time is too valuable (and I assume theirs is, too) to waste in listening to where the monolog occurs in the play, what's motivating the character at this particular moment, how the setting is supposed to look, and so forth. With a tidy, well chosen piece there should be "no need for *Cliff's Notes*," as William Anton puts it. [9] Acting, please. Cut to the chase — "anything else is the kiss of death." [10]

In this regard, bear in mind that the audition piece will always be regarded as only a part of your total audition, from the time you enter the space to the point where you exit. So the scene or monolog should be "complete" and self-explanatory. As Director Doug Johnson of the old Stanford Rep once advised me: "You want to leave those auditions people with a little nugget, a little gem that's polished and complete, so they'll be able to pick you out of the crowd when they cast." [11] Your audition pieces — your entire performance, in fact — should say it all about you.

This also implies that your pieces must connect and relate well. You can achieve this by paying special attention to their contrasting features — comic and serious, light and heavy, ballad and belt. Be certain that these contrasts are sharp: that a certain emotional quality, mood, or character trait in one piece is not also found in the next piece. You waste time in your audition by repeating yourself.

Remember that versatility and variety mean simply covering your range. If you haven't got a great range, don't pretend that you do. Do only what you can do well, what you can perform with honesty and authenticity, and no more. Eliminate everything in your audition performance that is not designed to present yourself as an actor. And remember that the shorter the piece the better — you don't have to take the maximum two-three-four minutes allowed. Show your best, then end it.

The sixth and final criterion of a good audition piece is that it be something with which you can strongly identify, a dramatic situation in which you can personally invest yourself. In fact, many directors and coaches regard this as the single most important criterion of a good audition piece! (Maybe I should have listed it first?) By this they mean that you've given the selection the personal stamp that you alone can place on it. You're not there to recite properly, you know! Your audition pieces become remarkable *only* when you've poured yourself into them, taken a hand from start to finish in shaping them.

This is not easy work, believe me. In the first place, you've got to "live" with an audition piece for months and months; you can't just grab it from somewhere at the last moment (like from an anthology!) and work it up fast for a tryout. Get started early to locate and survey possible choices and develop them in order to let them "percolate" in your soul before going ahead with them. It always irks me when students come to me a month before ACTF's or summer stock auditions and ask, "Can you find an audition piece for me to use?" They're lazy and haven't done their homework; they've waited until the last minute. I do it, of course, because even a last minute shot is better than none at all, and the audition in itself is valuable. But as a general rule, these students rarely have any success (especially where dollars are involved), and as a rule I never recommend them for URTAs because laziness is not the mark of a professional.

In brief, you take out what you put in. One of Great Britain's most successful writer-directors gave me this piece of advice for selecting material:

> The greatest mistake I encounter is where the auditioning actor has chosen a speech, somewhat at random, from a published selection of audition speeches. Often the extract has been taken entirely out of context, with the actor having done little or no research into the play from which it is taken. Inadequacy is almost always quickly evident. It's far preferable for the choice to be of a speech by a character they would like to play, in a play which they have read and thought about. They should have developed ideas about why the speech is appropriate for them. The fact that it is "well known," or "my drama teacher suggested it," or "I found it in an audition book" strike me as being potential death knells! [12]

The surest guideline for achieving uniqueness in your audition is the degree to which you can identify with your character's situation, his or her mood in the scene, the depth and sensitivity of feeling, the stakes of the struggle. Your gut reactions to the dramatic circumstances are, of course, something that a player has always been expected to bring to the stage: you must personally "own" the dramatic struggle in the monolog or scene.

This is just common sense, right? Can you "act" or can't you? To quote Sydney Walker again: "Choose audition material that you love, so that the belief is already there, and you don't have to whip yourself into a frenzy to sell yourself on material you don't really believe in. This is one of the few instances where the actor is in the driver's seat in terms of choosing material, and it should be meaningful to him." [13]

A character's life is only partially sketched in by the playwright who knows that the remainder — the center, the key element of the characterization — must come from the actor's own personality. This is just as true of finished performances as it is of auditions: the director *wants* to be touched, affected, somehow moved by a good, believable reading. He or she *wants* to behold *you* living and breathing a dramatic moment up there, instead of performing some collection of "character traits" like a trained circus monkey. [14] As I mentioned in the last chapter with regard to using and revealing yourself onstage, learn to bring yourself personally to the role in order to give the audition your unique personal stamp.

So regard all your audition selections as blueprints that you must follow but that need the personal skills of a master builder in order to bring them to life. Use others' opinions as tests for these qualities; invite criticism from your acting class, your teachers, even your roommates. Do some personal evaluation with a videotape if you can. The best feedback, of course, will come from a good coach, but more about that in the next chapter. As Monte Davis of the Milwaukee Rep once remarked to my audition class: "You have to really want to do it. It just means more to you than most things in life, being up there onstage." [15]

After locating potentially good audition material according to the suggestions in chapter 2, and after following the six guidelines mentioned above, you'll normally encounter three choices: *to use the selection as-is, extracted directly from the play; to condense or cut the selection in order to shape it appropriately for time limits or your own acting strengths; or to adapt a two-character scene into a one-character monolog by editing-out the second character's lines.* Let's explore each possibility.

The first option, using the selections as they stand, requires little discussion. So long as you're convinced that they allow you to use your talents in the strongest and most personal way, that they conform to the limits of time and appropriateness set by the particular audition, and that they work well together, then you should go directly to chapters 5 and 6 and begin working them up. Just be sure that you've read the whole script at least once from which the extract has been taken. You need to understand as much as you can about the background context and gain clues for your interpretation.

The second option, condensing the piece, is trickier than it sounds. What exactly do you cut? How do you determine what goes and what stays as you do this? There are four guidelines to follow — in sequence, order of importance — in order to accomplish this.

First, avoid simply cutting off the beginning or ending of the piece. No kidding, you'd be astonished to learn how many students try to cut scenes or monologs down to a manageable length by simply lopping-off the intro or ending sections! Madness! Don't make this mistake. You're not dealing with numbers of words or numbers of seconds, you're dealing with heartbeats; and you can't just lop them off according to a stopwatch. A monolog or scene, that is, makes *emotional* and *psychological* sense. It "tracks." So you must first determine what that track is — the heart and central action of the monolog — in order for the piece to remain emotionally and psychologically consistent after you condense it. In short, most often you must condense the monolog or scene *internally.*

The second guideline in condensing material is that some repetition can normally be sacrificed in order to shorten the piece. Find where this occurs within the scene or monolog, and cut some or all of it. *Third, you should eliminate ideas that are subordinate or inessential for expressing the central action of the monolog.* We call these "strategic" items. You want to retain the main items or strengths of the piece, its "substantive" or important core. *Finally, cut all sections of the monolog or scene that fail to highlight only one of your acting strengths.* "Play to only one of your strengths in each selection," William Anton advises in his audition videotape. "Then use contrasting audition pieces to demonstrate your versatility … Shorter is better. Determine when the piece has shown your strength, then end it." [16] If you find that one of your selections is somewhat more complex than the other (numerous discoveries, several decisions, two or three nagging questions or conflicts, multiple emotional shocks), you might focus it more effectively on one of your acting strengths by trimming some of the "extraneous" dialog. Remember that you're not auditioning in order to render the play; you're there to sell yourself.

Exploration #24: Condensing the Monolog

Using some of the guidelines just mentioned, take the following two comic speeches (one for a man, the other for a woman) and edit them down to no more than two minutes speaking time. If you've never edited any piece of writing before, then you should definitely enlist the help of English, creative writing, and journalism teachers as well as drama teachers to test your results. Editing-down a selection while retaining its central core action is not an easy job! In the first piece, *Duck Blind*, a teenage girl has been accidentally "abandoned" in a duck blind during a family outing; the second selection, from *Pee-Pipe*, is spoken by a young airman who is training as a combat fighter pilot in WWII.

Duck Blind by Shirley Barrie [17]

1 **Whoooo.** *(A duck quacks. JENNY jumps in fright.)* **Ahhh!** *(She*
2 *almost falls off the edge.)* **Geeeeeez!** Now *you* **almost had me in**
3 **the water.** *(Duck quacks.)* **Don't worry. I don't have a gun. Just**
4 **a stupid crazy family. I mean I'm hanging off the front end of**
5 **the boat, right, trying to see the channel through this**
6 **blinking fog when wham — Dad drives into this duck blind**
7 **and I'm gone. I thought I was a goner. I had this split second,**
8 **you know, when I was actually grateful Mom made me wear**
9 **this stupid life jacket. But then I hear her screaming, "You've**
10 **lost my baby! Why aren't you backing up, you monster!" He**
11 **wasn't backing up because he thinks I'm in the water and he**
12 **doesn't want to catch me in the motor. But that's a bit too**
13 **complicated for her tiny brain. Not that he's much better.**
14 **"You all right, Kiddo?" he calls. Kiddo — like I'm still eight**
15 **years old like stupid Lucy who just blubbers. So I didn't**
16 **answer. Well, I couldn't, actually. I kind of got the wind**
17 **knocked out of me when I landed. Anyway, I just figure they**
18 **can look for me for a while.** *(The duck quacks disapprovingly.)*
19 **Well do you think I** *wanted* **to come on this stupid moonlight**
20 **cruise? If they'd let me go over to Doug's house tonight they**
21 **wouldn't be riding around in the fog looking for me. But, oh**
22 **no. "It's a school night, Jenny. You know we don't allow that**
23 **sort of thing." Like what do they think? That we're having**
24 **some kind of kinky sex and it's okay on the weekend? I**
25 **doubt it. They probably couldn't imagine kinky. Anyway**
26 **two hours later, Dad's bouncing around the house, getting**
27 **Lucy out of bed. "Great night for a family moonlight cruise.**
28 **Could be the last one of the year. All hands on deck." Yeah,**
29 **sure. When it's something** *he* **wants to do it doesn't matter**
30 **what frigging day of the week it is. I told him I didn't wanna**
31 **come. I hate it when they ask why in that tone of voice. Like**
32 **it doesn't matter what you say, presuming you even wanted**
33 **to say — they're not gonna buy it. I mean, I've got my stupid**
34 **period — for starters.** *(Duck quacks.)* **What do you know about**
35 **it? You lay eggs. They lock the bathroom at night at the**
36 **cheap-o marina. And this dumb new boat of Dad's might**
37 **have a cabin but there's still no toilet. I'm gonna be a**
38 **flooding mess by the time I get home.** *(She feels her bottom,*
39 *struggles out of the life jacket, sits on it.)* **If I get home ...** *(Duck*
40 *quacks.)* **Yeah, I know. Fogs always lift. Eventually.** *(She*

1   *shivers.)* **It's gonna be a real barrel of laughs explaining to**
2   **Katie and Sue that I'm in the hospital with raging**
3   **pneumonia because I spent the night on a stupid duck blind**
4   **'cause my crazy father has this retarded idea about family.**
5   **"You used to enjoy it," he says with that sort of sappy look in**
6   **his eye. Yeah, sure, that's what he thinks. I could die of**
7   **exposure. And this rotten old blind could break loose and**
8   **float through the reeds.** *(With increasing theatricality.)* **And**
9   **drift towards the marina. Everybody's lined up along the**
10 **dock. But I'm beyond this world, floating towards them like**
11 **the Lady of Shalott. Okay so I'm not dressed like her, but my**
12 **face will be so beautiful and serene that they'll see me with**
13 **robes of white fluttering in the breeze. Just like in that song**
14 **Mom likes. She'll be crying. Buckets. Lucy, the little brat,**
15 **will be remembering all the times she was so mean to me and**
16 **got me into trouble by playing all cute and innocent when**
17 **she's really a conniving little monster. Katie and Sue are all**
18 **teary — even Katie who's tough as nails. And Doug is there,**
19 **struggling not to break down. But he lets out a heart-rending**
20 **wail as my raft slides into the dock. He leaps forward,**
21 **throwing his arms around my limp body. Mom and Dad are**
22 **devastated. "Forgive me, Kiddo," Dad cries. I'm dead and**
23 **he's still calling me some stupid baby name. But his face is**
24 **all lined with worry and grief. "We should have been more**
25 **understanding," Mom sobs. "If only we had another**
26 **chance."** *(Duck quacks.)* **Yeah. Only in my dreams. You know,**
27 **for one tiny infinitesimal second, I thought of asking if Doug**
28 **could come with us tonight. I must have been mad. How**
29 **could I even think of bringing somebody I really like into**
30 **contact with my crazy family. Doug'd never speak to me**
31 **again. For sure. Dad is just sort of pathetic, but Mom ... !**
32 **She's afraid of everything. She's specially afraid of the boat.**
33 **She's forever pulling Lucy and me back over the side and**
34 **wringing her hands when we water ski. She can't even swim!**
35 **Well, if it's** *really* **hot and we're anchored out at The Point —**
36 **where the sandbar is, you know — she'll get in the water and**
37 **do this truly embarrassing dog paddle. She doesn't always**
38 **come, but when she does she brings these amazing lunches**
39 **— stuff we love to eat whether it's good for us or not.**
40 *(Catching herself:)* **And she moans a lot. When Lucy was really**
41 **small we used to gang up on her, Dad and me. We'd do all**
42 **this dumb stuff to scare the pants off her. One time — I was**

1 about eight, I think Dad let me drive the boat right into the
2 busy marina. She freaked! And he'd let me ski when there
3 were waves. Anything more than glassy smooth and she's
4 having a hemorrhage! Even when she doesn't say anything, I
5 can tell. He understands what a thrill — *(Duck quacks.)* Okay,
6 okay. So maybe we used to have some good times. It's just
7 not the same any more. But they think it is. You are so lucky.
8 Weather starts to get down around freezing, you just spread
9 your wings and fly away down south. Wish I could fly. Far
10 away. *(She waves her arms. Stops.)* Course, you do have to run
11 the gauntlet of those asshole hunters trying to shoot you out
12 of the sky. Kind of like parents, right? Aiming to shoot you
13 down at every move. Kapow! Any attempt to do something
14 new. Kapow! Kapow!! They should all be banned. *(Pause.)*
15 Course, if there were no hunters, there wouldn't be any duck
16 blinds, and I would have landed in the water which is
17 frigging cold and ... Having a rational mind can be a real
18 pain. *(She recognizes her hunger.)* I could use some hot
19 chocolate about now. Mom always brings real baby
20 marshmallows to sprinkle on top. Not those stupid dried up
21 ones that come in the packet. And she made her "crazy dip".
22 It is *so* good. She won't tell us what's in it. "It's a secret," she
23 says. "Maybe when you have children ... " *(She registers*
24 *silence.)* Did you hear something? A motor? *(Pause.)* No?
25 Where are they? They wouldn't go and ... Mom'd never let
26 him leave me here. *(She calls.)* Mom! *(She frantically struggles*
27 *back into the life jacket. Louder:)* Dad!!! It's me. Jenny! *(Beat.)*
28 Your Kiddo! *(She looks out.)*

From *Pee-Pipe* by Sandra Dempsey [18]

1   If ya wanna know what flyin' is all about, here's the gumph.
2   Flyin' is all about stuff that ain't supposed to, fallin' from the
3   sky. 'Doesn't matter what th' job is, if there's an aeroplane up
4   there, ya know there's gonna be stuff comin' down here. I
5   mean, sure, there's the obvious stuff like guys parachuting an
6   bombs gettin' dropped. But I'm talkin' all the other stuff
7   nobody ever mentions. Like throwin' out any an' everythin'
8   that ain't nailed down t' help lessen yer weight an' gain altitude
9   — like dumpin' fuel t' lessen yer chance o' fire; bombs, too,
10 getting' dumped where they weren't meant to be dumped. An'
11 guns — whew-wee! It's not just th' actual bullets that rain
12 down eventually, but the shell-casings, too! Thousands of 'em!
13 Oh, an' o' course, there's always guys pukin' — I mean, why
14 puke into yer lap when ya kin just lean over … ? They just
15 never show that kinda stuff in th' picture-house news-reels —
16 all's they show is good-lookin' flyboys all manners an' snappy
17 salutes. But ya never see all th' poor saps duckin' fer cover on
18 th' ground! Ya just never know what's gonna come down on yer
19 head in this war. But I'll tell ya the biggest secret in the whole
20 flyin' world. One o' th' first things ya get introduced to in the
21 cockpit — any plane — Tiger Moths, Harvards — doesn't
22 matter. They all got … well, it's a … a kind of … Well, it's a pee-
23 pipe is what it is. Y'know, so's a guy can let go if he has t'. I
24 mean, it's not like ya can just pull over to th' side of a cloud …
25 It empties right out the bottom o' th' fuselage — usually out of
26 a fancy-lookin' pipe. You'd think it was some kind of
27 sophisticated mechanism, stickin' outa th' aircraft like that …
28 well, I guess it is vital! 'Problem is, the flyin' hours are so short,
29 even th' long-haul trainin' — y'know, cross-country 'n all that
30 — well, none of us ever gets a chance to figure out how t' use
31 th' pee-pipe before we go off solo. Now, in my case, *(He nods*
32 *towards the aft cockpit)* me an' my instructor are just wrappin' up
33 maybe our third-t'-last dual-instruction together … Dual-
34 instruction — yeah, that's where th' ham-fisted student pilot,
35 me, tries to figure out how t' fly this brand new bird, harness
36 th' six hundred horses behind th' prop and make her soar
37 sweet, like a hawk — while the flight instructor, *(He indicates*
38 *behind)* him, pretty much guzzles Milk o' Magnesia an' holds on
39 fer dear life. *(He begins to land the aircraft.)* So I bring me an' my
40 instructor down in that Harvard just as pretty as th' press in his

1   pants. An' just as I bring us into th' flight line, he throws back
2   the perspex, an' starts climbin' out, before I've even got her to a
3   stop, an' yells, *(He imitates the instructor, yelling above the engine*
4   *noise)* "Yer doin' alright, kid! Go on! Re-trim an' swing her
5   round an' take her right back up fer a circuit! She's all yours!"
6   An' he gives me a good hard slap on my back an' jumps down
7   off the wing. My solo check-out! Holy jumpin'! First in my
8   class! All th' guys are crowdin' around t' watch! My heart's
9   thumpin' so hard, I could spit! An' by now, the ground crew an'
10   everybody are startin' to get mighty interested in how come I'm
11   sittin' there like a dope in a flight-hot kite an' not getting' her
12   chalked an' re-fueled. *(He does the following.)* So I re-trim … an' I
13   gun her good an' loud just t' make sure I got everybody's
14   attention … I taxi out … an' they clear me an' give me th' green
15   right off … I give her full throttle … an' … I unstick … An' I'm
16   soarin' like a friggin' bird! Solo! *(He does the following.)* Gear up
17   … retract flap … I'm so excited! … ho-hoooo! … *(His bladder*
18   *suddenly fills.)* … Oohh jeeze! I gotta go! I had t' take a leak
19   when we landed, but I didn't wanna say anything an' get him
20   browned off … Oh jeeze! I gotta go so bad my back teeth are
21   floatin'! What'll I do? I can't hold it! I'm gonna wet my pants!
22   Wait! Th' pee-pipe! Where's th' pee-pipe!? There! *(As he ducks*
23   *down and fumbles for the pipe, the plane dips.)* Whoah, jeeze, keep
24   her nose up, man! *(He recovers control with his right hand on the*
25   *stick.)* Straight an' level — everybody's still lookin' — keep her
26   straight an' level! Oh, but jeeze! You idiot! He said do a circuit,
27   not fly to China! Jeeze! Th' kite's fuel tanks are near empty an'
28   mine are gonna burst! Wait! I know! I'll put her into a nice,
29   three-sixty orbit 'til I figure things out down here — they'll
30   think I'm just show-boatin'. *(He inclines into the left-hand turn.)*
31   Oh jeeze! I'm gonna burst! *(He fumbles to unzip his fly.)* C'mon,
32   c'mon, c'mon! Jeeze, th' zipper … I've never been so left-
33   handed! Oh jeeze! C'mon! Jeeze, I don't remember it bein' so
34   small … ! I am not climbin' outa this bird with a wet monkey-
35   suit! *(As he connects the pipe:)* Oh thank you! Thank you, lord!
36   Oh, thank you! Oh … *(While he continues his jettison operation, he*
37   *glances casually out at the ground below.)* Huh! 'Looks like a
38   farmhouse. 'Looks kinda familiar — Hey, wadd'ya know —
39   Dad's got an old red Chevy just like that one! An' a vegetable
40   patch beside th' house — we've got the same thing at our place!
41   An' there's a lady — huh, looks like she's hangin' out washin'
42   on th' line — I guess everybody's mom does th' laundry on

1   Monday! ... now she's, she's lookin' up here — look at that!
2   She's wavin' to me! *(He smiles and nods his head at her.)* **Yes,** I see
3   you! Hello to you, too, Missus! I'd wave back, only I kind o' got
4   my hands full at th' moment. Uh-oh — Maybe she's not wavin'
5   to me after all. Looks more like she's shakin' her fists? She is!
6   She's mad as a hornet! *(He laughs.)* What's th' matter, lady? My
7   aeroplane too noisy for ya? Did I wake ya from yer beauty
8   sleep? Well you just take a good look at my registration
9   number under th' wing an' see if they pay any attention to ya
10 when ya complain! There's a war on an' this happens t' be
11 official airforce trainin'! Hoo-hoo! Get a load o' those chickens
12 runnin' all over th' place! Hey, lady! Am I scarin' away yer
13 dinner? Hey, wait a minute — we've got chickens at our place!
14 *(Recognizing the woman:)* **Oh my gosh! Mom!?** *Mom!?* *(He*
15 *simultaneously loosens his grip on the pipe and the control stick.)*
16 **Whoa, jeeze!! Don't let go now, ya jerk!!** Oh, jeeze! I knew our
17 farm was close to the airbase, I just never realized how close ...
18 Oh, please don't remember the registration numbers, Mom!
19 Please don't! Oh my gosh — how many other guys have been
20 doin' th' same thing?! If th' war isn't over soon, our own
21 civilians are gonna drown! Oh, jeeze! I'm piddlin' on my own
22 mother!! I gotta stop ... Oh, like I can stop ... *(Pause.)* Here I am
23 gettin' ready to serve my country, an' all this time, I thought it
24 was th' hard water makin' our sheets yellow ... !

Wasn't that fun? Did you get it down to two minutes or less? These exercises always drive my students crazy! The task is always maddening and heart-rending, because sometimes you just hate to part with such good material! But, alas! It has to go! Learn to be ruthless and practical when it comes to working-up your audition pieces, and shortening or condensing a selection is very commonly done.

The third way of preparing an audition piece that you've chosen, "editing-out," involves adapting a two-character scene to a one-character monolog by eliminating the lines of the second character and connecting the other character's lines as a single uninterrupted discourse.

There are two reasons why some of the best coaches recommend this approach for devising good audition material for yourself. First, you're guaranteed that no one else is likely to come up with the same piece. And second, the material's original form, as give-and-take dialog, provides built-in reactions, turns, and developments in the other character's discourse that a monolog might ordinarily lack. This means that a character speaking in conversation reacts constantly to the other person's statements, so that the character's "collected lines" by themselves might display a lot more sparkle, surprise, and vitality than if he or she were speaking alone.

Not all scenes from plays can be edited in this way, and this method really only works best with two-character scenes (not three- or four-character ones). But you must be careful about a couple of technical things here. One is to be sure that your finished monolog has only one character speaking, otherwise your acting will seem muddy and confused. And second, you must be sure that the monolog you're developing follows the track of *emotional* logic of the character who is now speaking alone, and is not "crowded" by the *conversational* logic ("give-and-take" of the original dialog). The auditioning guidelines published by the URTA organization summarize this process very well:

> Selections should be self-explanatory with an overt beginning, middle, and end. Take liberty in editing for clarity. Two or more speeches may be combined to form a monologue as long as necessary connectives are smooth and logical. Test the clarity of your monologue by reading it to someone unfamiliar with the play. If there is any confusion regarding the who, what, why, when, or where of the piece, be sure it can be eliminated through editing or staging. Otherwise consider another selection. [19]

In other words, you must turn that two-character interchange into a one-character train-of-thought, borrowing the energy and development contained in the original piece. This is one reason why exposing yourself to plays, videos, and written scripts on a constant basis (Chapter Two) can be so important: you acquaint yourself with a lot of dramatic possibilities that you can use as audition material at a later time. [20]

Exploration #25: Editing-Out Characters

Take a look at the following scene by the English playwright Neil Duffield and the monolog adaptation that follows. It's set in an English prison where Liam, the Irish hero of the play, is being interrogated and taunted by a British detective. Notice how the adaptation "tracks" psychologically and emotionally, and how the final version presents a good range of emotion, a lot of development, strong energy, and several discoveries on the part of the interrogator without losing any dramatic tension found in the original scene. Can you see how omitting Liam's lines gives the actor portraying the Englishman opportunity to "play off" these lapses with silences, new discoveries, new tactics, mockery, self-doubt, etc.? And where would you now locate those "pregnant pauses" while the Englishman waits for an answer from Liam (that never comes)? Try on your own to speak the new monolog, keeping the pace and energy up as you relentlessly build the argument to its point of maximum dramatic intensity in the very last lines!

From *Lilford Mill* by Neil Duffield [21]

1 ENGLISHMAN: **Prisoner K561?** *(LIAM drags himself to attention.)*
2 **Sit down, K561. No need to stand.** *(LIAM ignores this. Remains*
3 *standing.)* **You may speak if you wish.** *(A pause.)* **I'm here with**
4 **the governor's approval. You have permission to speak as**
5 **much as you wish.** *(LIAM hesitates a moment.)*
6 LIAM: **Who are you?**
7 ENGLISHMAN: **Please sit down. I understand you're on**
8 **punishment. Forty days solitary, isn't it?**
9 LIAM: **I'm not complaining.**
10 ENGLISHMAN: **I admire your endurance, Mr. Mulcahey.**
11 **Five years they tell me you've been in here. Special rules**
12 **are not easy. Not everyone manages to last so long.**
13 LIAM: **I don't know who you are, but would you stop beating**
14 **about the bush?**
15 ENGLISHMAN: **They tell me you were quite a well known**
16 **figure in Dublin five years ago.**
17 LIAM: **They seem to have told you a lot.**
18 ENGLISHMAN: **Home Rule by peaceful means. That's what**
19 **you stood for, isn't it? It's funny how things turn out, isn't it?**
20 LIAM: **What's that supposed to mean?**
21 ENGLISHMAN: **What seems anathema to one set of**
22 **politicians becomes acceptable to another. Personally I**
23 **never trust any of them.**

1 LIAM: Is this some kind of game you're playing?
2 ENGLISHMAN: I'm here because the government are
3   currently discussing a bill to bring about the very thing you
4   campaigned for ... Irish Home Rule.
5 LIAM: What?
6 ENGLISHMAN: Of course, there will have to be certain
7   conditions. There's the thorny problem of the North. And
8   there's no way it can happen overnight. Negotiations will
9   be needed. These things take months. Sometimes years.
10 LIAM: So why me? Why are you telling me this?
11 ENGLISHMAN: You've always insisted you were innocent of
12   the charges against you.
13 LIAM: It's true! And there were people at my trial who knew it!
14 ENGLISHMAN: I know it.
15 LIAM: What?
16 ENGLISHMAN: You aren't naive enough to believe in
17   natural justice, are you, Mr. Mulcahey?
18 LIAM: You've got some bloody nerve.
19 ENGLISHMAN: Politics will always define justice. But
20   political climates change. And when they do, it seems a
21   shame that a man as intelligent as yourself should have to
22   spend a further three years locked in a place as grim as this.
23   After all, it would be much more useful to all concerned if
24   you were able to help influence decisions about the future
25   course of events. Don't you think?
26 LIAM: I think you'd better say exactly what you want.
27 ENGLISHMAN: Not everyone in Ireland thinks as you do.
28   There are those who have no interest in peaceful discussion
29   or legal means of any kind. They think the British
30   government is not to be trusted.
31 LIAM: Now, don't you find that truly amazing?
32 ENGLISHMAN: For these people violence is a way of life.
33   Sadly their influence is more than we would wish. There is
34   a real danger they could undermine the peace process.
35 LIAM: What's that got to do with me?
36 ENGLISHMAN: We'd like to know who they are.
37 LIAM: I think you'd better leave.
38 ENGLISHMAN: The people I'm talking about are no friends of
39   yours, Mr. Mulcahey. They're out to destroy everything you
40   ever stood for. One name. That's all I'm asking for. One name.

Monolog adapted from *Lilford Mill*

1 ENGLISHMAN: Prisoner K561? Sit down, K561. No need to
2 stand. You may speak if you wish. I'm here with the
3 governor's approval. You have permission to speak as
4 much as you wish. Please sit down. I understand you're on
5 punishment. Forty days solitary, isn't it? I admire your
6 endurance, Mr. Mulcahey. Five years they tell me you've
7 been in here. Special rules are not easy. Not everyone
8 manages to last so long. They tell me you were quite a well
9 known figure in Dublin five years ago. Home Rule by
10 peaceful means. That's what you stood for, isn't it? It's
11 funny how things turn out, isn't it? What seems anathema
12 to one set of politicians becomes acceptable to another.
13 Personally, I never trust any of them. I'm here because the
14 government are currently discussing a bill to bring about
15 the very thing you campaigned for ... Irish Home Rule. Of
16 course, there will have to be certain conditions. There's the
17 thorny problem of the North. And there's no way it can
18 happen overnight. Negotiations will be needed. These
19 things take months. Sometimes years. You've always
20 insisted you were innocent of the charges against you. I
21 know it. You aren't naïve enough to believe in natural
22 justice, are you, Mr. Mulcahey? Politics will always define
23 justice. But political climates change. And when they do, it
24 seems a shame that a man as intelligent as yourself should
25 have to spend a further three years locked in a place as grim
26 as this. After all, it would be much more useful to all
27 concerned if you were able to help influence decisions
28 about the future course of events. Don't you think? Not
29 everyone in Ireland thinks as you do. There are those who
30 have no interest in peaceful discussion or legal means of
31 any kind. They think the British government is not to be
32 trusted. For these people violence is a way of life. Sadly
33 their influence is more than we would wish. There is a real
34 danger they could undermine the peace process. We'd like
35 to know who they are. The people I'm talking about are no
36 friends of yours, Mr. Mulcahey. They're out to destroy
37 everything you ever stood for. One name. That's all I'm
38 asking for. One name.

Now turn to Chapter Six and try your own adaptation using the scene from R.N. Sandberg's play *Convivencia* (focusing on the character Ytzha); do the same with the scene in appendix A from Gustavo Ott's *Minor Leagues* (focusing on the character Goosey). *Convivencia* is an historical play set in a renaissance Spanish city inhabited by Jews, Muslims, and Christians. The city has just been conquered by Christian forces, and the frightened young boy Ma'el is hiding from Christian soldiers by Ytzha's house, where she discovers him. *Minor Leagues* is set in a contemporary South American hotel room, where the older American Goosey negotiates with the fifteen-year-old South American Vanessa for a valuable baseball card he wants to purchase from her and re-sell to a rich North American collector. The night before he had a heart attack and she saved his life by bringing him his medicine. He also confessed to her that his son, Michael, was not really alive but had died years ago.

In the scene from *Convivencia*, you'll have to do more than simply eliminate Ma'el's lines of dialog; you'll also have to decide which of Ytzha's own lines to eliminate in order to focus the monolog on a consistent set of her reactions to the young boy. Additionally, not all the subjects they discuss in the original scene can be retained in the monolog, and a number of stage directions will have to be ignored as well. But I think you'll find that the resulting speech for Ytzha gives her a large number of choices for physical actions to perform and a wide range of emotions to play in response to the boy demanding refuge from her and attempting to threaten her.

In the scene from *Minor Leagues*, Vanessa has already told Goosey a cock-and-bull story about her family and where she found the card, but in this scene Goosey insists that she tell him the truth, and he becomes profoundly touched by what appears to be her "true" situation. You'll find the scene challenging to reduce to a single monolog, because only the first part will lend itself to such a condensation. This means that you'll have to decide what quality of Goosey the first part of the scene can best reveal, and then how much of Goosey's original dialog you can retain in order to accomplish that and make it sound consistent when pasted together.

Now that you have a good handle on what you might have to do in order to locate good audition material for yourself, and how to adapt it for the tryouts, let's look in the next chapter at the steps you have to take in order to rehearse it for performance.

Review and Reflection

1. **What are the three most common mistakes that inexperienced actors make when selecting their prepared audition pieces?**
   - They choose pieces simply because they liked the play or the film without asking whether or not the selection presents their strengths or suits the play being cast.
   - They choose vulgar or bizarre pieces in order to get noticed.
   - They select pieces from one of the many popular monolog and scene books currently on the market.
2. **What are the six tests of an audition piece that will help to make it suitable and appropriate for you and for the play being cast?**
   - You must search out at least a half-dozen scenes and monologs to start with.
   - The selection must conform to your physical type, your vocal range, and your age.
   - Be sure that your piece is strongly dramatic so that it reveals your best traits.
   - It should be out of the ordinary.
   - The total audition package should be tidy, self-contained, and complete in itself, covering the range of your talent.
   - A good audition piece should be something with which you can strongly identify, a dramatic situation in which you can personally invest yourself.
3. **What makes a good audition piece "strongly dramatic"?**
   - Some kind of character development or "discoveries" the character makes.
   - One or more climactic points.
   - A strong and clear conflict (either internal/psychological or external).
   - A good range or "palette" of emotions.
   - Enough turning points or shifts in direction to permit the ideas to develop and change with variety and interest.
4. **How can I edit-down a scene or monolog to a shorter length?**
   - Be certain that the thought and emotional logic of the condensed selection "tracks" in a consistent manner.
   - Eliminate all repetition in the piece.
   - Eliminate all ideas that are not vital for expressing the central action.
   - Eliminate sections that do not reflect your strongest acting qualities.

[1] Internet conversation with the author, 26 March 2002.

[2] *The Student Actor's Handbook* (Palo Alto: Mayfield, 1975), 196. The "five minute" time limit here is merely a suggestion for practice. Many auditions will allow you only one minute or three minutes. But you should begin with five.

[3] As I mentioned in the previous chapter, many educational theatre directors are often forced to cast students in roles that are radically different from their type, but I'm speaking here of pieces that you actually select for prepared auditions. If you get to auditions, however, and the director gives you something to read for a ninety-year-old hermaphrodite with green hair and two heads, then go right ahead and do it. He or she must have seen something in your general prepared audition that makes you seem "right" for this!

[4] Quoted in Dennis Powers, "You're too fat...You're too thin...You remind me of my first wife...Thank you and goodbye," *Playbill* (Los Angeles) January 1984, p. 9.

[5] Tom Markus, *The Professional Actor* (New York: Drama Book Specialists, 1979), p. 42.

[6] Videotape, *Auditioning for the Actor* (New York: Theater Arts Video Library, 1989).

[7] I'll never forget the first time I heard a young woman zing me with Lewis Carroll's JABBERWOCKY as an audition for a children's theatre production. She got the part.

[8] Interview, 25 February 2003.

[9] *Auditioning for the Actor*, op cit.

[10] Bill Oliver's phrase, a director with the One-Act Theatre Company of San Francisco, in conversation with the author 13 April 1984.

[11] Interview, 2 February 1974. Many acting coaches will carefully point this out to new students because directors are constantly evaluating actors from the first moment they appear in the room. Are they focused? Are they jabbering? Are they observing? Attentive? How do they approach the stage when called? In his professional acting handbook, Tom Markus describes the importance of this as a mini-scene in itself, assigning acting objectives to each part of it for a good overall performance: "First, you must arrive at the audition hall ... The second part of your audition performance is your entrance ... The third part of your audition is the interview proper ... The fourth part of your audition performance will comprise the presentation ... Your fifth and final part is your exit." (*The Professional Actor*, op. cit., pp. 36–43)

[12] Frank Whately, Associate Writer and Director, National Youth Music Theatre of Great Britain, Internet conversation with the author, 25 February 2002.

[13] Dennis Powers, op.cit., p. 10.

[14] Michael Leibert, interview, Berkeley Repertory Theatre, 29 December 1981.

[15] Interview, 17 September 1980.

[16] *Auditioning for the Actor*, op cit.

[17] *Duck Blind* by Shirley Barrie, © 2000 by Shirley Barrie, all rights reserved. Reprinted by permission. Information concerning rights should be addressed to the playwright, 462 Clendenan Avenue, Toronto, Ontario, M6P 2X6, Canada, E-mail: Shirleybarrie@sympatico.ca.

[18] *Pee-Pipe* by Sandra Dempsey, © 2000 by Sandra Dempsey. ATTENTION: this play is fully protected under the copyright laws of Canada and all other countries of the Copyright Union, and is subject to royalty. Changes to the script are expressly forbidden without prior written permission of the author. Right to produce, film, or record, in whole or in part, in any medium or any language, by any group, amateur or professional, are retained by the author. Inquiries regarding performance and publication rights should be addressed to the author at: 1203-750 5th Street SE, Calgary, Alberta, T2G 5B4, CANADA. (403) 228-0363. sd@SandraDempsey.com., www.SandraDempsey.com.

[19] *URTA Handbook for Actors and Coaches* (New York: University Resident Theatre Association, 2002), p. 2.

[20] You must be careful about doing this for certain competitive festival auditions such as the American College Theatre Festival, which prohibits you from using anything "adapted" from the original script as an audition piece because of copyright reasons.

[21] *Lilford Mill* by Neil Duffield. Copyright © 1999 by Neil Duffield. All rights reserved. Reprinted by permission. Information concerning rights should be addressed to the author: Neil Duffield, 2 Gorses Mount, Darcy Lever, Bolton BL2 1PQ, UNITED KINGDOM.

Chapter Six

Preparing the Audition
"No excuses, please!"

Work on Your Own

As I've already pointed out in earlier chapters, you must develop the discipline of working alone at every stage of the rehearsal process. If you constantly expect your teachers, directors, and coach to tell you what to do with your audition piece, you really have no business doing it at all. Only by committing a lot of your own time and investing yourself personally in your monologs and scenes can you expect your audition to reflect the best of your abilities, projecting confidence and purposefulness when you present your selections. [1]

What should you develop on your own? The selection, interpretation, blocking movements, business, and vocal expressiveness should all be self-devised, otherwise you'll come across as a robot performing someone else's mechanical instructions. Your coach can sharpen your choices and suggest others, but only you should be making the choices.

So discipline and commit yourself to a systematic method of preparing your pieces on your own, just as the play director expects you to memorize lines and rehearse with scene partners before turning up for rehearsals. Remember that acting is work, and you should always take pride in that work. Here's a pearl of wisdom from Jane Alderman, Chicago director and casting agent:

> Think of acting as a business — your business. Never lose your training, your craft, your art: learn to use it in all the various curves that get thrown at you. Your training is yours, it's no one else's business how you work or prepare. And mind your own business — someone else's ladder and rate of progress has nothing to do with you. But remember: if you lay back, the next guy will overtake you! [2]

The approach laid out in this chapter covers all the necessary bases for preparing your audition pieces by yourself and then working with a coach. The specific exercises, however, are only general methods that are commonly employed in many conservatories and universities. They assume that you've already had some classwork in acting fundamentals, because no handbook like this can teach you how to act. So treat these exercises as reminders, as summaries of techniques that you've already encountered and mastered.

Whether or not every exercise will work for you is unimportant; each actor develops techniques over the years that work best for him or her and that may or may not be useful for someone else. I've found these approaches to be fairly standard in my classes and workshops because they seem to offer something to most of the young actors I work with. Try each at least once. Never omit the fundamentals: paraphrasing, eventing the script, identifying goals and obstacles, identifying the pattern of beats.

A couple pieces of advice for scene partners: First of all, you want to find a partner for your two-character scene who's a good actor. Avoid choosing a friend just because he or she is available and wants to do it. You wouldn't want to choose an accompanist who couldn't play the piano just because he or she's a friend, would you? So don't make the same mistake when choosing an acting partner. *Cast* that person, make sure that he or she is right for the role and can act well. Trying to do your best onstage with a wooden block is just going to ruin your own performance. Second, be sure your partner is willing and able to make rehearsals *and* (most importantly) performances. If he or she fails to turn up, then you've blown your audition, right?

Preparing Your Script

Your first step in working up an audition piece is to prepare three copies of the monolog or scene. These should be the final copies of your piece, after you've trimmed the original to an appropriate length, edited out the other characters, stage directions, etc. Word-process the monolog double-spaced, leaving room for notation. Two of these copies will be used for working rehearsals; the third will be your final draft. Always make notations in pencil.

Next, you should be prepared to mark up or "score" your script in pencil as you rehearse so you won't forget ideas about movement, emotions, business, vocal expressiveness and the like; you'll also want to incorporate suggestions of others. You'll refine these impulses, of course, as you move closer to a final version, but it's important at first to let the ideas flow and to note them in the script so you'll remember them.

At the same time, however, you want to avoid crowding your acting version with too many margin notes, underlines, etc. Your goal as you rehearse is to flesh out the text as you go with necessary technical points and then settle upon the best concrete choices you've discovered, discarding the other "experiments" you don't use. The final acting version should contain a minimum of notes for you to "skim over" in order to briefly refresh your memory prior to each performance. Operative words, beat changes, blocking movements, and business are the key elements here.

Paraphrasing

The next step in preparation is to do your paraphrase of the text. A paraphrase is a restatement of the character's language and feelings into your own words, and it should always be longer than the original. You want to be sure that you explore and utilize both the literal or surface meaning of the words and images as well as the underlying, subtextual meanings that the piece contains. These are commonly called the denotative and connotative meanings; both are important to consider, and both need to be paraphrased.

On the literal level, **there are many words and idioms in both modern and classical plays that only a dictionary or a teacher can explain to you.** Don't presume that you only have to "get the gist" of unfamiliar words that you encounter in the text. Even modern plays contain slang, jargon, regional, ethnic, and foreign terms that you must understand before you can make complete sense of the piece and understand the character. Nor should you assume that you understand the piece simply by reading it over a couple of times like a pop magazine — plays aren't like that. You'd be surprised how even experienced actors fail to read closely and look up terms in audition material and finished performances. So get a dictionary, get to the library, or ask someone who knows. *Any* clues you can dig up about the character's language will be useful to you.

Again on the literal level, **you must also pay attention to the way in which the character's speech pattern differs from yours.** Philosophers established long ago the connection between thought and language. In fact, the debate rages today whether or not we can even think of something without thinking of it in language, or to put it another way, if our language lacks the ability to express a phenomenon, then that phenomenon — whether a feeling, object, or relationship — doesn't exist for us, receives no notice from us. This implies that the way you think and speak are intimately and inextricably related, and in the hands of a skilled playwright, dialog gives you enormous clues about the way a character thinks. This is the main reason why actors — especially in

Western theatre — have always found it most helpful to begin their work with the play's language.

Noting the different ways in which you and the character speak helps you to objectify, to clearly see, the character, and this is the first step to building the role. Why does he or she speak in verse? Use "flowery" language? Speak in short, clipped sentences? Employ slang or vulgarity or regionalisms or foreign words? Why does she hesitate at this point or seem to use twice as many words to express what may be obvious in fewer? The answers to all these questions and others like them will help you enormously to enter the mindset and value system of your character, and this is how the literal or denotative paraphrase can be useful. **Never accept language at its face value.**

The connotative meaning is less easy to identify from a dictionary, although you'll find in the entry all the subordinate meanings of a word and these can be helpful. But word meanings are only partial clues. You'll find the subtext of your monolog or scene will emerge much more clearly as you rehearse it, because you'll begin to sense what underlies the character's spoken words. **These connotations are the hidden emotional dynamite that can energize your performance!** Do you call your boyfriend your "friend," your "main squeeze," your "hunk," your "main man," or something even more descriptive? They all mean approximately the same thing, but the distinctions are very important, right?! And those distinctions can reveal as much about you as about him.

This is why it's especially important to read the entire play if you have the chance. Words are only the tip of the proverbial iceberg underlying the lives of dramatic characters. The world of a well-written play provides a universe of context for understanding what emotional energy is appropriate in the scene, what words and phrases are implying, what goals are actually being sought, what feelings are being concealed or expressed. How often do *you* say what you really mean in real life? How adept are *you* at controlling and manipulating your own feelings and those of others by means of what you say? Well then, how much more likely is it that the character — designed by the playwright, don't forget! — has a lot more to say in the monolog or scene than his or her words are literally expressing?

Connotative meanings are especially revealing, and your paraphrase should seek to open up the worlds of nuance, suggestion, and levels of meaning that you'll need to bring to life in the scene or monolog and that audiences take so much joy in

experiencing. This subtext can be either in agreement with or in opposition to the spoken text, but it is always more complex and much closer in tune with the character's true emotional needs. The beginning actor, of course, just wants to get the words out and get them right, "to get through the bloody thing." But avoid this pitfall. Spoken language is only a partial clue to what the character truly intends to communicate.

Use your connotative paraphrase to tap this subtext and read between the lines of a scene. Ask yourself what the character really means by a word or phrase. The more questions the actor asks, the more creative and "layered" the scene will then become. Is your character forced to phrase his words carefully? To whom is she speaking? What is the real issue at stake here? How might the environment or situation be influencing what the character says?

To conclude, your denotative paraphrase must reveal all the surface meanings of the character's words. This is the "strategy" — the outward means your character employs to get what he or she wants. Your connotative paraphrase must reveal the character's deepest, strongest motivations. It must fire you up with vivid suggestions for concrete actions — what to do, how to move and actually play the scene. When you're in command of the subtext, you'll be able to fill the words with energy and drive, using them to create a more compelling performance.

Study the following speeches from R.N. Sandberg's *Convivencia* and John Webster's *The Duchess of Malfi* and the sample paraphrases following each. Remember that these paraphrases are done in the words of one student actor and that yours would be phrased differently because your language style and personal associations are unique.

From *Convivencia* by R.N. Sandberg [3]

1 **YTZHA: Blessed art Thou, Lord our God, King of the**
2 **Universe, who has commanded us to kindle the Sabbath**
3 **lights.** *(She lights the menorah. As she does so, she stops and*
4 *listens. She hears something. She calls into the distance, away from*
5 *the house.)* **Father? Father??** *(She gets no response. She senses*
6 *something behind her in the shadows. She quickly finishes lighting*
7 *the menorah and goes back through the gateway. Surreptitiously,*
8 *MA'EL, his face and clothes smudged with dirt and soot, comes out*
9 *of the shadows. He creeps forward, trying to make sure YTZHA is*
10 *gone. A voice comes from the darkness.)*

1 YTZHA: *(Off)* **What are you doing?** *(She steps into the light.)*
2   **Why were you hiding?**
3 MA'EL: **Please.**
4 YTZHA: **Are you Ahkmed's son? Have you come about the**
5   **fish? My father —**
6 MA'EL: **No, please, be quiet.**
7 YTZHA: **Why? What's wrong? Why are you so frightened?**
8 MA'EL: **Help me.**
9 YTZHA: **I ... Come back at dusk tomorrow. My father —**
10 MA'EL: **No.**
11 YTZHA: **It's the Sabbath. There's nothing we can do tonight.**
12 MA'EL: **I can't leave.**
13 YTZHA: **You have to.** *(Awkwardly, MA'EL thrusts out a knife in*
14   *his shaking hand.)* **Oh God.** *(She stays very still and quiet. With*
15   *the knife nervously quaking in his hand, he motions to the*
16   *menorah.)*
17 MA'EL: **Blow the candles out.**
18 YTZHA: **You know I can't.**
19 MA'EL: **Blow them out.**
20 YTZHA: **It's Shabbat.**
21 MA'EL: **Do you want me to —**
22 YTZHA: **You know our law. No work on the Sabbath.** *(They*
23   *are both shaking.)*
24 MA'EL: **I know your law. Blow them out.**
25 YTZHA: **No.** *(She seems immovable. MA'EL begins blowing out the*
26   *candles himself.)*
27 MA'EL: **No wonder we have to teach your children.**
28 YTZHA: **You teach us because we pay. And your prophet**
29   **Muhammad would have had no Qur'an if it weren't for our**
30   **Torah, so you learn from us, too.** *(MA'EL glances nervously*
31   *towards the house.)*
32 MA'EL: **That's enough. Someone will hear.**
33 YTZHA: **What do you want?**
34 MA'EL: **Quiet.**
35 YTZHA: **Why are you here? Why aren't you in your —**
36 MA'EL: **Enough, I said.**
37 YTZHA: **Have the Christians come?**
38 MA'EL: **If you speak again, I'll ... I'll cut out your tongue.**
39   **I've ripped them from peacocks with one slice. I'll do the**
40   **same to you.** *(MA'EL brandishes the knife at her, but his hand is*
41   *shaking and he almost drops it. YTZHA laughs.)*
42 YTZHA: **You've never cut off a peacock's tongue. Their beaks**

1   are sharp, and you hold that like a bar of soap. And it's a
2   kitchen knife not a butcher's. It'd take you an hour of
3   sawing to cut out my tongue. If you could keep your hand
4   steady. My father says "Respect the Muslims; they're great
5   thinkers." He should meet you. *(Deflated, MA'EL slumps*
6   *against the archway. YTZHA watches him for a moment.)* **Has**
7   **something terrible happened? I saw smoke all afternoon**
8   **and wondered if it was the Christians. After seven hundred**
9   **years, to have come back. They're very angry, aren't they?**
10   **Has there been fighting? Have you been in a battle?** *(MA'EL*
11   *is trying not to think about what she's saying.)* **Your people made**
12   **a mistake, you know. You should have just settled here**
13   **peacefully like we did and not fought with anybody. Then**
14   **you wouldn't be having the trouble you're having now. I**
15   **mean, we've been here a thousand years, and are we being**
16   **attacked? Of course, a battle must be very exciting.** *(It seems*
17   *that he's not even listening.)* **If you like excitement. Well, I**
18   **guess I'm going to go in now.**
19 MA'EL: Don't.
20 YTZHA: Why? I can talk to myself inside.
21 MA'EL: Stay for a bit.
22 YTZHA: Why should I?
23 MA'EL: You … you probably shouldn't.
24 YTZHA: Yes, well, I think my father'd prefer I go in. He gets
25   upset when I'm gone for more than five minutes.
26 MA'EL: He does?
27 YTZHA: He's got a horrible temper, too. He's sitting right by
28   the door. To hear any troubles in the street. If he knew I
29   were talking to you … if he knew you were here by our
30   house … you should see the knife he has. I've seen him slit
31   open stomachs and empty innards before you can say hello.
32 MA'EL: Oh God.
33 YTZHA: In fact, maybe I should call him since you tried to
34   threaten me. *(MA'EL grabs her and holds her tightly.)*
35 MA'EL: Don't. Don't. If you bring him on me —
36 YTZHA: I'm sorry. I was joking. He won't come out. He's …
37   you've nothing to fear. *(They stare at each other for a moment.*
38   *He releases her. But he holds the knife firmly.)*
39 MA'EL: You're not going in.
40 YTZHA: I —
41 MA'EL: You're not. You're staying with me. *(MA'EL'S head*
42   *sinks down on his chest. His arm falls to his side as he sleeps, and*

1   *the knife clinks on the ground. YTZHA carefully opens her eyes.*
2   *She sees that MA'EL has fallen asleep and the knife is on the*
3   *ground. Slowly, YTZHA creeps to MA'EL and takes the knife. She*
4   *stands over him, holding the knife easily in her hand.)*
5 **YTZHA: I've never touched a peacock, but I've gutted my**
6 **share of fish.** *(She laughs softly. The darkness begins to envelop*
7 *them.)*

Denotative Paraphrase (Ytzha) of *Convivencia*

1 **Blessed God, the king of all, I follow your command in**
2 **kindling these Sabbath lights. Is that you, Father? What are**
3 **you doing over there? Why were you hiding in the darkness?**
4 **Are you the son of Akhmed who wants to buy some of my**
5 **Father's fish? My father handles that business, not I. Why**
6 **should I be quiet? Is something wrong? Is there some new**
7 **danger? Why do you act so frightened? I'll come back at dusk**
8 **tomorrow. My father will be angry if I'm late. You must**
9 **understand that it's the Sabbath today and we are Jews so we**
10 **cannot do any work tonight. You must leave now. God save**
11 **me! You have a knife! You know I can't blow out these holy**
12 **candles in the sacred candle-holder. It's the Sabbath. You**
13 **know our law. We cannot do work on the Sabbath. No, I**
14 **won't blow the candles out. You Muslims are teachers to our**
15 **children because we pay you, not because you're smarter.**
16 **And your prophet Mahomet wrote his famous Koran using**
17 **our text of the Torah, so you Muslims learn from us Jews, too.**
18 **What do you want here? Why are you here? Why aren't you**
19 **in your own quarter of the city? Have the Christians come?**
20 **You've never cut off a peacock's tongue, you're lying. Their**
21 **beaks are sharp, and you're holding that knife like a bar of**
22 **soap! In fact, it's just a kitchen knife, not a butcher's. It'd take**
23 **you an hour of sawing to cut out my tongue — if you could**
24 **keep your hand steady. My father says to respect the**
25 **Muslims because they're great thinkers. Ha! He should meet**
26 **you! Has something terrible happened? All afternoon I saw**
27 **smoke and wondered if the Christians were burning the city.**
28 **To think that they've come back after seven hundred years!**
29 **They're very angry, aren't they? Has there been fighting?**
30 **Have you been caught up in the battle? You know, you**
31 **Muslims made a mistake. You should have just settled**
32 **peacefully in this city, like we did, and not fought with**

1 anybody. Then you wouldn't be in this trouble with the
2 Christians. I mean, we've been here a thousand years and
3 we're not being attacked. But I guess a battle must seem very
4 exciting to you. If you like excitement. Well, I'm going inside
5 now. Why shouldn't I? If you won't speak to me, I can just as
6 well speak to myself inside. Why should I stay? Anyhow, I
7 think my father would prefer that I went in. He gets upset if
8 I'm gone for more than five minutes. And he's got a bad
9 temper. He's sitting right there at the door to hear of any
10 trouble in the street. If he knew I were talking to you, or if he
11 knew you were hiding here by our house, he'd get angry. You
12 should see the knife he has. I've seen him slit open stomachs
13 and empty out the innards before you know it. In fact, I think
14 I'll call him because you threatened me. I'm sorry, I was
15 joking. He won't come out because he's busy praying. You've
16 nothing to fear. I think I'll go in. I've never had to carve a
17 peacock, but I have gutted my share of fish.

Connotative Paraphrase (Ytzha) of *Convivencia*

1 Blessed and Most High God of all, I light these Sabbath
2 candles as You have directed, keeping sacred Your holy day
3 ... three ... four ... five — what's that? What's that noise? Is
4 someone there? Is it dad, I wonder? Hmmmm ... no answer.
5 Maybe no one. But I'd better finish up out here and get back
6 inside. No telling who or what's skulking around at night
7 these days. Six-seven — there! I'm outa here. But wait —
8 there is a noise! What's going on out there? Hey — come out
9 here in the light where I can — who's that? Some kid? About
10 my age? A Muslim kid? What's he want? Oh! Maybe he's
11 Akhmed's boy, come for the fish he wanted from dad. Hey,
12 listen, it's too late now. The Sabbath is here and my dad's
13 already praying — help you? Whadda you mean? What help?
14 I can't help, we're Jews. We don't do anything on the
15 Sabbath. Wow! He seems really frightened. No, look, you've
16 got to leave because today — *Whoa! A knife!* Oh-kay ... oh-
17 kay ... just stay calm, Ytzha. Noooo problem, guy, nooo
18 problem, see? I'm not doing anything ... you got the knife,
19 right. No panic, Ytzha, no panic. What's he want? To rob us?
20 Rape me? Murder? What? Now what's he doing pointing at
21 the menorah? You want me to blow out the candles?!?! Like,

1   what is it with you? Don't you understand? Tomorrow — I'll
2   be here tomorrow and then ... No ... like — are you from
3   Mars, or what? You know the law. Jews don't do — What!?!
4   Blow out the Sabbath candles? Like, no way, guy! Who the
5   hell do you think — No! You can kill me if — now what's he
6   doing? Blowing out the candles himself!?! And what's he
7   say? Jews are so stupid that we even send our kids to be
8   educated by the Muslims!!! You little snot! You stupid Arab-
9   kid! Hey, buddy-boy, just a friggin' minute here! You educate
10 our kids because we pay you. That's what you're good at,
11 right? You Muslims will do anything for money, right? And
12 anyhow, you wouldn't even have a crappy Koran if your
13 precious Mahomet hadn't stolen all of it from our Torah! So
14 don't get all — whadda you mean, 'quiet'? I won't keep
15 quiet! Forget it, Jack! And what the hell are you doing over
16 here in the Jewish quarter anyway? Trashing our religious
17 services and everything? Why aren't you in your own quarter
18 — oh! I get it! The Christian soldiers are on your case, right?
19 Well, buddy, lemme tell ya — *You'll what?!? You'll cut out my*
20 *tongue?!?* Like a peacock?? Oh yeah, right, like I'm sure
21 you've butchered all these peacocks before, you wimp! You
22 wuss! You couldn't even cut your toenails with that little
23 kitchen paring knife! And your hand's shaking like some old
24 man! Hey ... what's wrong with him? Is he hurt? Maybe he's
25 hurt or something? Maybe I came on too strong there a
26 second ago ... hmmm ... he's kinda cute, in a way ... Hey —
27 has something bad happened? Are the Christians burning
28 your houses? Like, I saw a bunch of smoke this afternoon?
29 Hello? Are you listening? I said, are the Christians — well, it
30 stands to reason. You Muslims keep them outa the city for
31 seven hundred years, and the Christians are bound to be
32 pissed at you when they take over again. Hello? Do you hear
33 me? Why doesn't he say anything? Are you, like, tuning me
34 out or something? You know, you Muslims brought this on
35 yourselves, right? I mean, we Jews have been here for a
36 thousand years never making any trouble, and then you
37 people with your crazy jihads and battles and everything —
38 well, it just stands to reason. You like battles? Were you in a
39 battle today? Hey — answer me, turkey! Maybe you're in
40 trouble now because you like kicking Christian butt or
41 something? Well ... well — well, hell! I'm going inside. I'm
42 tired of this monolog. I mean, if you're not gonna say

1 anything ... Why shouldn't I go? I can talk to myself just as
2 well outside ... Stay for a bit? A bit? He wants me to stay
3 with him? Well ... at least he's asking now. But what for?
4 What does he want? Hey — maybe if I tell him my dad gets
5 all uptight if I stay out, and he's got this huge butcher knife,
6 and he's listening inside the door for trouble on the street,
7 and he slits fish and animals with their guts all over the place
8 — so maybe I should call my dad and — *Oh wow! He's*
9 *grabbed me and I can't ... get ... free!* He's ... too ... strong ...
10 I've never been this close to a boy before. Okay ... okay ...
11 listen, I was just ... just kidding about my dad ... he's not
12 listening ... and I won't call him ... just relax ... don't be
13 afraid ... you can let go of me, I won't cry out ... He's letting
14 go of me ... he has the deepest, deepest blue eyes ... I guess
15 ... I guess ... yeah ... I should go in, but ... well — hey?
16 What's he doing? Collapsing on me? What's he mumbling ...
17 that I should stay with him? He wants me to stay with him ... ?
18 Hey — I think he really is asleep there. Or maybe he's hurt.
19 And there goes the knife. Maybe I could ... sneak over and
20 grab it ... without waking him — got it! Got it ... now what?
21 He sure looks all helpless lying there like that ... and me
22 standing over him with this dumb knife. Like, what would I
23 do with this knife? Stab him or something? I just can't leave
24 him here ... even if it is the Sabbath ... of course, if I just lie
25 down here with him I'm not really doing anything on the
26 Sabbath, am I? I'm just ... staying with him until he ... if he
27 needs me ... maybe dad will come out looking for me. And
28 me with this dumb knife ... I've never even touched a
29 peacock ... the boy's kinda cute, like a peacock ... maybe I
30 could touch him while he's asleep, without waking him ...
31 like that ... he's so warm ... and smooth ... and his hair ...
32 and me with this dumb knife! Of course, I've gutted my
33 share of fish over the years! Har! Har! Well, just sitting here
34 by him isn't really doing anything on the Sabbath ... just
35 watching over him ... .

From *The Duchess of Malfi* by John Webster

**The misery of us that are born great!
We are forced to woo, because none dare woo us;
And as a tyrant doubles with his words
And fearfully equivocates, so we
Are forced to express our violent passions
In riddles and in dreams, and leave the path
Of simple virtue, which was never made
To seem the thing it is not. Go, go brag
You have left me heartless; mine is in your bosom:
I hope 'twill multiply love there. You do tremble.
Make not your heart so dead a piece of flesh,
To fear more than to love me. Sir, be confident,
What is it distracts you? This is flesh and blood, sir;
'Tis not the figure cut in alabaster
Kneels at my husband's tomb. Awake, awake, man!
I do here put off all vain ceremony
And only do appear to you a young widow
That claims you for her husband; and, like a widow,
I use but half a blush in it.**

Denotative Paraphrase of *The Duchess of Malfi*

It's really hard to be rich and to have an important family. I have to be kind of aggressive because men think I'm sort of aloof and untouchable, and that I can probably have everything I want. And like some kind of hypocrite with two-faced words I have to hide my love and my feelings, I have to joke around and tell stories, I have to be dishonest — as though anyone can be honest anyway! You're probably going to run out and tell everyone how hard-up and what a pushover I am. Well, you've pushed me over, all right. But it's just that I really love you, and I hope you feel the same way. Hey — you're trembling! Chill out, it's okay. What's wrong? I'm just a woman, a real person and not some news photo of someone praying at my husband's grave. Hey, come on, you know what I'm saying. Okay, so I'm a widow, but. And I really want to go out with you. And, yeah, I'm not blushing or too shy to say so.

Connotative Paraphrase of *The Duchess of Malfi*

1 God! This is such a downer! Like, what is happening to me??
2 What am I doing? I must be crazy — why the hell should I feel
3 guilty about being sexually aggressive if I want to? If I need to?
4 I mean, what's wrong with that?? At least I'm honest, even
5 though this sexist, conservative society doesn't want to think
6 about that. Doesn't believe women should be that way. But
7 haven't I got a right to express my needs like everyone else?
8 Especially like men do? Even if I am a duchess, I'm a person,
9 right? And so I have to use polite words to hit on you. But I'm
10 doing what I feel I have to, even though I may sound kind of
11 stand-offish and formal. Hell! You don't understand, do you?
12 Freaks you out, probably. But you don't really understand me
13 as a person either, do you? Can't you understand? I really want
14 you — so much!! Don't you get it? Can't you believe that? Well,
15 come on and grab me, why don't you? Just jump me! I'm
16 talking like a woman, a female — not a "duchess." Let's just cut
17 through all the crap and get on down to it! Let's be real, let's be
18 up close and personal and all that stuff. I mean, what's
19 "nobility" anyway? It's leadership, isn't it? Courage, guts,
20 going for it — more than the average person, right? So let's do
21 that! Are you that kind of guy or aren't you? I think you are.
22 That's why I'm coming on to you now! Have you got the guts
23 to do it with me now, or would you feel "safer" just keeping it
24 all "comfortable" between us?

The denotative paraphrase of Ytzha's words tries to retain a note of hesitancy and curiosity as she speaks, while the subtextual paraphrase captures her fear, outrage, and then her growing sense of motherliness, eventual control of the relationship, and feminine curiosity. The literal rewording of the Duchess' speech tries to capture the ideas of a young woman who is a very good-looking, wealthy, and attractive widow in her twenties, while the connotative rewording reveals the emotional sources of the spoken text. Notice how the student's paraphrase has also captured the urgency of the Duchess' need to win this man's love *right now.*

In each case the denotation solves any difficult problems with word meaning and helps you to personalize the speech by putting it into your own words. The connotation taps these characters' gut reactions and basic needs, thus giving you a driving force for acting the words.

Exploration #26: Exercises in Paraphrasing

Look over the speeches in appendix A by Beth (if you're a woman) from Max Bush's *Voices from the Shore*, and by the Boy (if you're a male) in Bob Mayberry's *Written in Water*. Write a denotative paragraph of the speech, followed by a short commentary listing at least three ways in which the playwright's language differs from yours and why that's important. Next, write a connotative paraphrase of the speech, followed by a short commentary listing three reasons why the character's original words conceal the powerful emotional currents you found between the lines.

Exploration #27: Exercises in Classical Paraphrasing

When you've completed these projects, turn to the more difficult selection in appendix A by Puck from Shakespeare's *A Midsummer Night's Dream*. For the denotative meaning you'll need to visit the library and use an annotated edition of the text, containing a glossary of word meanings and suggested line interpretations. You should also read or view the entire play if you're not familiar with it in order to understand the context, which is all-important for this speech. Once you've completed your denotative and connotative paraphrases of Shakespeare, compare your restatement against the original by speaking all of them aloud. Try to appreciate some of the advantages of using verse language instead of prose. Have your coach or a teacher help you with this step. You should ignore the obvious difference of "old fashioned" language. Focus instead on such things as economy of words, the rhythm of the lines, or the phrasing. What does the poetic form enable you to achieve as an actor that everyday prose fails to accomplish? And be sure to ask yourself whether Puck is concealing some hidden emotions underneath his words. What does Puck feel about Oberon? About the humans? About each of the different humans? About himself or herself (Puck has often been played as a gender-neutral character)?

Exploration #28: Paraphrasing and Improvisation

This fun exercise is designed to help you fine-tune at least one of the above connotative paraphrases you just completed. Select any of those monologs to work on: The Duchess, Puck, Beth, or The Boy. Read the original text aloud several times using an obviously false and unreal "character voice" from your favorite cartoon character. Donald Duck, Porky Pig, Scooby-Doo, SpongeBob, and others can all be excellent choices. Let yourself go and have fun with this improv. In fact, the more serious monologs might even be the most fun of all when done with a ridiculous character voice! Each time you finish a reading, note down in your journal what bizarre images or situations or "double-meanings" or interpretations of the text the cartoon voice brought to mind. If you do this exercise correctly, you should find some different spots to note each time you read the monolog, and some of those connotations should also be retained in the finished paraphrase as valuable insights into what's happening in the monolog. You might also bring one or two of these cartoon readings into class and present it publicly to a group in order to get some feedback from others. [4]

Exploration #29: Speaking the Denotative Paraphrase

The next step is to **practice all these speeches aloud, trying to keep only the literal meanings clearly in mind as you speak**. Avoid the temptation to rush and to run together words and phrases, especially in the Renaissance selections. Don't pantomime anything except in the most difficult passages. "Savor" the images in your mind before they enter your mouth. Try to deliver the speeches with as much clarity of expression as possible and motivate your delivery so it seems natural. When you feel you're ready, test yourself by having someone listen to you. Ask that person how much of the speech was understandable the first time through (75 percent is a good average with the classics). Also ask how much of the speech seemed believable.

Exploration #30: Speaking the Connotative Paraphrase

The final step is to **deliver the monologs while keeping only the connotative meanings in mind** and asking your listener how the literal sense of the speech seemed to change. This is by far the most difficult part of the exercise. You might begin by whispering the subtext several times before gradually moving into a whispered delivery of the text. Gradually increase your volume until you can speak in a full stage voice without losing touch with the subtext. You can also practice this with a tape recorder. Record the connotative paraphrase with great intensity, and allow it to play alongside you (or even better, with an earphone plug in your ear) underneath your delivery of the lines. Most importantly, give in to all your impulses for moving and gesturing and for radical vocal delivery patterns that the subtext may suggest.

Goals, Obstacles, and Actions

The next step in your preparation is to identify the goals and obstacles of your character in the scene or monolog and choose concrete actions to express them. Identifying and then playing objectives and obstacles effectively are the hardest things to master in acting and auditioning, but this skill lies at the heart of a compelling performance.

Michael Schulman, one of New York's most respected acting teachers, points out that goals and obstacles "and the uncertainty they generate with regard to outcomes ... constitute the basic structure of a dramatic event." [5] This means training yourself to spot what you're struggling to win in the scene (the goal, the intention, the objective) and what prevents you from obtaining it (the obstacles). Then you'll find it easier to devise concrete actions to play onstage moment by moment that will express those intentions clearly and overcome the obstacles.

To begin with, you should realize that *a character's objectives in a scene can be either single or multiple and that you have to be as specific as possible in pinning them down.* Your character will likely shift objectives in a scene or monolog as it develops, as he or she learns something new, encounters different obstacles, makes decisions, and so forth. Monologs or scenes will usually have one main goal that motivates the character to speak the speech, which must then be broken down into a series of other objectives that lead you moment by moment through the speech.

Once you divide the speech or scene into sections reflecting these objectives, you have what are called "beats" or "bits" of the monolog or scene; these are the spine of the scene, its building blocks, the events. You can say that you've "evented the script." You need to label each of these beats with a clear statement of its objective. This is critically important because you must play the scene as you develop and change moment-by-moment, i.e., you must play beats. And when the beat changes, you must know what objective you now seek in the beat coming up. You label each beat with clear, simple infinitive verbs to reflect these objectives: you want "to guilt" the other character, "to mock" him, "to seduce" her, "to mislead" him, "to shame" her, "to comfort" him, and so forth.

One of America's most experienced professional actresses and coaches, Pat Dougan, explains the process this way:

> You actively try to get something from or do something to the other character ... We see you in pursuit, trying to get something from the character you're talking to ... Your

choice is exciting, alive, and believable, not fixed or phony. Each time you choose an action, make a personal commitment to achieve it ... At first you may find that the choices you make are flabby, not strong. Or they may not really be playable or active. For example, choosing "I want to tell you" is much less active than "I want to excite you." "Tell" is more passive. This technique requires thought and patience. It requires practice ... The best actions are directed to another person and depend on that person's response, even if you have to create the response ...

Pat Dougan refers to these action objectives as "wants," and she lists some vivid ones an actor might assign to the beats in the scene or monolog in order to play each part of the scene — each beat — effectively:

I want to challenge you.	I want to tease you.
I want to quiz you.	I want to convince you
I want to entice you.	beyond a doubt.
I want to grab you.	I want to thrill you.
I want to embarrass you.	I want to share this secret
I want to surprise you.	with you.
I want to make you feel better.	I want to excite you.
I want to cheer you up.	I want to encourage you.
I want to justify my position.	I want to reassure you.
I want to charm you.	I want to dazzle you.
I want to compliment you.	I want to win you over. [6]

The next step is to devise a chain of specific actions you can play onstage that express those objectives. Occasionally, one or more such actions may be found in stage directions: the way a character speaks, gestures, or moves onstage may be directly suggested by the script. Although stage directions might be helpful at times, never follow them religiously, because they were most likely inserted by the stage manager at the first professional performance of the play, not by the playwright. That's why they're included in the script. Most frequently you'll find nothing indicated in the script, and you'll be required to improvise and invent them at the audition. In either case, keep in mind that the concrete actions must always reflect the objective.

One repertory theatre director of wide experience, William Glover, stated this very emphatically for auditionees at the Colorado Shakespeare Festival:

"What do I want? And how am I going to get it?" That's the whole excitement of acting. It comes spontaneously at the time when you meet the other person and the other person says, "No, you can't have it," and you try to get it. And you may have to bully, yell, scream, plead, cry or whatever you have to do in order to get what you want. [7]

When Molière's Arsinoë wants "to dominate" Célimène in *The Misanthrope* (Arsinoë's overall goal in the scene), does she begin with a smile ("to trick") and then a casual remark ("to hint"), and then follow up by crossing behind Célimène to deliver mild accusations ("to dig at"), before facing her and giving her the real zingers ("to dump on")? These are some *concrete actions* that might reflect Arsinoë's objectives in each beat of the monolog, all of which add up to fulfilling Arsinoë's goal. They are things an actor can play moment by moment as the monolog develops, and they add clarity and shape to the performance (either at an audition or in a performance of the play). When you can identify the character's goals, objectives, and actions, then you have something concrete to play onstage, and you look strong and purposeful! Events seem to be happening!

You have a lot of latitude in deciding the best objectives to play. One trick to remember here is that objectives come in two basic forms, internal and external. For example, you may decide that Arsinoë simply wishes to hear herself talk or plant suspicion or parade her knowledge (internal/psychological goals). You may also decide that she wishes to provoke Célimène to anger or cause her to cry or drive Célimène from the room (external goals). It helps to distinguish between the two so you can devise a clear pattern of verbal and physical actions that the director can see working in the scene or monolog.

Now you need to identify obstacles to your goals in much the same way, internally and externally. Take this same speech by Molière as an example. Perhaps Arsinoë's words are somehow forced or pointed because of an external obstacle (the social conventions of politeness and manners that Arsinoë is required to observe) or an internal one (her caution to conceal her lust for Célimène's lovers while insulting her). Again, you don't need to invent or discover anything complicated; the best choices are always the simplest and most direct, and are often found in the text. An obstacle may be as simple as a character's fear of failure (Claudio's reluctance to speak to Desdemona about the punishment Othello has imposed upon him) or even a physical defect mandated by the script (Laura's limp in *The Glass Menagerie*).

Why are obstacles so important? Dramatic characters are never permitted to move toward their goals unimpeded. Drama is conflict. In everyday life, our obstacles are rarely "dramatic," but in plays the obstacles energize the scene or monolog by intensifying the struggle, "upping the stakes" of the conflict, enlarging the events onstage. Michael Shurtleff often remarked to us: "Each and every scene you will ever do onstage is about relationship. Ask yourselves: 'This character and I are involved in a love relationship. What is the problem we're having?'" By "love," of course, he meant more than just romantic love. He meant *any* kind of need that binds you in a relationship with that other person in the present moment of the scene or monolog.

"Plays are written about the most important moments in people's lives," Shurtleff explains, "not about their everyday humdrumness ... What an actor must look for in a play is something unusual. Something important ... That attitude toward being alive without which you would long ago have jumped off the Fifty-Ninth Street bridge."[8] The stronger your struggle with obstacles in your audition piece, the more pizzazz you'll lend to the events you're creating onstage!

Your vital struggle to overcome your obstacle and accomplish your objective helps to compel the spectator's (and the casting director's) attention by conveying the importance of relationships. Moreover, it's what we expect from dramatic writing. "They're all vampires out there!" Broadway director Aaron Frankel points out. "They come to the theatre because things are so much more alive there, because their own lives are incomplete. They want to feed on you because of your vitality — your blood courses so much hotter and fuller than theirs. That's why they're vampires."[9]

Whether or not you actually win the struggle in your monolog or scene is unimportant; the greatest dramatic characters — Oedipus, Desdemona, Hedda Gabler — never do. What we want to see is that you try as hard as possible to do so, because nobody pays money to come to the theatre to see unambitious, uncourageous losers who won't even try. Do you want a piece of advice about why this is important in auditions? Try this, from one educational theatre director: "The single most common mistake of student actors at auditions," he remarked to me, "is not going far enough with the choices they've made — not playing contrasts vividly, or changes in mood and in pacing."[10]

Learn to work goal-obstacle combinations into your scenes and monologs so that your audition develops with punch and with urgency from the very first moments, and so you make events happen.

A handy way to begin looking for these elements in the material is by asking yourself what changes by the end of the piece. Your character can never end up at the same point where he or she began. There must always be some development. What events (external or internal) have occurred? Has she resolved a problem with the other character? Has he reached a decision? Has she suffered some setback? Has he discovered something new? Then ask yourself what difficulties your character encountered in reaching these new points. In this way, you can begin to nail down concrete actions to play, event by event. Remember to *always choose the most urgent objectives for your beats, the most tenacious obstacles, the most direct goals that you want to win.*

Examine this comic speech by Launce Gobbo from Shakespeare's *Two Gentlemen from Verona*, where the young servant explains to the audience how he saved his dog, Crab, from a whipping following a dinner party. Launce's final line suggests that the character's goal in the speech is to persuade his listeners that he's a good and generous master to his dog. In short, Launce wants "to win approval." Now, what obstacles must he overcome? Well, one general obstacle would be his listeners' ignorance of the facts. The audience doesn't know how Launce rescued Crab from drowning, educated him, tried to potty-train him, put up with his awful table manners, and even just now took Crab's beating on himself. These are all things he must explain to the audience; each is a separate event in the story fully and distinctly played — in sequence — to lead the thought through the speech. So he will "plead," "dump," "brag," "rage," etc., in order to win approval from his listeners. These are concrete verbs that tell an actor just what he's doing at each moment.

> When a man's servant shall play the cur with him, look you, it goes hard: one that I brought up of a puppy; one that I saved from drowning, when three or four of his blind brothers and sisters went to it! I have taught him, even as one would say precisely, "thus I would teach a dog." I was sent to deliver him as a present to Mistress Silvia from my master; and I came no sooner into the dining chamber, but he steps me to his trencher, and steals her capon's leg. He thrusts himself into the company of three or four gentlemanlike dogs, under the Duke's table: he had not been there — bless the mark — a pissing while, but all the chamber smelt him. "Out with the dog!" says one; "What cur is that?" says another: "Whip him out," says the third:

"Hang him up," says the duke. I, having been acquainted with the smell before, knew it was Crab, and goes me to the fellow that whips the dogs: "Friend," quoth I, "you mean to whip the dog?" "Ay, marry, do I," quoth he. "You do him the more wrong," quoth I. "Twas I did the thing you wot of." He makes me no more ado, but whips me out of the chamber. How many masters would do this for his servant?

Now study this breakdown done by one student actor, with the objectives written in the margin alongside each section. Note that the student has also clearly divided the speech into beats for rehearsal purposes with a boldface line through the text. You should always do this, too, with monologs and scenes. This helps you in rehearsal to remember where the beats change, so you can discover and attack ("play") each new one vividly as it presents itself, adding development and dynamism to the performance.

When a man's servant shall play the cur with him, look you, it goes hard: one that I brought up of a puppy; one that I saved from drowning, when three or four of his blind brothers and sisters went to it! I have taught him, even as one would say precisely, "thus I would teach a dog."	**to brag**

I was sent to deliver him as a present to Mistress Silvia from my master; and I came no sooner into the dining chamber, but he steps me to his trencher, and steals her capon's leg. He thrusts himself into the company of three or four his gentlemanlike dogs, under the Duke's table: he had not been there — bless the mark — a pissing while, but all the chamber smelt him. "Out with the dog!" says one; "What cur is that?" says another: "Whip him out," says the third: "Hang him up," says the duke.	**to shock his listeners**

I, having been acquainted with the smell before, knew it was Crab, and goes me to the fellow that whips the dogs: "Friend," quoth I, "you mean to whip the dog?" "Ay, marry, do I," quoth he. "You do him the more wrong," quoth I. "'Twas I did the thing you wot of." He makes me no more ado, but whips me out of the chamber.	**to play the hero**

How many masters would do this for his servant?   **to win applause**

Thus, the actor's overall goal in speaking the speech has four objectives connected to it, all of which add up to or develop the meaning the audience will understand. You don't have to concern yourself with that meaning as you're acting it — an actor can't play "meaning"; he or she only plays actions. "Meaning" is the spectator's job or the critic's. **An actor simply makes choices to play actions that vividly express the truth of his or her character's intentions, as he or she sees them.** That's what actors do, and that's all they should do. Leave the rest — the meaning — up to God or the onlookers' imaginations. Don't play the critic; you're an actor.

In a two-character scene you can follow the same procedure, but you find the changing events, the objectives and the obstacles in the pattern of conversation, the give-and-take of the dialog. This reveals the change in subjects as the dialog progresses: the questions and answers, the contradictions, the surprises, the discoveries — all such comments point to the major steps your character takes on his or her way to achieving his or her objectives. Use your vis-à-vis to pose those obstacles, throw you off-balance, offer or deny you the support you need; make eye contact with him or her and bring him or her into the scene with you (even though it's not their audition). You break down and lay out on the page a two-character scene the same way in which the student broke down the monolog in the exploration above.

Exploration #31: Beats and Objectives

Return now to the speech you used for the earlier exploration on paraphrasing: either The Boy from Bob Mayberry's *Written on Water* or Beth from Max Bush's *Voices from the Shore*. With the character of Beth, use as your overall goal "to win his love and commitment," and with the character of The Boy, "to find a way to convince Grandfather." Tape record a preliminary reading of the speech before analyzing it as though it were handed to you for the first time. Then divide the speech up into the different thought sections or beats and assign objectives in the margin beside each beat. When you're done, practice the speech aloud several times to **see if the thought really does change at the points you noted, and if you can keep your mind clearly on the different objectives as you play the text, the different events you're trying to create for the spectator**. Revise the beats or objectives so they make more sense to you, or when you feel they need to be strengthened, and repeat the readings accordingly. When you're satisfied with the train of thought, tape record yourself a second time as you read the speech, trying to "attack" each new beat sharply, making the monolog develop through discoveries, changes in intentions, surprises, etc.

Once you're satisfied with the dramatic shape of your audition scene or monolog broken down into beats and objectives, prepare one "final" copy and set it aside. Use a second clean copy for the explorations in the next section.

Vocal Rehearsals

Now that you've done the brain-work of analyzing the scene or monolog for your prepared audition, it's time to get it rehearsed! *The purpose of vocal rehearsal is twofold. Obviously you want to get your actual performance set, but also keep in mind that rehearsal is a further exploration of the text.* Rehearsing your audition pieces is a journey of *discovery*, not just finalizing what you've settled upon intellectually. So analysis is not done yet, you need to further explore the selections you've chosen.

I always recommend *three approaches for exploring the vocal interpretation of speeches: identifying operative words, sharpening your sense of vowels and consonant sounds, and attuning yourself to rhythm and pace of delivery.* Let's look at these one by one.

"Operative words" refers simply to those words and phrases in the piece that are the most important, the ones that should carry the most emphasis as you speak. This may sound simple and elementary, but it is not. You'd be surprised how many actors — often in the heat of performance — fail to stress operative words in ordinary sentences or place their stress in a strange and confusing location, such as on prepositions, indefinite articles, and so forth. If you succumb to "machinegun mouth," you'll simply rattle off the words and nothing will receive any emphasis. And if you succumb to stage fright (inability to concentrate on the situation), your voice may tighten up into a dull and lifeless monotone that drains the text of all energy.

Take a look at the following speech by a prison guard abusing his victim with bullying, mockery, and insults:

From *Lilford Mill* by Neil Duffield [11]

1 **OFFICER: Prisoner K561! Abo ... out turn! Qui ... ck march!**
2 **Left right left right left right left right ...** (*Marches LIAM back*
3 *to the bedroom.*) **Halt!** (*LIAM stands at attention. The OFFICER*
4 *relaxes. Takes stock of LIAM.*) **Well, Michael. Here we are. This**
5 **is where you spend the next eight years ... if you manage to**
6 **last that long. It's quite a pleasant little cell is this. Too**

1   pleasant some would say. People don't like it if we let things
2   get too pleasant, see? If things got too pleasant we'd have
3   every idle paddy in the country clamouring to get in here,
4   wouldn't we? That wouldn't do now, would it? We've got
5   enough of your lot already. *(LIAM'S face betrays some interest.)*
6   Oh, you didn't think you was the only one, did you? We've
7   had dozens like you. All as thick as pudding. Do you know
8   what happens to them — all these fellow countrymen of
9   yours — once they get in here? They lose their wits … Every
10   one of them. Go mad as bleeding hatters. *(Pause.)* Do you
11   know what it's like, Michael, not being able to speak to
12   anyone? Day after day? Week after week? Year after year?
13   'Course you can always talk to yourself. That's what they do.
14   We've heard 'em jabbering on for hours some nights. Laugh?
15   They've had us in tears. *(Pause.)* "They'll never drive me
16   insane." That's what you're thinking, isn't it? "Not me.
17   Never me." I wonder, Michael. I wonder if the name
18   Gallagher means anything to you … ? It does so. Good. You
19   know who I'm on about then. Gallagher had this cell,
20   Michael. I can see him now, sitting on that bed snivelling
21   and whimpering, chewing on his blanket. The man couldn't
22   even pee straight. Do you know what happened to him?
23   Gallagher? We found him one day in the carpenter's shop.
24   He was kneeling on the floor and he had this little wooden
25   board there in front of him. On it was a pile of something
26   that looked like salt. There he was stuffing it into his mouth.
27   Great handfuls of it. Swallowing down into his stomach. Do
28   you know what it was, Michael … ? Glass. Crushed glass.
29   Now I ask you, who in the world but a paddy'd eat glass?
30   "You carry on eating that and you're going to kill yourself."
31   I says to him. Do you know what he turns 'round to me and
32   says? *(Mimicking Irish accent:)* "A pound of it'd do you no
33   harm." *(Laughs loudly.)* A pound of it'd do you no harm!
34   *(Pause.)* You'll end up the same, Michael. Same as Gallagher.
35   One year. Two if you're tough. But we'll break
36   you … We'll break you piece by piece.

First off, a hasty and unshaped reading might proceed by
emphasizing the following words in the text (read this aloud, stressing
the italicized words): "*Well*, Michael. *Here* we *are*. *This* is where *you*
spend the next eight years … if you manage to *last* that long. It's *quite
a pleasant little cell* is this. *Too* pleasant some would say." Now try

stressing the following words that I'd recommend as "operative" in the same passage: "*Well*, Michael. *Here* we are. *This* is where you spend the *next eight years* ... *if* you manage to *last* that long. It's quite a *pleasant* little cell is this. *Too* pleasant *some* would say."

Is the second choice radically different from the first? Not especially; the meaning comes across in both cases. But is the second choice a little more focused? Does it pick up more on the central action of the monolog: to sadistically torture the prisoner? I think so. For example, it stresses more effectively the phrase "next eight years." It also tends to inject some tension and fear by stressing the word "if," and it raises uncertainty in the prisoner by hinting that "some" might consider the miserable little cell too good for the likes of him.

As you can see, deciding upon operative words is a very subjective process and depends a lot upon your own general literary sensitivity to the language of your audition piece. But never forget that it can also be tied to the central action of that piece and reinforce it — or it can scatter focus away from that action, sometimes radically, by failing to emphasize the important words or cluttering the line with unwanted emphases.

Exploration #32: Operative Words

Return now to the speech you used for the earlier explorations on paraphrasing and beats and objectives: either The Boy from Bob Mayberry's *Written on Water* or Beth from Max Bush's *Voices from the Shore*. Work through the entire speech now, underlining the important words and phrases you feel should definitely receive emphasis. Your point is not to memorize all these underlinings, but to **attune yourself to the presence of important ideas** in the audition piece. Rehearse the piece aloud (not memorized, simply read off the page) each time you get it marked up, in order to see if your operative words are really effective and whether you need more or less of them (the fewer the better!)

Exploration #33: Exploring Vowel Sounds [12]

In the very best writers you'll find more than simply a literary command of words in the form of vocabulary, sentence structure, narration, and such things; you'll also find a strong and vital command of the sound of words as they ring in the listeners' ears. This is, of course, particularly true of great poets and playwrights, and you should always read poetry and plays aloud in order to fully appreciate them. In the following exploration you should return to the speech you just used for operative words: either The Boy from Bob Mayberry's *Written on Water* or Beth from Max Bush's *Voices from the Shore*. Speak it very, very slowly, noting your identification of operative words and phrases as you talk, and "stretching" or elongating unnaturally all the vowel sounds. It will sound very odd to you, but don't be put off; stay with it! Roll the sounds around in your mouth, let them resonate and trill as you deliver the words until you feel like you're almost making opera music! This should sensitize you to any hidden vocal qualities of the language that the playwright has embedded in the writing. Then gradually bring your delivery "up to speed," and try to stress a little more those words and phrases where you just discovered the vowel sounds to have special importance in adding emphasis to the ideas.

Exploration #34: Exploring Consonant Sounds [13]

In the very best writers you'll also find a strong and vital command of the consonant sounds in words as they ring in the listeners' ears. Again, this technique is particularly true of great poets and playwrights, and you can attune yourself to the consonant sounds in dramatic dialogue in the very same way you just did for the vowels. In the following exploration use the same speeches either from Bob Mayberry's *Written on Water* or Max Bush's *Voices from the Shore*. Speak very, very slowly, noting your identification of operative words and phrases as well as vowel sounds, and over exaggerate the consonant sounds in the text. Again, it will sound very odd to you, but don't be put off; stay with it! Chew out the consonants and sensitize yourself to any hidden vocal qualities of the language that the playwright has embedded in the writing. Then gradually bring your delivery "up to speed," and try to stress a little more those words and phrases where you just discovered the consonant sounds to have special importance in adding emphasis to the ideas. By stressing the consonants in this way you'll find not only that you can greatly enhance the meaning of the text, but also that your stage speech is becoming more clear and projects better, without raising the volume of your voice! Why? Because it is the actor's pronunciation of the consonants that accounts more than anything else for the quality of his or her projection in live performance!

Once you've completed these vocal explorations, take the second clean copy of your script and note all the vocal dynamics you've just uncovered. You should now have two semifinal versions of your monolog or scene: the beats with their intentions penciled into the margins and the vocal interpretation you want to keep in mind (as well as the paraphrasing that you've done in your journal). Let's hammer out now the third and final version of the script you're going to use.

Movement Rehearsals

You're now at the end of your rope! The piece is ready to be staged in physical space. Bet you couldn't wait for this, eh? I understand exactly what you've been feeling, because any talented actor will have lots of imaginative ideas right off the bat on what he or she might look like, what to do, and how to move and gesture. But you really must resist the impulse to start "acting" right away, as though performing a monolog were the easiest thing in the world! Just get up and do it, right? Well, this ain't the gong show or late-night improv; it's live theatre! You've gotta understand the structure of the thing first, get a handle on the subtext, and learn about the words you must speak.

By the time you've done all that, you'll be in an even better position to stage the monolog or scene effectively because all these explorations will continue to stimulate your imagination. And at this point, too, you'll be less inclined to add all those nervous, unnecessary moves and gestures that just clutter up your performance and distract your audience from the action you're supposed to be playing. In other words, **now and only now can you make decisions on when and where movements will enhance your performance.** Who knows? Maybe no movements at all will be best for some pieces.

The following explorations will guide you on how to begin devising movement for your pieces in a step-by-step process, and the final exploration will give you a sort of "checklist" for the most common movement pitfalls to avoid. You should try them all, much like warmup procedures, doing each exploration for thirty minutes. And this means thirty minutes actually doing it, not just thinking about it! You'll likely discover after trying these explorations that only three or four will be most useful. That's fine, too.

Throughout the explorations — and even before this point — you should pay special attention to those tiny "impulses" to move and gesture as you speak. These are your instincts rearing their head, and they're often right on the mark. So note them in your journal, because you may want to return to them if you ever become "stuck" at any point and feel you need some new or different blocking in your monolog or scene.

Exploration #35: Whispered Movement Improvisation

Walk uninterruptedly in a wide circle or even at random in a large rehearsal space while whispering the lines or speaking them softly (you can do this with a partner for two-character scenes). Simply let the words "sink into you" without adding any expression to them. Avoid acting all over the place at first. Your words should be barely audible. Repeat your selection three or four times until physical responses to the text begin to surface. Then go with them.

Exploration #36: Exaggeration Improvisation

Begin to silently walk, first in a circle in your rehearsal space and then after several minutes in random directions. Try to concentrate on moving in slow motion, and exaggerate all of your movements: your steps, your arm swings, the movements of your shoulder, hips, etc. After five minutes of gaining control of *all* your movements in slow motion, begin to speak the text very slowly, also exaggerating the pronunciation of all the words in slow motion (elongating vowels, chewing consonants, etc.). Your goal is to eventually connect the flow of the text with the flow of your steps, gestures, arm swings, etc., until the text delivery becomes integrated with these dancelike or pantomimic physical actions, and until you can deliver the entire piece — gradually increasing the speed — until it seems more and more natural. If you're successful, you should discover many impulses to move, gesture, and facially express during the piece, and your movements will become less exaggerated, more selective, and more natural. Try to use these impulses now in physically expressing the text wherever possible as you speak it.

Exploration #37: Dance and Pantomime Improvisation

Tape record your selection or have someone read it to you as you perform this improv. Begin to move randomly in a large open space with the tape recorder playing or someone reading the selection. Concentrate on the words and images, and allow yourself to exaggerate your movement responses to the text by creating dance or pantomimic gestures, postures, movements, etc. If you've never explored physical, nonverbal expression of words and images before, then you might find this exploration challenging and extremely difficult. You should use whatever physical and nonverbal expression pops to mind: hand claps, foot stomps, falls and rolls, in addition to dancelike turns, steps, spins, leaps, etc. Your goal in this exploration is not to find specific actions you might actually use in performance, but to uncover those "cues" in the text that seem to spur you to do something in response to the ideas and imagery, to physicalize what you're saying.

Exploration #38: Life Gesture [14]

Before beginning any movement, spend a few minutes thinking about the dramatic character and his or her physical appearance. Ask yourself if there is some distinguishing manner, attitude, posture, muscle tone, mannerism — a "life gesture" — that seems to characterize that person. We all have such life gestures: hooking our hands on our belts, flicking hair away from our face, standing with arms akimbo, moving our mouth, holding our hand, something. Try to discover something of the sort that's appropriate for the dramatic character based upon everything you know about the entire play. The gesture may or may not be performed in the actual monolog; you should make the choice whether or not it actually becomes overt. Experiment with several possibilities using different lines from the monolog or scene until you hit upon one that seems right to you — one that seems to encapsulate the character's attitude best. The final step is to try to perform the scene or monolog with this gesture in mind (or even physicalizing it here and there) to gain a sense of physically characterizing: of building a character physically or "physicalizing the role." If you're successful, this physicalization should feel somewhat (or possibly very!) different from your normal physical attitude. And many acting coaches suggest that until you gain a very concrete sense of how physically different the dramatic character is from your real self, you haven't gone far enough in your characterization! [15]

Exploration #39: Physical Objects Improvisation

Fill your rehearsal space now with as many different large objects and pieces of furniture as you can locate: chairs, stools, tables, a broom, a bicycle, several large cardboard boxes, a sofa, a laundry basket, etc. As you speak the monolog or act the scene with your partner, try to make physical contact with everything in the room at least once, including the walls and the floor. This doesn't mean that you necessarily have to use the object extensively such as sitting in the chair, riding the bicycle, or folding the laundry. Simply touching it or relocating it will often suffice. The point is to make the ideas concrete in your own mind, to ground the text in some sense of physical, spatial reality. In actual performance, of course, you will have no props or furniture to use, but you should find that introducing physical objects to your movement improvisations now will stimulate even more ideas for staging the piece later.

At this point, your imagination should be fully charged and ready to put the monolog or scene into real space! *As you devise movement patterns, you must always keep this basic rule in mind: never move just for the sake of moving; all stage movement must be purposeful and reflect the action taking place in the monolog or scene.*

I find it most helpful to begin staging a scene or monolog with the beats in the selection, each of which might need to be reinforced with blocking movements. Remember that this series of beats is the spine and structure of your piece, and so each beat or event might be accompanied by a different physical action: a cross to another part of the stage, an approach to or withdrawal from the other character (either real or imaginary), or even something as simple as a change in posture or a body lean or a strong gesture. In other words, physical action can underscore and can sculpt the change of intentions as you move through the piece, thus adding a stronger sense of clarity, focus, and development to your acting.

Second, the pattern of beats you've established in the scene can also dictate the changing tempi both vocally and physically. All scenes and monologs have what directors call "peaks and valleys" of intensity where the character's energy changes and shifts as the piece develops. Look to underscore these dynamic energy patterns in the structure of the scene or monolog both physically and vocally so your audition has variety, contrast, and development.

Third, look at which physical actions are dictated or implied by the script, and include these in your staging. The stage directions, as I mentioned earlier, may give you some helpful hints about what you need to do, but remember that you're not staging the play, you're creating a vivid audition piece. So, many scripts that are chock-full of stage directions won't always be helpful. More importantly, look for the relationships in a scene to dictate certain kinds of movements that could be very effective. For example, is there any point where physical touch of some kind would be wonderfully expressive of what's happening in the relationship? How near or how far from your vis-à-vis should sections of the scene or monolog be played? When and how to make eye contact with your imaginary or real vis-à-vis can also be profoundly expressive.

Fourth, you want to be sure that the range of emotions in the selection is being adequately reflected vocally and physically. Because we've spent so many more years in learning how to read language to ourselves rather than to speak it, we tend to "intellectualize" our responses as we read or recite from memory. In short, most people tend to become dead, monotonous, talking heads.

Of course, exactly the opposite is needed for acting! Ask yourself what you *feel* at this point in the text? In fact, the explorations immediately above should have tipped you off to the strong images that need physicalization. These images may now dictate some movements here and there during the scene, but more likely than not they'll suggest a change in your gestures, body energy, facial expressiveness, or the like — *small* physicalizations rather than large ones.

Be sure that you feel "loose" and uninhibited when you, or you and your partner, are beginning to stage the piece so that you can feel free to experiment with anything and everything that comes to mind. Of course, you'll gradually reduce all of this improvised, exploratory physical action to more comfortable and natural proportions. But at first, it's very important to just "let yourself go," exploring every impulse you have for staging the piece and vocally interpreting it. And always remember — whatever you do, it should always be connected to the text.

When rehearsing the blocking movement patterns, the gestures, the changes in intensity, and so forth, you want to be careful to *avoid crowding your enactment with too much movement*. Normally, you'll have nothing to work with in an audition but a chair or two, and you'll never want to use any costumes or hand properties. Avoid a lot of movement, because people want to see you act — not fuss with the props or the furniture. Too much movement is distracting and gives the impression that you're "acting all over the place" out of nervousness, desperation, or lack of focus. **Remember that in the audition you must always seek to create a relationship onstage!**

This last sentence, "always create a relationship," is absolutely crucial for your work at this stage in preparing your audition piece. *If you forget to do everything else in this chapter, you must never, ever forget to ask yourself this one very important question: "To whom am I speaking these words, and why?"* The great American actor and coach Uta Hagen reiterates this very simply: " ... determine what you are doing there *besides* talking to yourself ... You do *not* come into a room in order to talk to yourself. You do *not* sit down or rise to talk to yourself." [16]

Actor/director and coach Angela Paton of the American Conservatory Theatre makes this same point, reminding actors that it applies just as much to two-character scenes — where it may *seem* like you're talking only to the other character onstage in the scene with you — as it does to monologs: "The actor *needs* someone to listen. He *needs* to reach out off the stage and get a response. It should seem as though he could not *not* express his thoughts." She further suggests that when you rehearse a monolog you must visualize the responses you may be getting from the other imaginary character, just as you actually do get responses from your acting partner in a two-character scene. By visualizing feedback from your words in this way, you tap into the character's *need* to relate, to connect, to express his or her concerns. [17]

"Need" is so all-important in staging and presenting your monolog that too much cannot be said about it. You absolutely *must* believe in the words you're speaking, nothing less will suffice. You absolutely *must* win the goal you're fighting for in the monolog or scene; nothing less will satisfy you! The stakes have got to be high! That's why I mentioned earlier in the chapter that's it's so important to choose audition material to which you can personally relate, material that tends to turn you on emotionally. Many directors and actors refer to this as the real "inner life" of the character. To quote Broadway director Aaron Frankel again, who was fond of using Shakespeare as an example,

> Shakespeare provides the vehicle, but you supply the gas. You're the driver, and the words are there only to help you act on your impulses. If you really saw your Juliet, your action would be obvious and your ability to get there would be increased, and poor Juliet, you know, hardly could defend herself against the onslaught. That's what we're talking about! [18]

Visualize the character and his or her relationship in the most concrete details possible, believe in his or her need to speak these words, and then allow your inner impulses to take over and move you forward. Remind yourself that focusing upon that inner life without allowing yourself to respond physically is just as deadly as too much movement and gesture all over the place that lacks justification by proper belief and emotional involvement.

Staging your audition piece takes *a lot* of energy. You're probably going to push yourself at this point harder than you've ever worked before if you're doing it right! This might also be an excellent test of your talent as an actor, to see if you've the ability to stick with it! But the commitment, tenacity, and energy required of you in preparing your selections is nothing compared with the energy that you'll need to do a solid audition performance. Take it from Robert Goldsby, prize-winning director, actor, and coach at the American Conservatory and Berkeley Repertory Theatres, who advises auditionees of the following:

You look very much for swiftness of attack, and the swiftness of feeling, the swiftness of body movement — energy, energy, particularly energy. Where is the energy: vocal? emotional? intellectual? I want somebody who really has energy because acting takes tremendous energy. Most students don't have any idea how much energy it takes to do a play. The student has a lot of physical strength but he doesn't know how to focus it. It's dispersed, or else he thinks it doesn't matter so the script and the moments are underplayed, somehow understated. Actors are, like Artaud said, athletes of the heart. You've got to have lots of energy, and auditions really require that. [19]

Exploration #40: Checklist for Staging

Once you've settled upon the staging of your scene or monolog, review the following "checklist" for movements and stage positions. It will help you to sharpen the choices you've just made and avoid any basic pitfalls before you present your work to your coach.

1. Always face downstage when you introduce yourself and your audition selections, in your performance (as much as possible), and in the concluding "thank you" before exiting. This will give auditors maximum opportunity to look at you and see you as a person; they're not interested in your back or your profile.
2. Search for ways to "open" the scene or monolog to the audience whenever possible, and avoid playing to empty chairs or imaginary characters to the extreme sides of the space. Share your decisions, frustrations, choices, fears, doubts, etc., with the auditors.
3. Never deliver your piece to the director as the imaginary listener or audience. He or she has enough to do considering your acting skills without being made to feel obliged to give you a response.
4. Be certain that your acting partner in two-character scenes is visible to the auditors, and be sure to involve him or her in the scene.
5. In a monolog, place your imaginary listener, the vis-à-vis, downstage of you, either to left or right of the auditors. Fix the location of that listener definitely in one place and always speak to him or her at that point. Never try to speak your monolog to an imaginary listener who is supposedly moving about, or your audition will tend to lose focus.
6. You may have moments in a scene or monolog where the character is "speaking off into space": dreamlike, nostalgic, recalling events, etc. Be certain at these moments that you speak out to the house, over the auditors' heads. Find one definite place in the auditorium in order to "anchor" your visual focus at such moments.
7. Never pantomime actions such as drinking, smoking, applying makeup, fighting, etc. Either discover a way to eliminate these actions, or, if worse comes to worst, bring a small hand prop with you for the purpose.

8. Play the monolog or scene as far downstage as possible, and avoid body positions toward the extreme left or right sides of the stage. Use what furniture there is in the space, but beware "hiding" behind it or having it block you.

9. In two-character scenes, be sure that your acting partner is turned away from the auditors as much as possible during the scene in order to leave you strongly in focus.

10. Always rehearse with only a single chair, and if they give you more to work with at the actual audition — another chair, a table, or a stool — by all means be ready to use it somehow.

11. Consider carefully whether or not you should actually sit in a chair. Most actors find that sitting will rob them of energy during the audition.

12. Rehearse your scene in very different spaces: small, large, a stage, an empty classroom, etc. Not only will this prepare you for whatever space you encounter at the actual audition, but it will help add variety to keep you "on your toes" so your audition pieces stay fresh.

13. Rehearse your personal introduction as carefully as your audition piece, including your movement to and from the stage. The casting people are *always* watching you for clues! Never take more than a few seconds to begin your piece, and avoid fussing about with the furniture!

14. Remember that at every audition, the other "character" you're presenting is you! So make a confident but relaxed entrance, introduce yourself and your pieces pleasantly and clearly, and when you're finished, a simple "thank you" and a businesslike exit will suffice. Don't forget to smile!

15. Never stare at the stage floor! There is nothing there! Create a relationship with someone!

16. If you bobble a word or a phrase, never go back and start again, and never, ever apologize! Crash right on!

Working with a Coach

Once you feel comfortable with the way you're presenting your audition piece, it will be time to find an experienced and qualified coach to help you. He or she can be that necessary outside eye, giving you a more objective opinion of your work than anyone else, and perhaps also suggesting acting choices you may not have considered. Never try any audition without getting some good coaching, if only to be sure that you've "covered some of the bases" you may have overlooked.

What sort of people make the best coaches? Those who love acting and seem to know something about it are certainly good bets! Also look for someone who has the time and is willing to work with you on an extended basis: at least once or twice a week for a month prior to your audition date. Another useful quality in a coach is someone who's knowledgeable and willing to help guide you through all the necessary administrative requirements: applications, resumes, appointments, references, etc.

A good coach is someone who's primarily an *observer* of what you're doing, someone who tells you exactly what he or she is seeing while watching you onstage. This means a kind of person who doesn't try to dictate everything he or she wants you to do, but who supports and validates the choices you've already made and suggests others for you to explore.

Student actors should avoid falling into the "obedient student" trap with their coaches (relying on the coach to tell you everything and unquestionably doing everything the coach suggests). On the other hand, don't be too "fixed in your ways" when presenting your work to a coach. You know how easy it is to become "obsessed" and fixated on your own work and one way of doing things. Professional stage and screen actor William Redfield explains it this way:

> One need neither argue with a director nor 'take' direction with unquestioning, childish obedience. A proper instruction, carefully worded, would be: *digest* direction. Be in or out of agreement, as your intuition dictates, but *listen* to the direction. If you don't like it, don't do it, but taste it, savor it — roll it about in your mouth. Then swallow it, digest it — it may work out. It may stretch you to an achievement you did not imagine. Do not confuse stubbornness with integrity. Be blown by the wind. Imagine yourself a kite. [20]

Remember, too, that many casting directors will ask actors to change the piece a little here and there and then perform the audition again just in order to see whether or not the actor can "take direction" (more about this in the next chapter). Working cooperatively with your coach in rehearsals is good practice for this sort of challenge at an actual audition. After all, there is never only one way to play a scene or monolog effectively, right? How many great Hamlets have there been in the history of the theatre? There are always other options to explore, and becoming aware of these other performance possibilities will certainly enhance your audition.

In addition to exploring suggestions your coach makes and then bringing them in for criticism, you should set yourself the goal of bringing your coach your own different "versions" of your monolog or scene over a period of several weeks. This is a way of keeping the piece fresh in your mind and continuing to make new discoveries. In order to accomplish this, you should be sure to keep asking the traditional acting class questions about your piece and the character you're presenting, and then rehearsing it according to those new possibilities: what was this character (or characters in a scene) doing ten or fifteen minutes ago? what is he/what are they wearing or carrying at this moment? is he/are they fatigued, nervous, hungry, drunk, cold, dirty, harried? is he/are they speaking in a public place? among friends/strangers/enemies? or is he/are they very much alone and able to "let go" emotionally here and there?

All these possibilities are good sources of improvisation for you, or you and your scene partner, as you continue to rehearse your monolog or scene. The important thing is to avoid thinking that there's only one "right" way to play it. Be sure to keep your journal handy as you rehearse and improvise your pieces so you don't forget anything valuable that you've turned up. Also be sure to discipline yourself (and your scene partner) to rehearse regularly in order to get the work done. Remember, once you've got the piece memorized and staged (blocked), you've only cleared the first hurdle!

As you continue to develop and refine your audition pieces, you'll also be working on new ones; remember that you want to have more than just the "minimum" that may be required by a particular audition. In fact, it's fun to work on two or three pieces at the same time, because it adds variety and a little spice and surprise to your work. You'll also want to have more than just one coach. Run your audition material before others whenever you get the chance, because you can never audition too much. You always need the practice, so keep working at monologs and scenes on an ongoing basis, and show them to others for feedback when you think they're ready to present.

And a final piece of advice for all auditioners, "The Law of the 5 Ps": **Proper Preparation Prevents Poor Performance**. College students are notorious for their lack of preparation for tryouts. They wait until the last minute to do *any*thing, if they do it at all. Maybe it comes from some high school experience of "getting away with," doing nothing unless someone calls them on it or puts a bat upside their head. Maybe they're just extra lazy and think, "Oh, Professor X knows what I can do so I don't really have to work at it." Who knows what they think? Don't you fall into this self-indulgent trap: *Proper Preparation Prevents Poor Performance.*

Review and Reflection
Reflection

1. **What are the basic steps in preparing a monolog or scene for auditions?**
   - Prepare three copies of the monolog or scene.
   - Mark up or score your script in pencil as you rehearse with blocking, business, emphases, pauses, etc.
   - Perform denotative and connotative paraphrases of the text.
   - Identify the goals and obstacles of your character in the scene or monolog, and choose concrete actions to express them.
   - Identify the operative words, sharpen your sense of vowels and consonant sounds, and attune yourself to rhythm and pace of delivery.
   - Rehearse the speech in order to develop your vocal skills.
   - Rehearse the speech in order to develop your movement skills.

2. **What are the three goals of vocal rehearsals when preparing your audition pieces?**
   - To identify the operative words in the selection.
   - To sharpen your sense of vowels and consonant sounds in the selection.
   - To attune yourself to rhythm and pace of the delivery of the selection.

3. **What guidelines do you use for staging the monolog or scene with blocking and business?**
   - Begin staging a scene or monolog with the beats in the selection, each of which may be reinforced with blocking movements.
   - The pattern of beats you've established in the scene can also dictate the changing tempi both vocally and physically.
   - Some physical actions may be dictated or implied by the script, and these should be included in your staging.
   - Be sure that the range of emotions in the selection is being adequately reflected vocally and physically.
   - Visualize the character and his or her relationship in the most concrete details possible, believe in his or her need to speak these words, and then allow your inner impulses to take over and move you forward.

[1] Consider this piece of advice contained in the guidelines published on the website of the American College Theatre Festival Irene Ryan Scholarship Auditions: "The confidence, poise, and polish characteristic of an outstanding audition presentation is the result of dedicated, concentrated rehearsal and astute coaching ... A five-minute presentation should be rehearsed a minimum of six hours, excluding time spent memorizing the material and time discussing it with coaches." Again, some advice from Michael Kahn, the artistic director of the drama program at Juilliard, who auditions candidates for the conservatory: "I also listen harder to the pieces they bring in to see whether that person has the ability to make their own, something that is not their own." Excerpt from comments on the videotape *Juilliard*, directed by Maro Chermayeff, produced by WNET-New York ("American Masters Series" in the PBS catalogue), 2002.

[2] Interview, 8 October 1982.

[3] *Convivencia* by R.N. Sandberg. Copyright © 1998 by R. N. Sandberg. All rights reserved. Reprinted by permission. Information concerning rights should be addressed to the author: R. N. Sandberg, 160 Bertrand Dr., Princeton NJ 08540.

[4] Eric Bogosian uses this same technique for his monolog performances: "The most powerful way into a character is by assuming a vocal stance ... letting the vocal posture shape the improv from within. Try reciting 'The Gettysburg Address' in a Minnie Mouse voice and you'll get the idea." "Cutting Loose," op. cit., p. 19.

[5] "How to Approach a Scene," in *Contemporary Scenes for Student Actors*," eds. Michael Schulman and Eva Mekler (New York: Penguin, 1980), p. 27.

[6] *Professional Acting in Television Commercials* (Portsmouth: Heinemann, 1995), pp. 59–68. See also a second very handy and extensive list of objectives and actions in Joanna Merlin's book on professional auditioning, *Auditioning: An Actor-Friendly Guide* (New York: Vintage, 2001), pp. 59–60.

[7] Quoted in the film *Borrowed Faces* (New York: McGraw-Hill, 1979).

[8] Audition, op.cit, pp. 53–67.

[9] Interview, 3 May 1982.

[10] Dr. William James, interview, 18 December 1981.

[11] *Lilford Mill* by Neil Duffield, op. cit.

[12] This exercise was first presented to me by Dr. William Oliver, director with the now-defunct San Francisco One-Act Theatre Company. Oliver decried the blunt, plosive monotone that so many young actors seem to have developed from movies and television shows. He led actors towards more musical speech patterns and a broader range of inflection by forcing them to twist the sounds of individual words and phrases.

[13] More advanced versions of this exercise can be found in Arthur Lessac's excellent textbook, op. cit., pp. 63–121.

[14] This exercise was suggested to me by Broadway director and acting coach Aaron Frankel in his movement workshop, New York, 3 May 1982.

[15] In her recent book on professional auditioning, Joanna Merlin refers to this exercise as "psychological gesture." Op. cit., p. 58.

[16] *Respect for Acting* (New York: Macmillan, 1973), pp. 122–123. An excellent chapter devoted to monologs in this book is entitled "Talking to Yourself" (pp. 119–123). Although some of Uta Hagen's rehearsal methods are best taught in a long-term class, there are a few valuable hints in this chapter for auditions preparation.

[17] Interview, 30 December 1981.

[18] Interview, 3 May 1982.

[19] Interview, 2 January 1982.

[20] *Letters from an Actor* (New York: Viking, 1967), p. 59.

Chapter Seven

Performing the Audition
"Your little nugget"

Staying Fresh or Going Stale

Every actor reaches a point working on plays or audition pieces where the material seems over-rehearsed. You know what I mean. In the theatre we call this "phoning-in a performance," "going stale," "getting mechanical," and so forth. And it takes many forms. If you regularly feel bored or uninspired about rehearsing or presenting your audition piece, if you feel it's lost excitement, or if you just plain feel that it isn't challenging you anymore or going anywhere — then you need a dose of "stayfresh" medicine!

Don't be depressed about your moods. They happen to everyone. Think of those professionals who have to perform the same show eight times a week on Broadway! Auuuugh! What do *they* do? Remember, too, that you won't be able to predict your mood or feelings at the time you actually audition. What if you feel bored and listless then? What if you have to wait hours before your number is called? Be ready to deal with this problem of sustaining your energy during the rehearsal period, because it might very well recur at the audition.

Every actor has his or her way of dealing with this situation; here are six suggestions for improvisations.

Exploration #41: Pick-a-Place

Rehearse your selection in an unusual environment. Try a very confining space, or even a huge one. Try it outdoors, or perform it in a cemetery, an office, a classroom, a hallway, the kitchen, etc. In each location, open yourself to the influences of the new setting by letting the environment alter the way you had it "set" originally. You may not know what your actual audition place will be like until you enter it, so things like acoustics, lighting, ceiling height, and spatial relationships are some of the unknowns you'll have to be ready to deal with. In fact, in the "real world," you never know where a professional audition will take place: a hotel room, an agent's office, a darkened rehearsal hall! After a half an hour working in the new setting, return to your original staging and see what has changed!

Exploration #42: Pick-a-Star

In this exercise, let yourself go and "ham it up" by caricaturing famous actors as you perform the monolog or scene. Choose an actor noted for his or her "over the top" acting, for example, or perhaps one with a distinctive "one note samba" acting style. Movie and TV actors are good choices. People like Eddie Murphy, Renée Zellweger, Jim Carrey, Arnold Schwarzenegger, for example; or even movie classics like Humphrey Bogart, Lucille Ball, and John Wayne might be fun choices. You can also use well-known poptrash "characters" like Austin Powers, Xena, or Darth Vader. It can be great fun. After a half an hour working in this way, return to your original staging and see what has changed!

Exploration #43: Pick-an-Obstacle

Give your character a strong physical obstacle and struggle against it in the scene or monolog. For example, rehearse your monolog as if you were in your death throes from a couple of spears sticking in your back, or perform your scene as though you just had to go to the bathroom but couldn't leave the room! Act it like your stomach is getting ready to hurl from some kind of food poisoning or like you don't want to breathe because of some foul smell in the air. Perhaps you should just search the room continually for a lost $100 bill, or fumble with a stuck zipper as you perform the selection; or you and your partner could do the scene trying to free yourselves from sticky glue-like alien spit in one of the *Alien* movies, or while doing vigorous calisthenics in the gym. Of course, you never want to include such arbitrary obstacles in the finished piece, but after a half an hour working in this way, return to your original staging and see what has changed! Are you now playing the *actual dramatic obstacles* in the scene more sharply? Are you using the sounds of the language differently?

Exploration #44: Abandonment

There are many variations of this exercise, which basically involves nothing more complicated than completely letting yourself go, physically and vocally, in every direction that you possibly can. This can mean thrashing about and writhing wildly on the floor, kicking and screaming like a mad person as you perform the piece. (Be careful not to "screech" or strain your voice by producing "gravelly," grinding shouts.) You and your partner might outrageously exaggerate each and every line of the scene: bellowing in rage at each other, desperately horney, viciously bitter and vengeful, hysterically giddy, suicidal, tearful, desperate, ecstatic — whatever. In fact, this exploration might unlock some new emotional colors in the scene that you hadn't perceived before. Who knows? After a half an hour working in this way, return to your original staging and see what has changed! Is it "larger" now? Are the emotional peaks higher? Have you added some new blocking or physicalization?

Exploration #45: Grand Opera

This exploration is particularly suited to enhancing and unlocking your vocal interpretation of the scene or monolog. As the name implies, it simply means singing each and every word of your selection in the style of grand opera. Never seen an opera? No problem — go and catch a live performance somewhere or rent a video/DVD of something by Verdi or Puccini (tragic) or Mozart (comic). Then do your impression of grand opera using your audition selection as the material. You're going to feel very stupid attempting this exploration, so be sure to do it in a place where no one can see or hear you. But keep at it for at least a half an hour; it's even more fun if you're a lousy singer! Be sure to "milk" every syllable of the words, even the indefinite articles in phrases, and exaggerate all your postures, gestures, and vocal sounds. Hold that note *forever*! Open those arms *wide*! *Stride* across the stage like the potbellied baritone or the chunky soprano and *bellow out* those vowels; *spit out* those consonants! Two-character scenes are especially fun with this exploration. After a half an hour working in this way, return to your original staging and see what has changed! [1]

All these improvisations share one thing in common: they'll help keep you flexible and enliven your performance no matter what kind of situation you encounter in the actual audition. The spirit of improv — spontaneity, making immediate choices and then committing fully to them, risk-taking, invention — should inform all your acting, not only in auditions. Judy Jenkins, a casting agent at CBS in New York, remarked to me how valuable improv experience is for actors, especially in cold readings: "Mostly what it gives you is a certain confidence in working without the printed page. Actors should know they have the talent to perform without a script — without someone giving them Shakespeare or Shaw. Often you just have to read it, then get up and do it." [2] Southern California acting coach Robert Cohen agrees, recommending that you "try out your audition piece as often as you can in an acting class, at a party, in your home, or wherever you can get an audience of one or more to see you. Get used to performing amidst general inattention and extraneous noise." [3]

As you can see, improv skills are not only helpful for keeping you fresh and on your toes; many directors include improvisations as part of the general audition in order to learn valuable information that a prepared audition may not reveal. James Roose-Evans, West End and Broadway director, notes: "I may have them stand on their heads and sing 'Rule Britannia' or 'Mary Had A Little

Lamb' in the middle of a reading just to see how they take direction, work together, or perform under stress." [4]

Many directors, sensing a certain rigidity or "mechanical" quality in an otherwise interesting actor, will use improvisations to relax the individual and help him or her to shed preconceived notions. Jack Fletcher at the American Conservatory Theatre of San Francisco used audition improvs for just this purpose:

> You can see that they're locked into a certain way of doing it that is inhibiting them from discovering more about the piece or from achieving a certain spontaneity. I make them get up and I totally change the given circumstances. I make them run around and do it, or I make them do it as a six-year-old child trying to get a piece of cake off the table — anything that'll trick them into shedding a preconception about the piece. [5]

And will you ever be auditioning for an acting school or scholarship instead of a role in a play? Take note of this remark by Jane Armitage, director of International Activities for the Drama Studio, who auditions students worldwide for entrance into the school and who always runs them through improvisations following their prepared presentations: "I can learn if they're willing to take risks, if they can concentrate and react honestly, if they can fulfill their goals in the improv (can they take direction), and especially, can they deal with specific details: the place, the circumstances and so forth." [6]

Arrival and Preparation

At this point you have your audition prepared, you know the day and the place to turn up, and you've stayed fresh during the intervening weeks in order to get ready. Now let's take a look at just what you're going to have to do on the audition date.

The first thing you must do upon arrival at the audition is to get there early enough to have plenty of time to relax and shed the hassles of everyday life — "decompress from the rush to get yourself there," as one actress explains it. [7] Plan ahead for this and avoid arriving at the last minute, and by all means have your wardrobe ready to go the night before (see chapter 10). Locate the stage manager or person in charge and check in, learn the procedures of the day, and do everything you need in order to get registered for the event. This can be a formal or informal process. At regional auditions for summer work, or for scholarships and other competitive auditions, you may need your papers, resume, photos, etc.; while at your school play or community theatre an assistant might simply collar you, shove a form into your hand, and take your name.

Take a look around while you're doing all this and *examine your environment closely*. Can you see the audition space? If not, go and find it. What's it like? Where are the directors sitting? What furniture is available? What sort of lighting or acoustics are there? Notice everything you can and attune yourself to the locale. If you can get into the audition space (especially if you're there early!), go there, move around, hear yourself talk a bit, and get a feel for it. The more familiar you are with the audition space, the less anxious you'll be when you enter it to perform.

Remember that you are auditioning from the moment you walk through that door! I can't tell you how many times I've scanned the crowd of auditioners waiting their turn and noticed all sorts of unprofessional behavior that left me with a negative impression of individuals even before they were called onstage! Why cut yourself off at the knees like this? In fact, at many professional auditions, the casting people will wish to speak with you a bit at first in order to "break the ice." In such situations, Molly Thon advises:

> Present yourself professionally and with dignity. Friendly, but no unsolicited jokes or extensive chat. Introduce yourself and hand the director your photo and resume, stapled or clipped together. Some directors wish to review the resume before you begin, perhaps ask a question or two, such as: "What are you working on now?" Be prepared to answer, briefly. [8]

Then *locate a place to warm up.* **Under no circumstances do you ever walk out in front of people to perform anything without warming up!** You'll never find a professional doing this, but young actors usually don't treat warmups seriously. It takes a lot of energy to perform an audition well! Acting is not a natural activity, and the energy to perform well doesn't just flow automatically in supremely gifted and talented people like yourself! It needs to be aligned and on tap ready to go in order to function well when your instincts call for it.

There's absolutely no excuse for failure to do this because all drama students are exposed to warmups somewhere in their training, and there's always a classroom, practice room, or hallway somewhere that's available to you. (Keep an ear cocked for the stage manager calling your name!) And you need to develop a warm up "routine" that works well for you for pre-performance as well as for auditions. Usually three kinds of routines are necessary. A brief thirty- to sixty-second routine that specifically focuses you on the actual piece before going onstage, a ten- to twenty-minute routine to keep your motor running between "takes," and a longer thirty-minute routine that's fairly complete in order to get yourself started in the first place.

Avoid the common cop-out of whining, "There's no warm up space for me to use." If you ever attend professional auditions in New York, Chicago, or L.A., you'll find people crouched in stairwells, phone booths, on the sidewalk, and in closets warming up their instrument. They're hungry for a role, and they warm up physically and vocally. They're also refreshing themselves on their prepared pieces or running over the scripts they've been handed by the stage manager for "semi-cold" readings.

Avoid the other common cop-out of whining, "Well, everyone else is sitting there watching." They're sitting there and watching because they've already lost the part. They're worrying about how well they'll do, they're mentally sizing up and criticizing you, they're adjusting their hair or looking cool, they're afraid to do anything because of their self-image — in short, their concentration is scattered everywhere but where it should be: on their audition performance or on the script. Or else they're running over their monolog or scene in their heads — a totally useless and self-destructive activity. Ignore those people; get out there and rehearse your material. Focus. Concentrate. Avoid the worry-trap. [9]

Finally, while you're waiting to be called onstage to perform, ***think positively and develop a healthy, optimistic attitude.*** You must beware of one common pitfall that besets many actors at auditions: the attitude that you're "up against those people" behind the casting table who are putting you through this miserable, frightening experience. The "me and them" syndrome that encourages all sorts of negative thoughts about yourself, the directors, and the whole audition situation. "Go into an audition with the attitude you're making a new friend," one New York actress suggests. "That'll take the edge off feeling judged." [10] Keep your attitude and outlook positive and upbeat, and try to transform the stage fright you're experiencing into creative energy that can work for you.

How do you do this? Remind yourself that the directors really do *want* you to perform at your best in order to help them cast the play well! They're not your enemies. Actor-coach Pat Dougan, speaking of the mood she has encountered in countless commercial auditions, expresses it this way:

Always try to maintain a sense of confidence and professionalism. Don't look or act desperate or too eager to please. This is a business. Even though all of us have to start at the beginning, you are a whole, complete person who also happens to be an actor. You should be treated with respect. Don't settle for less. Find positive ways to ensure that treatment ... *Since the casting director and director are on your side and want you to do well,* they will do their best to make you comfortable. Believe it or not, they are not there to judge you. If you look good, they look good. But remember, they have been auditioning people all day and they get tired. Like the rest of us, they are only human. [11]

Whether or not they *want* that type of actor-character in their show is another matter, of course. That's up to them and God. And you really must avoid becoming sullen or resentful when responding to questions or presenting your audition pieces; that's the kiss of death. People can spot such attitudes a mile away and no one wants to work with that sort of person. All you can do as an actor is to remain confident, present your prepared pieces as strongly as you rehearsed them, and then get ready for the semi-cold and cold readings for a specific role that hopefully will follow.

You've got to trust the directors to know what they're doing in this highly vague situation we call "auditioning." Michael Shurtleff used to recommend that we remind ourselves how phony auditions are — everyone knows that! To look at dozens or even hundreds of people for only a minute or two (most directors are watching for only the first fifteen seconds anyway) and then decide whether or not they're appropriate for the role and if they should be called back for a longer read-through — how unreal! But it's the best way to cast a show, the only way we've got, so we all go through it: directors *and* actors. They didn't create the system, and they're trying to make the best of it just as you are. So keep your spirits up, your concentration focused, and your energy high, and give the casting people whatever it takes to help them make the best sense of you in this terribly artificial situation. Trust your material, trust yourself, and trust their professional judgment!

The Audition Performance

When your name or number is called, be businesslike about your two-, three-, or four-minute activity onstage by remembering what you're about: you're an actor presenting different features of yourself at all times — not just with dramatic material. *Make a strong, upbeat, and confident entrance to the stage,* because a good entrance doesn't just help directors, it can help you, too! Your remarks help you listen to yourself in the space before you start "acting," and setting up the furniture can physically relax you.

Many, many directors have remarked to me about how important these first few moments can be for an actor. They're watching you as you approach, they're waiting for "something new" (after who knows how many others have gone before!), they want to be entertained and to finally discover that actor they need. They're "experts" in body language and stage presence, so don't disappoint!

You have no idea how many actors have shot themselves in the foot by a wimpy or bumbling entrance, or especially by a weak and "shamefaced" exit that nonverbally shouts at the directors: *"I knew that was lousy!"* A poor entrance or exit can create a negative impression that few audition performances can overcome. Michael Leibert of the Berkeley Rep put it this way: "There's a certain chemistry to an actor when he walks onstage. He alters the state of the stage, he has the potential to make everything shift." [12] The great Stanislavski of the Moscow Art Theatre was fond of saying: "Let him who cannot sense the magic threshold of the stage, not presume to cross it."

So take control as you enter the stage with a pleasant smile and a relaxed confidence. Play your entrance fully by being sensitive to the space and your relationship to the "audience" of casting people. *As you enter, take a look at the lighting and be sure you're in the light at all times!* (You'd be surprised how many audition spaces can be poorly lit!) *Immediately locate your "fourth wall" just behind the auditors. Set your chair if there is one; if there isn't, then ask for one. Then come downstage as yourself and speak directly to the casting people.* I recommend the following script for personally introducing yourself in a three- to four-minute casting call where you must perform two pieces:

1. Enter and set up.
2. "Hello! My name is X [and this is my scene partner X], and I'll/we'll be presenting two pieces for you today. The first is the character X from the play X by X [the playwright]."
3. Go to your starting mark, take no more than a beat to concentrate, then attack the first selection. Finish with a very brief freeze or "button" (a gesture or pose held for just a beat or two as a finish or "cap").

4. "For my second piece I'd like to do the character X from the play X by X [the playwright]."
5. Repeat step #3 above.
6. "Thank you very much. My name is X."
7. Turn, collect your things, and exit.

Not everyone, though, will have the luxury of three to four minutes. For those common one-piece, sixty-second presentations, plan to do the following: *"Name — Number — Piece — Song — Name — Number — Exit."*

This format gives you several advantages. First, it's brief and doesn't waste time. Second, it gives you some extra moments at the start to move around and speak comfortably about yourself as that "extra character" you're presenting in addition to the two pieces you've chosen and prepared. Third, by introducing each selection separately, you can end-stop the first and have a little break without having to rush right into your second piece. Finally, by repeating your name at the end, you remind the directors who you are and present yourself one more time. You can modify this format by adding another song or audition piece or by announcing both your pieces at the outset and saving time (if you've unfortunately timed your presentation down to the last second!).

Be well-rehearsed and avoid rushing. You'll find that nervous tension always produces nervous rushing. Remind yourself that the directors want to see feeling, they want to see a relationship come to life up there. They're looking for your emotional and imaginative commitment to a situation and relationship onstage. This doesn't mean getting to the end of the bloody thing as fast as possible (one very good reason why you never want to time your audition down to the last allowable second, or you'll feel pressed for time-time-time!).

Leave yourself some spare time during the audition for two reasons: you don't want to feel rushed knowing that your well-rehearsed piece is already at the time limit, and you want to feel relaxed enough to explore and discover new things in the piece — every time through the piece should be a new experience. Demetria Thomas, a Chicago pro, recommends the following "actual audition times":

- 60 seconds = 45–50 seconds
- 2 minutes = 1:35–1:50 minutes
- 3 minutes = 2:40–2:50 minutes
- 4 minutes = 3:35–3:50 minutes [13]

Each step along the way of your monolog or scene is important.
Work it moment by moment right from the outset, feeling out the
relationship, the images, or the problem as you go along. Do not
play the end of a scene from the beginning. Avoid thinking of the
beat coming up while you're supposed to be fully playing the beat
at hand. Play each beat singly and fully before proceeding to the
next, and let yourself respond fully and honestly to the emotional
punches in your material.

*You should also pay attention to the ending moments of your
audition selections.* Let the auditors see your "recovery" between
selections and before your exit remarks. Make these transitions, too,
with emotional honesty and avoid cutting them off either technically
(in order to rush to the next thing) or self-consciously. Your recovery
process is far more engaging to watch than an actor who's just setting
up furniture for her next piece. Give yourself an edge.

And now a couple tips on starting your audition selections.
*Hopefully you'll have chosen pieces that are strong right from the
outset.* (I mentioned this in chapter 5.) You don't want to let the
directors fall asleep waiting for you to build to your "big moment."
The rule of thumb, again, is to grab their attention with something
in the first fifteen seconds. Now, this doesn't mean charging in like
Godzilla, but it does mean shaping and acting your pieces so that
something definitely *does happen* in the opening moments. "It's that
swiftness of attack they look for," remarks West Coast director Bob
Goldsby. "It's a kind of energy — what the French call 'verve' — the
presence the person shows right from the top of the audition. And
there are all sorts of ways for getting that: emotional recall, sense
memory, moment before, countdown — whatever seems to work
best for a person. But it's got to be there." [14]

Goldsby is referring to some kind of personal "trigger" that a
lot of actors use in plays and auditions immediately before their
entrance to quickly place them in the dramatic situation. "Find the
phrases, words or images that will give you an instant sense of
empowerment before you go into the audition. Imagine your
boyfriend, mother, teacher beaming with pride just looking at you,"
suggests one actor. [15]

Emotional recall and sense memory are classic Stanislavsky
techniques for substituting powerful memories from your own life
for those embedded in the dramatic situation. Simply recalling an
image from these can trigger psycho-physical belief in a person.
(Ever stumble across an old photo or souvenir from years past, hear
an old familiar piece of music, or encounter a smell or feeling that

can instantly throw you back to that time and place long ago?) "The moment before" is a Shurtleff technique that works by forcing the actor to begin the scene or monolog *from somewhere*, from something that just happened a moment before the action begins. This, too, can help lend the opening moments of your scene or monolog a vital energy without your having to start the piece "from zero" and then work yourself up to an emotional level of nine or ten. [16]

The Afterglow

Once you've left the stage you're ready for the big blow-out, right? A tremendous wave of relief washes over you, a tremendous burden seems lifted from your shoulders. All you have to do now is wait for that magic phone call! Of course, there may not *be* a phone call if you failed to get the role or win the scholarship. In casting, the usual rule is "don't call us, we'll call you." In scholarship or college entrance auditions, you'll normally receive the courtesy of a rejection call.

On the other hand, perhaps the conclusion of your general audition isn't "the end of the road." For example, there may be the "callbacks." As I explained earlier, the purpose of callbacks is to give the director a closer look at you, perhaps only by putting you in combination with other actors where relationships are important. If you didn't earn a callback, however, don't automatically assume that you were lousy. It may simply mean that the director is fairly sure that he or she can't use you for this play. And I have heard time and again from casting and stage directors that even though an actor may be turned down for *this* part, a good audition is *never* forgotten. There will be other directors and other plays in the future, and the theatre business is a very small world! You'll be remembered.

In chapters 7 and 8, I'll deal with the semi-cold and cold reading situations that you're likely to encounter in callbacks and the interviews that often accompany them. Right now I want to point out a few things about the aftermath of your *first* auditions, the general ones, that you need to pay attention to.

To begin with, you need to **be sure to record all the details of your auditions in your journal.** This is important for two reasons. A good self-critique is always valuable and necessary for your artistic growth because it reinforces what you may have discovered and done well, and it also helps you to avoid repeating any mistakes you may have made. Additionally, your *professional* career needs to keep track of whom you auditioned for and when, whom you met at the audition, and other mechanical details. You'll need to file this information in order to build up your "networking" as an actor just getting started, and refer to it time and again as you make the rounds looking for work. The world of live theatre isn't all that big, and you're bound to run into some of the same people again and again. So get into the habit of recording important info after each tryout, sort of like notes following a "business meeting."

A second thing you need to do after finishing your general audition (and any callbacks and interviews) is to treat yourself right. Instead of beating yourself up when you think you've done a bad audition, plan ahead to have a nice dinner somewhere special. Arrange a get-together with friends or with that special someone. Make sure that you couple in your mind the audition experience with something satisfying and pleasurable in order to reinforce your positive attitude towards auditioning and seeking work. This is especially necessary for those important scholarship and entrance auditions that a lot of very young actors must perform; I know there is incredible stress associated with those. The last thing you want to do is to come back to that motel room or face that long train ride home in grim and accusatory silence. "Auditions seem to happen very quickly," notes actress Joanna Merlin,

> especially an audition that didn't go well. You're in the audition space, you do your thing, you leave and it's over. There you are, out on the street, trying to remember exactly what you did, or didn't do, or should have done. Don't spend the day sulking or beating up on yourself. Go to the gym. Call a friend. Don't indulge in self-flagellation. Later you can evaluate the experience. [17]

So give yourself a break by scheduling a fun time for yourself afterward, because you've earned it!

You really must *work at keeping a positive attitude after the audition experience — especially after a rejection.* It's so easy and tempting to beat ourselves up, isn't it? "It was me, the *turkey,* who lost the role. *And everybody knows that now!*" Well, that ain't the way it is. Remind yourself that most of your friends and classmates would never even *think* of risking their self-image by going through an audition! Only us masochistic actors have *that* crazy desire for self-destruction! You know it's true, don't you? It takes a heckuva lot of courage to just get up there and do it. It takes guts, so pat yourself on the back, whether you won or lost!

In a similar vein, you must always *avoid bad-mouthing the*

casting people afterward and running them down. Remind yourself that you have no idea what influenced their decisions and that they were simply and sincerely interested in assembling the best possible cast, even if for some reason that cast didn't include you. Sandra Fenischel Asher, after years of scrutinizing actors and chatting with them in audition situations, made this point about some of the attitudes she unfortunately had to encounter:

> Do not take rejection personally. Do not "play the race card, the sexism card, the ageism card, the nepotism card, the favoritism card, the inside clique card" or any other cards. Such thoughts change nothing and damage your own self-esteem. Assume the director really was trying to assemble the best possible cast he or she could — according to his or her own perceptions and needs. Yes, another director would have called the shots differently. Rest assured: there will be other directors, and even other plays with this director. [18]

In short, put the audition experience behind you and get on with your life. What's most important for you now is the next audition, right? So focus yourself. Record everything in your acting journal, be businesslike and thorough. "Make notes of everything you learn from each audition," advises the actor Joanna Merlin.

> A less-than-perfect audition can be unsettling and prevent you from being objective immediately after the audition. If that's the case, wait to undertake this analysis until a few hours later, when you can be more objective about what happened. Your investment in post-auditioning checkups will make you aware of any particular problems you continue to have.

And remind yourself, she adds, that the results of each and every audition extend further than simply the question of whether or not you won the role, the scholarship, or the competition: "Auditions will teach you how to work quickly ... Auditions will help you explore your character range ... Every audition has the potential for opening the door to work ... Auditions teach you how to direct yourself ... Auditions provide you with a chance to act." [19]

Write it down, then set your sights on the next audition!

Exploration #46: Post-Audition

Get into the habit of recording your auditioning experiences in a professional manner following each tryout. Your goal is twofold: to record important information that you may need at a later date and to assess your own performance as objectively as possible. The following "Q&A" is a good starting-point exercise if you've never done this sort of thing before; you should try to develop your own post-audition checklist as you gain more experience.

- What is the name of the group, the date, the place, the play, and the roles you read for?
- What are the names of the important people in charge whom you met there?
- Which audition pieces did you present? What sort of things did they have you do in callbacks: prepared readings? cold readings? improvisations?
- What did you wear as an audition costume? Was it okay? Did it work? What were the other actors wearing?
- What feedback did you receive during the audition or afterward about your performance?
- What information did you learn from networking with other actors who were also auditioning? What prepared audition pieces did they use?
- What information did you learn about auditions etiquette, interviews, casting procedures, materials to provide, other actors competing for roles, etc.?
- What do you feel were the strong and the weak points of your audition, or how you presented yourself?
- What do you feel was strong or weak about your audition piece(s)?
- If the auditors suggested at the tryouts that you change your audition in any way and try it again, how would you present it now that you have more time and less pressure to do so? Try your audition again now, working in those suggestions on your own. Were you able to execute those changes? Did they help or hurt the audition? Do you think you can be ready to do those changes on the spot in the future?

Review and Reflection

1. What are the five steps to follow when arriving for an audition?

- Get there early enough to have plenty of time to relax and shed the hassles of everyday life.
- Examine your environment closely.
- Remember that you are auditioning from the moment you walk through the door.
- Locate a place to warm up.
- Think positively and develop a healthy, optimistic attitude.

2. What are the steps in a general, all-purpose "script" for presenting your audition?

- Enter and set up.
- "Hello! My name is X and I'll be doing two pieces for you today. My first selection is the character X from the play X by X [the playwright]."
- Go to your starting mark, take no more than a beat to concentrate, then attack the first selection. Finish with a very brief freeze or "button."
- "For my second piece I'd like to do the character X from the play X by X [the playwright]."
- Repeat step #3 above.
- "Thank you very much. My name is X."
- Turn, collect your things, and exit with an upbeat, confident manner and a smile.

3. What important things should you be sure to do following every audition?

- Record all the details of your audition in your journal.
- Treat yourself right with a good meal or social event.
- Keep a positive attitude after the audition experience — especially after a rejection.
- Avoid bad-mouthing the casting people afterward and running them down.

[1] One New York actress/playwright remarked to me about the value of a "musical rehearsal" of audition pieces: "Do your monolog to different pieces of music. The right music might reveal something you didn't realize was there!" Karen Huie, Internet conversation with the author, 15 March 2002.

[2] Interview, 4 March 1982.

[3] *Acting Professionally.* op. cit., p. 126.

[4] Interview, 5 May 2001.

[5] Interview, 4 January 1982.

[6] Audition workshop at ACTF Region III, 6 January 1984.

[7] Karen Huie, Internet conversation with the author, 15 March 2002.

[8] Molly Thon, op. cit., p. 26 March 2002.

[9] An essential feature of professional behavior that you should seek to develop is the ability to focus on your upcoming audition without bothering other auditioners who are also waiting or becoming distracted and falling into "the worry trap." It can be very difficult to "center yourself" while waiting with others for your name to be called: other auditioners will want to chat out of nervous tension, or share "important" tidbits of information about what's going on, or you may meet people at tryouts whom you haven't seen in weeks or months. In professional auditions, some people coming out from their audition may be talkative, but others might not want to say anything because, after all, you may be in competition with them for the same role. In any case, nervous "chatter" should always be avoided because it will distract the other auditioners, and often the sound spills over into the audition room itself. If you run into an old acquaintance at a tryout, excuse yourself by arranging to meet afterward. And if others try to engage you in nervous conversation, excuse yourself by declaring that you have to study the script a bit or warm up before you go on.

[10] Karen Huie, Internet conversation with the author, 15 March 2002.

[11] Pat Dougan, op. cit., pp. 94–96.

[12] Interview, 29 December 1981.

[13] Interview, 18 January 2003.

[14] Interview, 2 January 1982.

[15] Karen Huie, Internet conversation with the author, 15 March 2002.

[16] Joanna Merlin recommends what she calls a "pre-beat": "a preparatory moment immediately before you start your audition, in which you gather your concentration and focus … The pre-beat should trigger an energy source in the scene." *Auditioning: An Actor-Friendly Guide,* op.cit., pp. 68–69.

[17] Ibid., p. 192.

[18] Internet conversation with the author, 22 March 2002.

[19] Merlin, loc. cit., pp. 15–17.

Chapter Eight

Cold Readings
"The chips are down"

What Is the Cold Reading?

Probably the most dreaded audition situation is the "cold reading," where actors are given a scene they've never seen before and asked to get right up and read it. All actors hate doing this. And to the general public, it's this type of challenge that immediately pops to mind when they think of how fearful auditions must be.

It seems impossible that any intelligent casting decision could ever be made on such a basis — let alone the all-or-nothing decision that rides on the choice of the right actor for the role. If 80 to 90 percent of the success or failure of a production depends on proper casting (as most directors will tell you), how does *any* play stand a chance of succeeding when the casting decision is based on cold reading? Even veteran actors will tell you how terrifying a cold reading can be: knowing nothing of the play or the scene, nor anything much about how the director wants the role played, the actor must simply make a leap of faith and take his or her best shot at the unknown.

In all these cases, you must remember that *cold readings are only a part of the overall casting process* — a very important part, certainly, but ultimately only a part. In some cases, *initial* cold readings will serve the purpose of screening auditionees in order to single out those who deserve closer attention in callbacks. In other cases, only the callback takes the form of cold readings from the play being cast. Occasionally a cold reading may be the major type of audition used when the script is new and actors have no way of familiarizing themselves with the play beforehand. As you can see, in combination with prepared general auditions, a cold reading is mainly designed to test likely candidates with several types of scenes and partners.

There are really two types of "cold" readings: the absolutely cold and the semi-cold. Absolutely cold is when you've been given *no time whatsoever* to prepare — you're just handed the script and instructed to get onstage and do it. Semi-cold means that you've had *some* time to look the material over (two or three minutes or so).

Of course, nearly all the auditions that you'll encounter in school are likely to be cold or semi-cold readings. You may be required to bring *something* prepared for general tryouts in order to give the directors a basic idea of what they're dealing with and to gain valuable educational experience with self-preparation. But you'll certainly also be handed a scene or two from the play being cast and asked to read with other students for whatever roles the directors may feel you might be suited to play. In any case, you should bear in mind that *only a cold reading can reveal certain vital qualities of the actor to a director, so directors will always use them.*

In the first place, cold readings are a sort of "pressure cooker" that test an actor's ability to create under stress.* As such, they're a valuable tool at either the initial or final stages of the casting process. Your stress tolerance is very important for a director to know. I needn't remind you that there's going to be *a lot* of stress in the production process, and a director *must* be certain the actor can handle that pressure. No matter what other skills you may have, nothing can save you if you cannot work under pressure. If you tighten up, blow your lines, lose your temper, forget blocking, or "lose it" in any other way when the heat is on, your performance and the success of the show will certainly suffer.

In addition to performing under stress, the cold reading serves another very valuable purpose: *it helps a director explore some qualities about you that he or she may only just have noticed.* It's to some extent a "spur of the moment" thing, a "voyage of adventure" into your acting skills that you and the director can take together. So it gives you the opportunity to work at your best, before the director turns the readings toward those specific requirements demanded by the play at-hand. Many actors unfortunately take a "me versus them" attitude when placed under the pressure of cold readings, when they should instead welcome the opportunity to show the director some aspects of their talent that the director found interesting and wishes to explore.

One important thing that actors, especially young actors, tend to overlook is that *a cold reading is very likely to reveal what kind of a human being you are to work with.* A director can learn much about you from the way you respond to a stressful, cold reading situation. After all, he or she will have to live with you for a month or two throughout rehearsals, and doubtless the director has already spent "a month in hell" with an actor having some sort of personality problem. Neil Duffield, a writer-director who has worked extensively in England with young actors, makes this point very clearly:

> Theatre is a collective art form and most directors I've worked with are not only looking for a good actor who fits the requirements of the part, but they're also after people

who can work together as part of a team, people who can contribute positively in a rehearsal process and get on with other team members.

He concludes by reminding young actors that "workshop-type sessions in auditions are not only designed to test improvisational skills, they're there to sort out the attention-grabbers from the actors who can give as well as take." [1]

Remember that directors have enough difficulties getting the show on without having to deal with troublesome actors. What sort of attitude do *you* bring to the cold reading? Are you pleasant, trusting, and cooperative? Or sullen, defensive, and resentful? Are you ready to take risks? Confident and upbeat? Or do you seem to need a lot of "hand-holding," justification, and explanation?

In addition to testing your stress level and attitude, *the cold reading will reveal the extent of an actor's "basic skills training."* Without any preparation, do you have the ability to read material and play the relationship, rather than just trying to get the words right? Do you seem to lock into the given circumstances of the scene and what's happening? Can you speak clearly and interpret the text in a lively way? And can you relax physically, move and gesture, and begin to enter into the life of the character? These fundamental skills will always emerge in a cold reading. Whether they're done well or poorly will tell the director a great deal about the level of talent that he or she will be dealing with in the weeks ahead and for what kind of role you'll be most suitable.

In addition to basic skills, *the cold reading will often zero-in on more advanced skills that you may possess.* For example, are you listening and reacting to your partner and making eye contact? Or are you glued to the script and relating to the text? This presupposes that you understand the importance of relationships and that you know how to hold your script during a cold reading. Scanning the text a few words ahead of your spoken lines or cues in order to look up from the page and create some relationship with your partner is essential (see chapter 4).

Another advanced skill the director will want to see is the kind of choices you're making with the material. Are you aware of the events in a scene and how strongly to play them? Are you sensitive to the language of the play, exploiting the sounds, phrasing, and diction to some extent? Are you choosing some concrete actions to play that express your goals in the scene? Or is your acting muddy and uncertain, your vocal delivery bland and uncompelling, or your relationship with your scene partner unshaped and lacking energy? Conversely, are you so obsessed with one way of playing the material that you fail to take direction?

Finally, the cold reading allows directors to closely consider actors in roles for which they may be suited. In fact, as I mentioned above, the cold reading may be the *only* kind of audition used at your school for this very reason. You must understand that your castability might depend heavily upon how you look in relation to the other actors: Do you resemble the other brothers and sisters in the family (or do you seem from another planet altogether)? Do you look appealing and compelling side by side with the leading man (or does he clearly dominate you)? Do you fit in with the gang of Jets and Sharks (or do you seem too nice)? Additionally, it may reveal whether or not you can "play off" the other actors who are also being considered. Can you generate the necessary "chemistry" with the leading lady? Do you communicate the necessary "menace" when seen onstage within the group? Do we still experience that sense of whacked-out comedy when we see you in the scene with the leading man?

In brief, a cold reading unlocks certain doors into your acting skills that a prepared reading will not reveal. Look to and rely upon your whole development as an actor when you have to present an unprepared audition.

Preparing for Cold Readings

Okay — so if "cold" means unprepared, and if all you can do is trust your "basic instincts" as an actor, then what sort of "preparing" is an actor to do? Well, there's a lot you can do to get your acting muscles in shape for cold readings, so let's get started.

First on the list is practice: Get your friends together, find anthologies of scenes and monologs for actors in your range, and ***practice reading material right off the shelf.*** Stuff you've never seen before. I'm assuming that you've worked your way through the suggestions and exercises contained earlier in chapters 4 and 6, so you know what goes into making a good scene. This means the *mechanics* of reading fluently and expressively the words off the page, as well as moving and gesturing in order to *physicalize* what's happening. It also means *analytically* understanding and playing the beats, discoveries, developments, relationships, and so forth that the scene contains.

You really don't need trained faculty coaches to practice in this way; your fellow acting students will do just fine. They can watch a scene between you and your partner and see whether you've nailed the relationship in some definite way, whether you've picked up on all the events that seem to be contained in the text, whether you're moving and speaking clearly and purposefully, whether you're playing the given circumstances, and so forth. After a few weeks of this, you'll start to get the hang of approaching "strange" material and treating it in a workmanlike fashion instead of remaining paralyzed with fear that you might somehow get it wrong.

As you explore this first stage of cold reading preparation, you should also *test yourself after practicing by reading the complete play and comparing the choices you made cold with the whole play that you now understand.* Was there something in the scene you should have noticed now that you know the whole drama? Did your analysis miss some clues? Well then, don't miss those clues again. Were there some emotional "colors" in the relationship you might have introduced to make your acting more vivid? Where and how could you have introduced those? Perhaps your own choices were too timid, too bland, or too over-the-top? After reading the whole play, do you now think your character is more or less physical than you imagined? More or less impulsive? More or less moody? Frustrated? Wounded? Confused?

By first reading the scene or monolog cold and then reading the whole play, you'll remind yourself that a lot of acting is about the *choices* the actor makes. Any scene or monolog can be played in a variety of ways, and some choices are, of course, more vivid or effective than others. Notice I did not say "right" or "wrong." Once again, there is no "right" or "wrong" way to play a scene (short of completely misunderstanding or misinterpreting it, which rarely happens with intelligent actors). There are only "more effective" or "less effective" interpretations. How many people have played Prince Hamlet? Was one "better" or "worse" than the other? A moot point, 'nuf said. Make the most vivid choice *you* can, and perhaps comparing the whole play with your reading of only a small extract will reveal some *other* choices embedded in the material. You'll learn a lot from this.

Go back then and play the scene differently, according to the information and insights you picked up from reading the whole play. See what this different reading feels like. Now you'll have two possible interpretations. Try to develop a sense of several different options you can make in playing the scene so you don't get too locked into just one way of playing it. After all, you may do a very good cold reading the first time through, but the director will want you to play it slightly differently the second time. You'll want to have some other possibilities in mind for just that situation.

As you play this exercise with your friends, be sure to set yourself definite time limits for preparation. In most cold readings, you'll only have two to three minutes to look the material over (a "semi-cold" reading!). Of course, you might get more time, but try to nail your preparation down to just a few minutes, and then if you do get more time at the real audition, so much the better. Have someone sit with a stopwatch for this and time you.

Also *try to rotate your partner as you do this exercise; don't just act with your same buddy over and over.* You never know with whom you'll be reading at an actual audition — a bad actor, an actor competing for the same role, a stage manager, the class clown. Get used to playing off people with different personalities and different skill levels, and get used to reading with men and women.

Next, after a lot of practice, *ask one of your teacher/directors to "test" you by throwing some unprepared material at you.* Do it in a rehearsal hall or on an empty stage, as close to the real audition context as you can get. Have the director pick a few things of his or her own liking and give you and your partner some comments after your cold read. But only attempt this step after you've practiced the above exercises for a month or two, because you don't want to waste your director's time or your own. The advantage of testing yourself against a director is that a stage director can pick up on things that your friends missed and perhaps also have something to say about the context of the whole play. He or she can be more objective than your friends and can certainly give you more to work on and think about.

The last suggestion in preparing for a cold reading should be obvious by now: read the entire play beforehand. Unless it's an absolutely original script (and even new plays are often available for reading prior to auditions), no audition should ever be "cold." You may not know what scene you'll be asked to read, but at least you'll know what the play's about and who the characters are.

This is enormously important information, but you'd be amazed how infrequently actors (and young actors are the worst sinners) take the trouble to do that even with famous plays. These actors place themselves at a serious disadvantage at auditions, because they'll always look more hesitant or even silly by comparison with others who know what the scene's supposed to be about and what the characters are supposed to be doing. Practicing cold readings beforehand, reading the play beforehand — these things are so important because they represent *what you can do* in a cold reading situation. How you can get on top of it with a little effort. Remember there is so much that you *won't* be able to control in an audition, that anything you *can* do to make yourself more confident, more empowered, is absolutely necessary. Chicago-based stage and screen actor Bradley Mott expresses it this way: "The only thing you should be ashamed about is that you weren't prepared for the audition. You didn't have your monologs ready? You didn't pick up the script beforehand? Shame on you! Work on the things you have control over." [2]

How do you read a play beforehand in order to get ready for cold readings? Well, you try to note several things about it:

- *What happens in the play?* What's going on here, both on the surface and between the lines? Might I have to read some scenes that absolutely depend upon what went before or what's going to happen later on?

- *What is the tone of the play that I must somehow capture?* Is it a comedy? A melodrama? A wild farce? A murder mystery? What mood should I aim to create in the reading? You'll look awfully silly up there reading Ibsen's *The Wild Duck* like Neil Simon's *Barefoot in the Park*.

- *Which characters do I seem right for, that the director is likely to have me read for?* Which do I seem close to? Why is that? What is it in me that is unique and that I could bring to any of these characters? If you're aware of your strongest and most unique qualities (chapter 4), you'll be able to invest unfamiliar characters with a lot of life, rich details, and compelling, unusual traits.

- *What are the key relationships in the drama that I must understand?* What scenes bring out these relationships most vividly? Are these the scenes the director is most likely to choose for a cold reading? If so, what emotional challenges am I likely to face? Might I be called on to read a cheesy love scene? A bitter fight? A scene of terrible grief and loss? Of fear? Get ready for it, anticipate it.

- *What special skills does the play require that I must bring out?* Is it in verse? Is it a period play (historical) with special costume and movement demands? Does it require some specific physical or vocal skills? Consider how you will meet these special demands.

Performing Cold Readings

Once you're handed the script "to look over for a bit," *do not* try to prepare the scene or monolog according to the procedures explained earlier in chapter 6. You haven't time for that. Instead, follow these guidelines:

First, be sure to ask the director what he or she wants, or what the scene is about. It's crucial at this point that you listen carefully to how the director explains the scene in order to aim for that in your performance. Remember that no matter how *you* may want to interpret the scene or monolog, it's what *the director* wants that counts. You must shape your reading to conform to those instructions or you risk being rejected as an actor who can't take direction. And by the way, if you're ever handed a script and asked to "go ahead and just read it," *always* ask for a couple of minutes to look it over. You may not get it, but it never hurts to ask.

This is not the time to agonize over interpretation, either in your own mind or with the director. So don't start discussing the scene with him or her. Get right down to the three basic steps for approaching a scene in a cold reading, and *quickly decide upon and commit to your choices:*

1. *Who am I and who is my vis-à-vis (the other character in the scene)? (Relationship)*
2. *What happens in the scene or monolog? (Events)*
3. *What do I want from my vis-à-vis? (Goals and Physical Actions)*

Who is my vis-à-vis? Once again, *every scene you will ever act onstage or on camera will always be about relationship. If you do nothing else at an audition, you must create a compelling relationship with your vis-à-vis.* A lot of actors have told me they find it helpful to "concretize" this relationship in a cold reading by quickly calling to mind a similar relationship in their own personal lives. This easy technique of substitution is explained in chapter 6; it's great for cold readings because it works quickly to help you imagine and play a concrete relationship.

Also be sure to study the other character's lines. Many actors foolishly concentrate just upon what *they're* going to have to say, but the words of your vis-à-vis will reveal a great deal about you, the relationship, the given circumstances, and the developments in the scene. A lot of acting, I'm sure you've heard, is *re*-acting to your partner's statements, because other characters provoke what you say and do. If nothing else, familiarizing yourself with your partner's lines will make you attentive to your cues when it comes time to perform the scene.

A special note on reading monologs. In a monolog, of course, you don't have this "luxury" of another character's lines to cue your change of beats, to play given circumstances, to take reactions, and the like. Monologs require a slightly different textual analysis in order to determine where the vis-à-vis has done something, or may have done something to motivate a change in beats within the monolog. Refer to chapter 6 about envisioning the reactions of your imaginary vis-à-vis to what you're saying, and then make your vis-à-vis as concrete as possible.

What happens in the scene or monolog? Michael Shurtleff used to harangue us in his workshop sessions with his constant demand: *"Event your script!"* He wanted to *see* things happen in the scene, he wanted us to play actions that change and develop over the course of the encounter. And he would constantly challenge us to make ourselves different by the end of the scene or monolog than we were at the beginning. **Something has got to happen.**

In chapter 6 you learned that an "event" can be either physical or psychological, and the most important events are psychological ones. Your first task then, after deciding about your relationship with your vis-à-vis, is to *identify how you're a different person by the end of the scene than you were at the beginning.* Once you've done that, you look for two or three events that happen to you in the scene that have caused that change. Such things as discoveries, conclusions, and decisions always work well to add dynamism to your acting. It's very important that you play these events vividly and "attack" each new change — each new beat — with energy, because we need to *see* these things happening. You must compel our attention with such actions.

You'll find yourself at this point — and perhaps also when considering question 1 above — tending to "over-analyze" the scene, but such "psychologizing" is the kiss of death for an actor in cold readings. It wastes precious minutes at a time when quick decisions are called for. *You must quickly make choices about who you are, what relationship you're in, and what is happening in the scene, and then commit to playing those choices boldly and energetically when you're called.* In prepared auditions, you have the luxury of time to consider more profoundly your character's motivations and study his or her relationships with others. But this isn't the case with a cold reading, and that's why the unprepared audition will always bring the actor's instincts "to the fore." Like a snap judgment, you must swiftly and surely lock on to what you need to play. You must learn to make a decision, to "cut to the chase."

What do I want from my vis-à-vis? Save the answer to this question for last because it should emerge naturally from the other two steps you've just completed, and also because it requires less study of the text and more imaginative invention on your part. You need to decide what drives you forward in the scene. *What is it that the other character — and only the other character — can give* *you at this moment?* What you want from him or her should be something that you simply cannot live without, and this scene is the moment it's got to happen.

Ordinarily, as I explained in chapter 6, this objective will be apparent in the scene. You'll want him or her to kiss you passionately, to surrender the money you crave, to break down in tears and confess the truth, or maybe to quit the room in shame. Occasionally, however, the scene or monolog you're given to read might be somewhat opaque, in which case you must improvise or invent that concrete objective for yourself. But in either case, it should be strong.

This is vitally important at a cold reading, despite all the uncertainty that accompanies the situation. You don't know exactly what you're after in the scene, perhaps because you haven't read the play, or because your character's true motives are masked somehow. In any case, you've had no rehearsal for the scene, and perhaps the director is also unsure what he or she wants from the character at this point in the play. You've just got to choose a strong objective and play it — even if it's the wrong one. *The point is, the director must see you acting with energy and commitment.* He or she will have weeks of rehearsal with you (if you're cast!) to get the correct interpretation, but in the cold reading you must at least show the director that you can play an objective strongly.

Visualize that, make it concrete by using language as vivid as the words I just used above ("to kiss passionately," "to surrender money," "to quit in shame," etc.). And because your goal in the scene should be so important for you, you must pursue it any way you can: physically, vocally, gesturally. So make those strong choices! And this holds true for an imaginary vis-à-vis in a monolog just as it does for your acting partner in a scene. To quote Hollywood actor Henry Winkler again ("The Fonz" from *Happy Days*): "It doesn't matter what you're reading for. It's always about making a clear objective. Whether or not it's exactly what they're looking for doesn't matter. It will separate you from 99 percent of the people who don't know what it is to make an objective in the first place." [3]

With these three basic steps complete you're ready to perform the scene. If you have time left, be sure to set in your mind the points in the scene or monolog where the events must happen, so you can play these forcefully. And you can also practice reading the lines aloud while holding your objective firmly in mind. Finally, time permitting, try to get the first and last lines of the scene or monolog memorized so that you can maintain maximum eye contact at these critical points.

Exploration #47: Relationship in Cold Readings

Set a timer to "pace yourself" as you perform this exercise. It should begin counting as soon as you read the title and end as soon as you've written down two or three possible relationships. Your goal here is to read the scene (either for the male or female character) and decide on two or three vivid and distinct relationships that you would be able to play in the scene. The director has told you the following: "Look over the following scene for a few minutes. It's a play on U.S. history with numerous role transformations — the characters occasionally step out of their main role in order to play the role of another character for a scene or two. Here, the actor who normally portrays Christopher Columbus plays the part of Thomas Jefferson struggling to write his famous "Declaration of Independence," while Jefferson's African slave and mistress, Sally Hemings, looks on. Look it over for a bit and give it a try."

From *Turtle Island Blues* by William Borden [4]

1 COLUMBUS: "We hold these verities to be —" No, "verities"
2 isn't right. "We hold these ideas"? No. "We hold these
3 hypotheses"? *(SALLY HEMINGS enters with tea tray, teacups,*
4 *etc.)*
5 SALLY HEMINGS: Truths!
6 COLUMBUS: *(As if he had thought of it)* "Truths! To be ...
7 obvious." No. "To be ... clear as day." No.
8 SALLY HEMINGS: Do you want some tea, Tom?
9 COLUMBUS: "We hold these truths to be ... or not to be, that
10 is the ... ." Thanks, Sally. "We hold these truths to be — "
11 SALLY HEMINGS: It's self-evident.
12 COLUMBUS: *(Writing)* "Self-evident"! "Self-evident ... that
13 all people — that all men ... " *(He looks at her a moment.)*
14 SALLY HEMINGS: Why not all people, Tom?
15 COLUMBUS: Please. I'm busy.
16 SALLY HEMINGS: You said "people," then you changed it to
17 "men." Why?
18 COLUMBUS: Don't you worry your pretty little head about
19 it, Sally Hemings.
20 SALLY HEMINGS: You're writing that Declaration of
21 Independence, aren't you?
22 COLUMBUS: This doesn't concern you.
23 SALLY HEMINGS: It doesn't concern me?
24 COLUMBUS: Sally, I love you. I live with you as my wife,

1 even though it's illegal, even though you have no rights,
2 even though you are inferior to me.
3 SALLY HEMINGS: You find me equal enough when you
4 want somebody to talk to.
5 COLUMBUS: You're a good listener.
6 SALLY HEMINGS: When you want to bounce ideas off
7 somebody.
8 COLUMBUS: You understand me. Madison, Washington,
9 Hamilton — they've all got their own ideas about things —
10 they're not good listeners.
11 SALLY HEMINGS: When you want somebody to cheer you
12 up when you're sad.
13 COLUMBUS: I don't know what I'd do without you, Sally.
14 SALLY HEMINGS: Now what's this word you're looking
15 for?
16 COLUMBUS: I can find my own words!
17 SALLY HEMINGS: Fine! Find your own words!
18 COLUMBUS: Where was I?
19 SALLY HEMINGS: Men.
20 COLUMBUS: "All men are created ... " What shall we say?
21 SALLY HEMINGS: Dumb.
22 COLUMBUS: "The same ... " No.
23 SALLY HEMINGS: Endowed by their Creator ...
24 COLUMBUS: *(Writing)* "Endowed by their Creator ... "
25 SALLY HEMINGS: Whoever She is ...
26 COLUMBUS: *(Writing)* "Whoever She — " No, no. "By their
27 Creator ... with certain ... certain ... " What's a word, Sally,
28 that denotes that which cannot be taken away? *(SALLY is*
29 *silent.)* Come on, Sally. Sal-ly. Saaaallllyyyy. *(She ignores*
30 *him.)* "Certain ... rights?" But what kind of rights? I know
31 there's a word ... Sally? *(She ignores him.)* If I don't finish
32 this tonight, Franklin'll write it, and he'll go down in
33 history instead of me. Is that what you want? *(She ignores*
34 *him. He tries again.)* Fun rights. Swell rights. Cool —
35 SALLY HEMINGS: Oh, for God's sake, Tom! Inalienable
36 rights! *(He stares at her. Beat. He writes.)* All *men* have
37 inalienable rights! *(He writes.)* All *white* men! *(He writes, then*
38 *stops.)*
39 COLUMBUS: That won't look so good.
40 SALLY HEMINGS: It's what you mean.
41 COLUMBUS: Of course it's what we mean. What else could
42 we mean?

Exploration #47 (cont.)

Once you've written down three possible ways of playing this relationship between Jefferson and Hemings, stop the timer. As you practice this exploration with other plays, try to reduce your time to three to five minutes. Here are some suggestions you might have uncovered:

- (For Jefferson): **He is pompous and domineering** with his servant-mistress, demanding her assistance and bitter that he depends so much upon her; **he is weak and childlike**, depending upon her for and cajoling her out of everything, including his so-called "great" ideas; **he is generous and fair** with Sally, but romantically naïve, and only admits for the first time during the scene that he desperately needs, desires, and truly loves her.

- (For Hemings): **She is sullen and resentful** of the power that Jefferson exerts over her and that she has given into, never missing a chance to mock his foolishness or hypocrisy, but careful to never insult him outright; **she is good natured and familiar** with these "serious" moods he sometimes has, teasing him at such moments as a wife might do; **she is coy and flirtatious** with Jefferson, only realizing during the course of the scene that she desperately loves and desires him as completely as he seems to love her.

Play the scene several times with a scene partner, each of you using some of these different relationships (only one relationship per readthrough), and notice how the scene changes almost entirely each time you do it! If you feel the scene isn't changing all that drastically, keep working at it until you can play the relationships consistently throughout the entire scene and the scene *does* change drastically. Once you begin to develop some skill with influencing a scene by means of relationships this way, you can then try this same exploration with other scenes of your own choosing. It's important to keep in mind that in a cold reading you may not ever know which relationship is the "correct" one to play — which interpretation is the one the director prefers. What's important in a cold or semi-cold reading is only that you understand there are several ways to play relationships and that you do so consistently and strongly. The director may want you to change your interpretation during the reading, of course, but more on that below. And don't forget: look up from the page as you read it through! Make eye contact with your vis-à-vis! Relate!

Exploration #48: Eventing the Scene in Cold Readings

Read over the following scene for young audiences, and this time concentrate upon "eventing the script" — deciding what important events happen in the scene and where. *This involves two sorts of events, each dependent upon the other: how is your character different at the end than he or she is at the beginning, and what discoveries, decisions, or surprises occur "along the way" in order to cause that change?* Again, set a timer for yourself and begin timing when you read the title. Stop the time when you've written down one sentence describing the overall change from beginning to end and two sentences identifying what and where "internal" events should take place in the scene. The director has told you the following: "Look over the following scene for a few minutes. Salmonberry's the heroine, and she's sitting on a rock in the bay talking to her new friend, Teabag the seal. It's really a 'modernized' version of the Cinderella story, but don't let that throw you — just read it like any other scene. Look it over for a few minutes and then give it a shot."

From *Salmonberry* by Cornelia Hoogland [5]

1 TEABAG: Those are very good apples.
2 SALMONBERRY: *(Angrily)* Is food all that you think about?
3   Food, food, food. Here, have them all. *(SALMONBERY*
4   *dumps six apples on to rock.)*
5 TEABAG: Hey, hey. I was just commenting. Your Papa's apples,
6   you love talking about them. *(Breathless:)* You know —
7   favored by the King of France centuries ago. How your
8   Papa grafted a twig descended from the one in the king's
9   garden on to the apple tree right here in your back yard on
10   the west coast.
11 SALMONBERRY: You know what she did? She stole my
12   mother's picture! Right off the wall! She stole it!
13 TEABAG: What picture?
14 SALMONBERY: My Mother's embroidery. You know —
15   stitch, stitch. *(Mimes stitching.)* Dutch landscapes she
16   embroidered with linen thread. We have — we *had* — six of
17   them. Now five. I told her to give them back, but what's the
18   use? *(SALMONBERRY slumps.)*
19 TEABAG: Your Papa will make her give them back.
20 SALMONBERRY: *(Bolting)* Papa? Guess where he is?
21   Certainly not within talking distance.
22 TEABAG: Fishing?

1 SALMONBERRY: Of course! He dumps this witchy wife and
2   her witchy daughter and takes off in the "Sea Lion."
3 TEABAG: Hey, watch it. Sea lion's not my favorite relative.
4   *(SALMONBERRY makes a scary face, roars like a lion, flaps a*
5   *pretend flipper at Teabag.)* **For sure!**
6 SALMONBERRY: "Sea Lion's" the name of his boat, silly. It's
7   what fishermen do. Go out in boats and travel to
8   Desolation Sound, Prince Rupert. All the little points along
9   the coast. Anyway, I come home from work and there they
10   are gaping at the TV and stuffing fritos in their yaps.
11 TEABAG: Fritos — are they better than apples?
12 SALMONBERRY: Stick to apples is my advice.
13 TEABAG: Apples are better than herring. Your apples
14   anyway. Maybe better than salmon — although ...
15 SALMONBERRY: My mom had this recipe. *Appletaart.* A
16   kind of apple cake.
17 TEABAG: You could make it for me any time.
18 SALMONBERRY: I wonder what happened to the recipe.
19   *(Pause.)* What am I going to do? The two of them are taking
20   over the house. They're mean and boring, and make me do
21   all the work while they go ga-ga over the soaps.
22 TEABAG: Soaps.
23 SALMONBERRY: TV, you know. "The Young and the
24   Restless."
25 TEABAG: Not really.
26 SALMONBERRY: Well, it's dumb. Like eating nothing but
27   chips. Dumb.
28 TEABAG: And your Papa's gone.
29 SALMONBERRY: Yeah.
30 TEABAG: And your Mom's gone.
31 SALMONBERRY: You mean dead.
32 TEABAG: Yeah.
33 SALMONBERRY: Yeah, she's dead and I miss her.
34 TEABAG: And you've got this witchy Stepmother and
35   Stepsister taking over the house.
36 SALMONBERRY: And making me do all the work. *(Mimics:)*
37   You scrub the floor, Salmonberry. Scrubbing breaks my
38   nails. Dish soap wrecks my oh so t-e-n-d-e-r skin. *(Change of*
39   *tone:)* She shouts at me.
40 TEABAG: This after working in the orchard all morning.
41   *(Pause.)* At least there you work with friends.
42 SALMONBERRY: Lucy and Tom, Charlotte. My friends and I

1   **are going to the Festival Dance. At the end of the month.**
2   **On Hornby Island.** *(SALMONBERRY kicks her feet into the air*
3   *so her shoes are visible.)*
4 **TEABAG: Maybe I can do my tricks at the Festival** *(TEABAG*
5   *starts up with tricks again.)* **Enough nonsense. Alright, young**
6   **lady, we need to make plans together.**
7 **SALMONBERRY: Yeah. Kicking that witch out of the house**
8   **is one.**
9 **TEABAG: Visit me every day till we have this sorted out.**
10   **Wind will bring you to my rock whenever I ask. A sort of**
11   **secret voyage.**
12 **SALMONBERRY: I'll keep the boat hidden in the salal**
13   **bushes. Stepmother will never know. If she knew I had a**
14   **friend she'd —**
15 **TEABAG: That's right. Our secret. You bring the apples.** *(Lights*
16   *fade out as TEABAG calls. Audience response is invited here.)*
17   **Wind, Wind, over the sea, blow my friend to shore for me.**

Exploration #48 (cont.)

Once you've written down an overall change and two possible events to play in this scene, stop the timer. As you practice this exploration with other plays, try to reduce your time to three to five minutes. Here are some suggestions of events that you might have uncovered:

- (For Salmonberry): **She develops from sadness and depression to new and cheerful enthusiasm,** and along the way she finally admits that her mother has passed on and voices for the first time her frustration with her father who is always away from home. **She develops from angry and irritated to gleeful and rebellious,** and along the way she realizes what a great friend Teabag really is and confesses that she really, really misses her father. **She develops from listless and bored to energetic and gleefully conspiratorial,** discovering along the way that her father is working too hard to help her and reveling in her new sense of empowerment at outwitting her gross stepmother.

- (For Teabag): **He develops from casual and flippant to serious and commanding,** realizing along the way that he really, really loves her apples and that he'd better get serious and help her. **He develops from ravenous and starved to well fed and sassy,** shocked along the way that she can talk so casually about sea lions and discovering that he might be able to do some circus tricks at the local festival. **He develops from being obsessed with**

delicious apples to a naughty delight at helping Salmonberry's plot, finally figuring out along the way what's really irritating her and discovering his own role in her secret plot.

Play the scene several times with a scene partner, each of you using some of these events (only one set of events per readthrough), and notice how the scene changes almost entirely each time you do it! If you feel the scene isn't changing all that drastically, keep working at it until you can play only the one or two events consistently throughout the entire scene and the scene *does* change drastically. Once you begin to develop some skill with influencing a scene by means of eventing it in this way, you can then try this same exploration with other scenes of your own choosing. It's important to keep in mind that in a cold reading you may not ever know which events are the "correct" ones to play — which interpretation is the one the director prefers. What's important in a cold or semi-cold reading is only that you understand that every scene can contain numerous "events," that you should only pick out one or two major ones to play, and commit to playing them strongly. The director may want you to change your interpretation during the reading, of course, but more on that below. And don't forget: look up from the page as you read it through! Make eye contact with your vis-à-vis! Make these events *happen*!

Exploration #49: What You're Fighting for in Cold Readings

Read over the following scene and this time concentrate upon strong goals and physical actions that you can play. Some of this will be indicated by the script, but the *urgency* with which you want those goals — "the stakes" — are yours alone to determine. Learn to invest your choices, your goals, with compelling stakes, and physicalize those stakes with two or three physical actions you can perform. Remember that only your vis-à-vis, only here-and-now in this scene, can give those goals to you. In short, learn to *fight* for what you want. Again, set a timer for yourself and begin time when you read the title. Stop the time when you've written down two sentences describing two possible goals you might win and two physical actions you might perform in the scene. The director has told you the following: "Look over the following scene for a few minutes. The play's about these two teenagers, Roger and Ana, trying to get to know each other. He's Canadian and she's an immigrant from war-torn Croatia. Anyhow, look it over for a few minutes and see what you can do with it."

From *Boom* by Julie Salverson and Patti Fraser [6]

1 ROGER: When you lived in Croatia, did you see any?
2 ANA: Of course.
3 ROGER: What was it like?
4 ANA: What do you think?
5 ROGER: I don't know.
6 ANA: You must know. You get good marks in this class.
7   What do you think?
8 ROGER: Scary. Lonely?
9 ANA: Lonely, why? I had my whole family then.
10 ROGER: But when I'm scared it's like there's nobody. Even if
11   there is, you know.
12 ANA: What are you scared of? The math test? Your father
13   chewin' you out? Really scary stuff.
14 ROGER: Don't act like I'm a jerk just cause I'm askin'
15   questions. Don't think I'm stupid. Bosnia or Serbia, it's like
16   this mine thing, why should I have to know? I'm sorry. I
17   just know that you're from Europe and there was a war.
18 ANA: Your life's here, maybe nobody tells you anything. You
19   want me to make you feel better about that?
20 ROGER: No.
21 ANA: You want to know about my country, read about it.
22   You've got a million TV channels, do you watch them?
23 ROGER: But it's just TV. You know, you were there.
24 ANA: You see this experiment I'm designing? The molecules
25   have a strong attraction, polarized by the water and the
26   magnets. I have to learn what these instruments do, put my
27   hands on the cold metal, feel the tension in my body
28   waiting to balance the magnetic force. Carefully, so
29   carefully. A wrong move and it dissipates or explodes. My
30   breath learns to move with the water sliding down the tube.
31   I shut out the other noises in the room, I listen to the
32   crystals, the tiny particles moving. But first ... before I can
33   try the experiment, I have to read. Everything, all the
34   scientists. I learn how much the container can hold, I
35   respect the instruments, the delicate balance I must
36   achieve. The molecules are alive, they breathe, I know this
37   before I use them in my experiment. It's my life you're
38   asking about, Roger. Go find out something. Anything.
39 ROGER: Okay. Um, what about Saturday night? To work on
40   the story? I mean, my finals story.

1 ANA: I don't know. I have to babysit. I'm too busy.
2 ROGER: Busy doin' what? All you do is play around with
3   experiments, wanting to be a hero.
4 ANA: And what's wrong with that? *(ANA goes back to*
5   *computer terminal stage right where she works on her experiment.)*
6 ROGER: What'd I do? Just asked a question? What's the big
7   deal about a question? So the world's a lousy place, I'm not
8   blaming her! I don't care.

Exploration #49 (cont.)

Once you've written down goals and physical actions to play in this scene, stop the timer. As you practice this exploration with other plays, try to reduce your time to three to five minutes. Here are some suggestions you might have uncovered:

- (For Roger): He wants **to share** something with her about her past life. He wants **to thrill her** by telling her that he really likes her. He wants **to date her** where they'll work on his story together. He wants **to dazzle her** with his seriousness. He wants her **to open up to him** about a war she was involved in. As for physical actions, he may choose to sit beside her, fidget with his clothes, touch her hand, turn his back to her, remove his glasses, follow her every step around the room.

- (For Ana): She wants him **to really listen and understand** her seriousness about science. She wants **to avoid his flattery**. She wants **to avoid dating him**. She wants **to earn compliments** from him. She wants **to date him**. She wants **to test his sincerity** towards her. She wants him **to go away** and leave her alone. As for physical actions, she may turn away whenever he steps close, try to read her textbook, grab him by his shirt, adjust her hair, avoid eye contact, and so forth.

Play the scene several times with a scene partner, each of you using one of the goals and physical actions (only one goal and physical action per readthrough). Don't tell each other which you've chosen to play, let the other actor "play off" of it. Notice how the scene changes almost entirely each time you do it! If you feel the scene isn't changing all that drastically, keep working at it until it does. Once you begin to develop some skill with influencing a scene by means of changing goals and physical actions in this way, you can then try this same exploration with other scenes of your own choosing. You can also do two other things: learn to change those goals during the scene as the text dictates and as you encounter obstacles from the other character, and learn to devise more concrete physical actions that express your goals. It's important to keep in mind that in a cold reading you may not ever know which goals and physical actions are the "correct" ones to play — which interpretation is the one the director prefers. What's important is only that you understand that every scene can contain numerous goals and actions, that you should only pick out one or two major ones to play, and commit to playing them strongly. The director may want you to change your interpretation after the reading, of course, but more on that below. And don't forget: look up from the page as you read it through! Make eye contact with your vis-à-vis! Make a relationship *happen*!

Callbacks and Interviews

The callback is what you should be aiming for with your general audition. It's the situation in which you'll get to show your talents in more detail to the casting people and learn a lot more about them. Certainly you've shown a lot by your prepared audition, but, as I mentioned above, there are some acting skills that only a cold or semi-cold reading (and maybe also an interview!) can reveal. In any case, you should realize that the director will use the callback with its cold or semi-cold readings mainly in order to determine how well you take direction.

"Taking direction" from casting people during the audition really means showing the director how flexible you are in your acting choices, how skilled you are in changing on the spot some of the given circumstances of a scene or monolog, and how easy or difficult an actor you may be to work with. As I mentioned earlier, few directors outside of your school will ever cast actors simply on the basis of general readings. The callbacks will be a combination of free improvisations, an interview, and text readings. They may be brief (only a few hours) or very lengthy (perhaps even weeks and weeks!), and you should be prepared to "work with" the director every step of the way in order to give him or her a good idea of your suitability for the role.

In the previous chapter I discussed one aspect of taking direction during callbacks, the improvisation, and how you can be ready for that. What I want to look at here are three other forms of taking direction: the "overnight callback" with assigned material, how to "add" directorial suggestions during a cold or semi-cold reading, and how to conduct yourself in the interview.

An overnight callback is one in which the director gives you a scene or two from the play to look over and bring back the following day. This is often a valuable part of auditions when time permits, because it focuses on the play being cast and gives you ample time to prepare something, yet doesn't require you to "set it in stone."

The first thing to keep in mind about preparing a callback reading is to approach the scene or monolog as chapter 6 advises, without committing it to memory. As you rehearse aloud "overnight" again and again, you'll find yourself automatically committing some parts of the scene to memory, but you shouldn't make the effort to memorize it entirely word for word — only the beginning and ending lines.

What you *must* do, however, is **listen very carefully to what the director tells you about the scene before you go off and work on your own.** Is the director looking for a certain *quality* in the character? Is there a certain *tone* or spirit or mood to the scene that you'll be expected to capture? Is the *relationship* with your vis-à-vis somewhat complicated, and how much of that can you bring out in your reading? And certainly don't neglect to study the lines of your vis-à-vis for clues about your character, what's happening in the scene, and other information. Remember, you're going to have to play the scene with some other actor and you'll be expected to make that relationship work! Things like these are vitally important in order for you to "fit into" the kind of interpretation the director may have of the scene, the characters, and the play overall.

Once you return with the scene more or less prepared, you can expect to be able to perform it at least once the way you've interpreted it, but after that, the director will likely start to tinker with your interpretation and ask you to change a little here and there. The fundamental rule you must *always* follow when taking direction in this situation is to **never drop entirely the basic interpretation you've formed, only add to it what the director is suggesting.** Just as you must have done *some*thing well in the general audition in order to get called back, so too in the callback itself you must rely on your basic interpretation as a sort of foundation for whatever the director wants you to add or change.

You're bound to encounter directors now and then who don't understand this. They may tell you that what you've done is not really correct, or that they want you to try something "radically different," or that they want to "see how far you can take it." But what they really mean is to *add* the new direction to what you've already done. This is how we work as actors: we *modify* our basic instincts to conform to this or that production style or interpretation. Yes, the next reading may and should be different than the one you just did, but you play that difference as a *variation* upon your basic choices.

It's the only way we *can* work, you see? We don't ever create something from scratch, do we? Like turning on a faucet and suddenly there's water? Every "characterization" is a process of building up one detail after another, one clue after another about that role we're creating. Some of these details are text-based, and we discover those through textual analysis and rehearsals. Some of them are substituted from our own lives and experiences, as I explained in chapter 5. Some are freely improvised and invented by you or the director or ensemble during the rehearsals.

That's how we work through rehearsals, and that's how we must work in callbacks (albeit more quickly): by adding this and that to some of the basic, fundamental choices we've already made. And this is true whether you have "overnight" to consider your options and then make some choices, or whether you have just a few minutes to do so in a semi-cold reading. Moreover, we always leave some of these choices open, because we never know (at least in auditions) with whom we'll be playing the scene. An actor will play differently with a different vis-à-vis.

I should point out here that the vis-à-vis is the big "wild card" at a callback. We all know that "we play better tennis when we play with better players," and we're all hoping we have a great scene partner to work with. At the generals, you may not have this luxury because there are a lot of people reading there who will be screened out of the callbacks. I can't tell you how many times I've found myself reading off a stage manager or rehearsal assistant at generals, and I just had to make the best of it. But rest assured this isn't likely to happen at callbacks. There, the directors will only have the better actors reading for the roles in the show.

So when you're asked to take direction, always add it to or layer it upon what you've already done. Otherwise, of course, you run the risk of losing the good qualities you've already brought to the audition. You don't want the director to conclude, "Gee! She's lost all that spark I saw at the tryouts. I guess I was wrong. Or maybe she just can't take direction. Too bad!"

You can train yourself to do this by regularly practicing the three exploration exercises above. Each of them gives you a different way of playing the scene and changing your interpretation: through relationship, events, and goals/physical actions. If you become skilled with these methods, then you can easily translate what the director wants you to do in the callback to any of those three approaches and produce a scene with a radically different quality. Directors love this at auditions, believe me. They love to see an "acting machine" who can respond flexibly and creatively to their suggestions. And even if your callback interpretation isn't quite what they wanted, you're going to communicate to them that you've got the chops to deliver the goods after enough rehearsals. So make the director feel he or she can shape a good performance with you, given enough rehearsal time.

The final thing that may take place at a callback is the interview. This can be fairly brief and casual, like exchanging a few words with the director and stage manager just before or after a reading. Or it can be more lengthy and somewhat formal when it occurs in the context of an URTA audition or callbacks for summer and commercial theatre work. But no matter the context in which it may occur, you're still auditioning during the interview.

You can't really prepare for an interview, and you never should in the sense of "scripting" anything to say. Interviews should be natural, unforced, and spontaneous. *Above all, you must remember that the interview is an invitation for you to reveal your personal self to the auditioners.* It's one of several areas — like choosing your prepared pieces or making unique choices to play in the scene — where you, the actor, are in control of the audition situation. So make the most of it.

You see, directors often have a difficult time in interviews, because they don't know quite what to say or what to ask you. That is, they might be wonderful directors but lousy communicators. So help them out, perhaps, by asking them a question or two. How did they get started directing, as opposed to acting or writing? Or how do they find the energy to sit through fifty auditions each day and keep a clear head? Why did they choose this play to produce? Things like that.

In addition, don't be shy about speaking of personal matters during the interview if they pertain to the casting process. For example, did your audition piece ring some odd bells with you the first time you discovered it? Is a particular scene or actor's performance in a new feature film still on your mind? Does the play appeal to you for some special reason? It's the one chance you have to reveal something about yourself as a human being. You don't want to run on at the mouth, of course. But above all, don't be defensive and wear a mask at the interview.

There are, of course, some basic things you want to accomplish when speaking with the director and staff in a school situation in order to communicate to them that you're likely to be a pleasant and cooperative co-worker on the production team. You should always seem reasonably enthusiastic about the play and the production, happy to meet everyone connected with it, positive about the experience of callbacks, and curious about what happens next. You should also seek to know

- the names of all the staff people present,
- if there will be any further callbacks,
- if you can earn academic credit for participating in the play,
- when and how the cast list will be announced,
- if you can apply for some technical work if you don't get cast, and
- when or if the first rehearsal meetings have been scheduled ("just in case" you're cast, you want to keep those times available!).

When it comes to auditioning for plays outside of your school, you'll have other things that you'll need to know. At URTA interviews, faculty will question you on your suitability for professional training at their institution. You need to know from them

- when they plan to announce their acceptance or rejection decisions,
- what sort of financial aid they normally offer to new students,
- what sort of emphases their program offers by comparison with other schools,
- how many new students they accept each year,
- whether they allow their students to work outside their program,
- and what sort of commitment the school has to helping students find professional work after graduation (senior showcases with agents? professionals in residence who can serve as contacts?).

For commercial work and summer theatres, you'll find interviews a lot more businesslike. In addition to getting to a know a little bit about you as in the above situations, these producers may also want you to perform a few more prepared audition pieces, because they may be casting for several shows. Additionally, they'll want to know how much money you're expecting to receive if you're cast, and if you can work *fast* because they often have short rehearsal schedules on account of costs. From your standpoint, you need to know the following in addition to the basic casting information on the show you've just auditioned for:

- what are the exact dates their season begins and ends? Are these the actors' call dates?
- is the theatre union affiliated? If so, will you have to pay union dues to enjoy any union privileges and benefits?
- what do they pay, when do they pay it, and what arrangements do they provide for actors' lodgings or food?
- do their actors normally have day jobs, or does the theatre expect actors to be available more or less full-time for rehearsals and performances?
- are actors expected to do other technical or administrative tasks? (often the case in non-union companies)
- what is the normal work week at their theatre (one or two days off? how many performances?)
- will there be any opportunity for you to take classes or workshops, or is the group just a production company?
- what sort of audiences does the theatre play for?
- what shows are they considering you for (if the theatre does a "season" of different plays)?

Of course, all auditionees going into an interview situation also need to be prepared for questions *they* will be asked by the directors or casting people. This means you must do your homework!

- Know the plays from which you chose your audition pieces so you can talk intelligently about why you chose to portray that particular character in an audition.
- If you're auditioning for a single play, read the entire play beforehand so you can form an opinion of it and gain some idea of the roles you'd like to play.
- If you're auditioning for graduate school or scholarships, know #1 above, and learn something about the graduate school (why you picked that school instead of others, what you think the school emphasizes in its training, where the school is located, etc.).
- Study your schedule and know what dates you're available for work on a particular show or with a particular company's season and any conflicts you may have with the posted information about rehearsals, performances, etc. (*very* important!).
- If you're auditioning for commercial work or for summer theatres, know what shows the theatre has done in past seasons.
- Be prepared to talk articulately about your resume.

This last point is all-important. You will never know what specific questions the casting people will ask in an interview, but 99 percent of the time you can expect some version of the following: "So, tell me a little about yourself." Most commonly the question is asked in reference to your resume, which they'll have in front of them, so have something prepared. Keep your answers short and very focused. The director has likely read at least three or four entries on your resume after scanning it (directors rarely read everything there), but this doesn't mean he or she wants you to tick off everything you've listed on it. It means the director wants you to **highlight one or two items that excite you about what you have done or currently are doing.**

So you must think about the entries on your resume and identify the high points of your experience. Pick out one or two *roles* about which you could speak animatedly for twenty to thirty seconds. Identify one or two *workshops or classes* listed there that you could praise in an intelligent way for half a minute. Choose a *director* you worked with who taught you a lot about acting. Pick a *training program or workshop* you completed, are enrolled in, or are looking forward to that you can describe with interest. And then, of course, let the director lead the comments after that.

Exploration #50: Verbal Resume

Examine your resume as just described and write up a thirty- to sixty-second *verbal* version of it, in prose, like a monolog. Try to avoid making it "literary" and instead shoot for natural sounding and spontaneous. Get it solidly memorized so you don't forget anything important. Practice it for friends. Practice it for your teachers or coaches. Practice it sitting, standing onstage, riding in a car, or talking in someone's office until it sounds right to you. Prepare two to three versions of this verbal resume so you can continually keep them updated like your audition pieces themselves. Perhaps one could be tailored for a community theatre director, a second for a professional or commercial producer, maybe a third for a scholarship or school admissions committee wherein you also should articulate your goals and commitment to acting training. And be sure to get used to performing these for someone, just like your regular audition pieces. Your classmates make an excellent audience, and your teacher certainly shouldn't mind your asking for two to three minutes to run it by the class and get their feedback.

The Wrap

Rest assured that your unsettling feelings about callbacks, cold readings, and interviews won't end when you've finished the actual experience. More than in prepared readings, you're going to feel even more uneasy after such a session. This is where you must remember the advice I gave at the end of chapter 7: When they tell you "that's all," *you need to leave with confidence and poise.* Although your stomach is churning and your nerve endings are wired tight, you must communicate instead that you feel completely satisfied with your audition because you've nailed it.

Present a businesslike, workman-like attitude at the end of the session and avoid expressing hesitancy, fear, or even a suggestion that you think you've "failed the test." One auditions coach makes this point very emphatically in her book on auditioning for TV commercials: *"Do not ever, under any circumstances, apologize, visually or verbally, for your work!!!"* [7] You say brightly: "Thank you," or "Thanks for the chance to explore the material like that," and you collect your things and leave with a perky step.

Again, don't waste time at this point — theirs or yours. There's nothing more to say right now. They must make up their minds. You have other important things to attend to: another audition, a rehearsal, your all-important journal entries that record everything about this experience for future reference, whatever. Be professional, you've nailed it, you've wrapped it, and now it's up for grabs. Leave like a winner.

Review and Reflection

1. What are cold readings designed to accomplish?
- They reveal how well an actor is likely to create under stress.
- They offer directors a chance to explore interesting qualities they've noticed in actors.
- They give a good indication of what kind of a person you may be to work with in rehearsals.
- They will help to reveal the extent of an actor's basic skills training.
- They will often zero in upon more advanced skills that you may possess.
- They allow directors to closely consider actors in roles for which they may be suited in the particular play.

2. **How should I proceed when practicing cold readings on my own?**
   - Practice with friends reading scenes or monologs right off the shelf.
   - Test yourself after practicing by reading the complete play and comparing the choices you made cold with the whole play that you now understand.
   - Go back and play the scene differently according to the information and insights you picked up from reading the whole play.
   - Be sure to set yourself definite time limits for "preparation."
   - Rotate your partner as you do this exercise; don't always practice with the same person.
   - Ask one of your teacher/directors to "test" you by throwing some unprepared material at you.

3. **When reading a play before auditions, what questions should I ask myself?**
   - What *happens* in the play?
   - What is the *tone* of the play that I must somehow capture?
   - Which *characters* do I seem right for that the director is likely to have me read for?
   - What are the *key relationships* in the drama that I must understand?
   - What special *skills* does the play require that I must bring out?

4. **What must I do to quickly prepare a cold reading when I'm given a script?**
   - Be sure to ask the director what he or she wants and what the scene is about.
   - Quickly decide upon and commit to your choices: Who am I and who is my vis-à-vis? What happens in the scene? What do I want from my vis-à-vis?
   - Be sure also to study the other character's lines.

5. **What are some important points to keep in mind when attending callbacks?**
   - Approach the scene or monolog as chapter 6 advises, without committing it to memory.
   - Listen carefully to what the director tells you about the scene before you go off and work on your own.
   - You can expect to be able to perform the scene at least once the way you've interpreted it, but after that, the director will likely ask you to change a little here and there.

- Never entirely drop the basic interpretation you've formed, only add to it what the director is suggesting.
- At the time of the callback, be prepared for an interview, which is an invitation for you to reveal your personal side to the auditioners.

6. What information should I ask the directors for at a school audition?

- The names of all the staff people present.
- If there will be any further callbacks you should attend.
- If you can earn academic credit for participating in plays.
- When and how the cast listed will be announced.
- If you can apply for some technical work if you don't get cast.
- When or if the first rehearsal meetings have been scheduled.

7. What information should I ask the directors for at an URTA callback?

- When they plan to announce their acceptance or rejection decisions.
- What sort of financial aid they normally offer to new students.
- What sort of emphases their program offers by comparison with other schools.
- How many new students they accept each year.
- Whether they allow their students to work outside their program.
- What sort of commitment the school has to helping students find professional work after graduation.

8. What information should I ask the directors for at callback for a commercial theatre, summer theatre, or festival theatre?

- The exact dates their season begins and ends. Are these the actors call dates.
- If the theatre is union affiliated. If so, will you have to pay union dues to enjoy any union privileges and benefits.
- What they pay, when they pay it, and what arrangements they provide for actors' lodgings or food. What sort of benefits they provide.
- If their actors normally have day jobs. If the theatre expects actors to be available more or less full-time for rehearsals and performances.
- If actors are expected to do other technical or administrative work.
- What the normal work week at their theatre is.
- If there will be any opportunity for you to take classes or

workshops, or if the group is just a production company.
- What sort of audiences the theatre plays for.
- What shows they are considering you for.

9. What kind of information should I have ready to offer at a callback interview?

- Know the plays from which you chose your audition.
- If you're auditioning for a single play, read the entire play beforehand.
- If you're auditioning for graduate school or scholarships, learn something about the school.
- Study your schedule and know what dates you're available for work on a particular show or with a particular company's season and any conflicts you may have with the posted information about rehearsals, performances, etc.
- If you're auditioning for commercial work or for summer theatres, know what shows the theatre has done in past seasons.
- Be prepared to talk articulately about your resume.

[1] Neil Duffield, Internet conversation with the author, 30 March 2002.

[2] Bradley Mott, interview with the author, 30 September 2003.

[3] Henry Winkler, "Inside with Henry Winkler," op. cit., p. 13.

[4] *Turtle Island Blues* by William Borden. Copyright © 1991 by William Borden, revised January 1993. All rights reserved. Reprinted by permission. All inquiries regarding rights should be addressed to the author: William Borden, 10514 Turtle River Lake Road NE, Bemidji, MN, 56601. E-mail: Wborden@paulbunyan.net.

[5] *Salmonberry: A West Coast Fairy Tale* by Cornelia Hoogland. Copyright © 1999 by Cornelia Hoogland. All rights reserved. Reprinted by permission. Information concerning rights should be addressed to the author: Cornelia Hoogland, 19 The Ridgeway, London, Ontario, N6C 1A2, CANADA. Telephone: 519.434.7815. FAX: 519.661.3833. E-mail: chooglan@uwo.ca.

[6] *Boom!* by Julie Salverson and Patti Fraser. Copyright ©1998 by Julie Salverson and Patti Fraser. All rights reserved. Reprinted by permission. Information concerning rights should be addressed to the author: Julie Salverson, Dept. of Drama, Queens University, Kingston, Ontario, CANADA. E-mail: salverson@oise.utoronto.ca.

[7] Pat Dougan, op. cit., p. 97.

Chapter Nine

Musical Theatre Auditions
"Get the leg up"

The Allure of the Musical

It's very unlikely that a young actor can go through school these days without getting a shot at a part in musical theatre: Broadway-style musical comedies (*Cabaret, My Fair Lady, Into the Woods*), rock musicals (*Celebration, Godspell*), operettas (*Brigadoon, Pirates of Penzance*), light operas (*Sweeney Todd, Threepenny Opera, Phantom*), revues (*Oh, Coward!, Woody Guthrie's American Song*), or musical dramas (*1776, Mother Courage*).

Does that list sound complicated? Too many "categories" or "genres"? Well, today's musical theatre is the fastest-changing and most experimental theatre form in the U.S., so it needs a lot of description! It's also the most popular form of theatre and if you try to become a good, or even self-supporting actor without doing some form of musical theatre, you're going to have an uphill battle.

Shakespeare is music, song, and dance (among other things). So is classical Greek tragedy and comedy. New multi media performance art ensembles like the Blue Man Group and others incorporate music, mime, acting, and audience-interactive elements. Bertolt Brecht and Peter Weiss, the last century's most radical and successful political dramatists, wrote musical dramas, operas, revues, and the like to score their points. Many "straight" plays by writers like Sam Shepard, Caridad Svich, Martin McDonagh, and others incorporate music and often songs as part of their scripts. And theatre for young audiences — a huge and growing field, not only for kids — will often blend music, mime, acrobatics, song, circus technique, and creative movement in presentations like *The Lion King* or *The Wiz*.

What is it about musical theatre that makes it so popular and merits a place in your audition training? For one thing, the musical has developed into a tough and flexible theatrical form that can handle a wide range of subjects, which makes it an attractive but complicated beast to audition for. For example, it can be the vehicle for self-reflection (*A Chorus Line*), camp (*Oh, Coward!*), sentiment (*The Fantastics*), icon-bashing (*Urinetown*), social problems (*Rent*), the macabre (*Sweeney Todd*), and other themes. And don't overlook the fact that lots of plays are being done that have substantial musical elements in them but aren't ordinarily referred to as musicals.

Actors must perform these shows, which means that actors must know how to audition for them. What do you need for musical theatre auditioning besides the obvious requirement that you must be able to sing, and maybe also dance?

Well, the first thing an actor must know in order to audition well for musical theatre is the historical style of the genre. Up until the last century, stage plays always included music in some form. Sometimes that meant full-blown opera, while in other plays you might only have music and occasional songs accompanying the dramatic action (the "melodrama"). In the past century, however, we in the West developed a very popular body of plays that were largely "realistic." These dramas rejected the theatricality ("non-realism") of song-dance-drama, and instead tried to put on the stage a naturalistic "slice of life" to greater or lesser degree.

This is mainly how separate categories or genres came to be established for "musical" versus "straight" or "legitimate" plays. [1] Nowadays, however, the boundaries between "opera," "musical," "cabaret," and other forms have begun to shift and merge again as writers explore new forms and styles. This is why actors need to understand very clearly the kinds of musical tasks they'll be called upon to perform when they audition for this genre of shows.

A second thing you have to understand about doing musical theatre shows and auditioning for them, is that it's going to take a lot of energy. As Joanna Merlin explains,

> Music brings an energy into the theater that is unique to the musical-theater form. The music of the overture, the songs, the dance music, the music scored under the dialogue, all create a theatrical energy that becomes a defining element for the actor who performs in the musical theater. You may not have heard the score if it is a new musical, but you must pay attention to that heightened energy when you are preparing your audition. [2]

If you've ever done this kind of a show, you know what she means: You really have to work at it! You must act, sing, and dance — often at the same time. The scenes and emotions are somehow bigger than you'll find in "straight" plays. The stage action is faster, the encounters more compressed and intense, the characters more cleanly developed, and the physical action more vivid. It's the kind of play that lots of people want to be in because it's fun. One New York director nailed it down in these terms: "The musical's arena is the outrageous, the wondrous, the screwball — life at its full rhythm — and more common than we think. As Martha Graham puts it, the creative problem is not to be larger than life, but as large." [3]

Bear in mind that musical entertainment is real bread-and-butter for actors nowadays, and there's lots of opportunity at the entrance level for young performers. Probably more young, new actors are employed in musical shows every year than in all straight plays combined because of the wealth of musical opportunities in summer theatres, dinner theatres, resort theatres, theme parks, and other venues. So if you can understand the many forms that musicals assume nowadays, and if you've got the energy and commitment for these kinds of shows — *and* if you can read music, sing, and learn choreography in addition to your other acting skills — then you've got a real edge on landing yourself a part in a show of this kind!

Building a Healthy Attitude

Musical shows, while ever in demand, in many ways also present the most difficult audition challenges for actors. For example, when you try out, you'll have to convince directors that you truly are a "triple threat": someone who is able to act, sing, and dance. Michael Shurtleff reminds actors that a musical audition "needs everything an actor gives to drama and yet it needs more. More force, more economy, more relationship … more humor, more of everything an actor has to offer." [4]

In addition to overcoming the challenge of competition, young students sometimes feel poorly equipped and self-conscious about their skills. In brief, you'll need to feel comfortable with the following:

- The ability to sight read music
- The ability to carry a tune, both rhythmically and tonally
- The ability to sing with a clear, strong voice within a reasonable range
- The ability to project feeling, meaning, and belief into the lyrics
- The ability to work in a disciplined fashion on dance routines and other forms of choreography
- The ability to work in a variety of dance styles

I know that all of this sounds like work, and it is. But you have to remember that many, many young actors are entering the field today well trained from B.F.A. and M.F.A. programs where they've honed these skills. In fact, if you've ever attended ACTF auditions, you'll have seen a lot of well-trained individuals competing there with musical pieces! That's the level you have to aspire to if you're going to earn a living in this profession.

If you're already enrolled in a B.F.A. or M.F.A. program, don't assume that your school is automatically supplying you with all the training you need. Look critically at your program and examine how it's preparing you for musical drama. You may find it lacking in musical production opportunities or certain kinds of classes (dance styles, movement for actors, singing voice, etc.). No matter how well you think you're doing on campus, you may have to get off campus or get involved in summer productions in order to remedy those deficiencies! "Many students come to New York," comments one professional acting coach, "with their M.F.A.'s in hand, their glowing reviews in a portfolio, and their talents very sketchily developed through a too-casual acceptance of their (misleadingly) high campus status." [5]

In short, don't fall into the trap that snares a lot of students who think themselves "actors" just because they can get cast in realistic plays. That's basic, of course, but it's only a notch above poptrash TV shows. Take your cue from a song in the famous musical *Company* about all the wannabes out there: "And another hundred people just got off of the train." You want to be equipped when you step off your academic train.

An additional problem that student actors frequently have with musicals is that song and dance — while fun — seem artificial and "phony." Students sometimes feel awkward singing and dancing onstage, as though it's unnatural. If this is your situation, you simply must overcome it. It might help you to think of some of the big movie musicals, something like *Singin' in the Rain* or *Grease*. Singing is just as natural for those characters as the crazy behavior of Shakespeare's fools is "real" for them, or the antics of clowns in commedia dell'arte, or the bumbling confusion of otherwise normal people in a Feydeau farce.

In musicals, characters sing and dance because this is the only way they can express their "big" emotions. In the world of this play, it all seems logical and natural, and actors must play it that way. Song is just a heightened form of human communication similar to, but not the same as, poetry.

After all, ordinary people sing all the time to themselves, because singing is a natural human activity, right? You might catch yourself whistling and humming tunes as you do chores or walk along, or singing along with the radio as you drive, or singing karaoke-style in bars and maybe in the shower. You also sing in many formal contexts as well: in church, for birthdays, at school assemblies, at athletic events when the national anthem is played, etc. So singing has a lot of real-life "dramatic logic" behind it, and you can certainly learn to identify with it if you try. As one Chicago-based actor recommends: "Don't close the door because you think you can't sing. Find a song that you can sing and work on it, and use that as your audition piece." [6]

Music and dance, too, are parts of our everyday life — from muzak in the supermarket to the expensive sound system plugged into your ear or sitting on your shelf at home. And because you're listening to music, your behavior will change, right? Music shifts your moods, awakens strong emotions, and makes you move and gesture in different ways. You may simply tap your fingers or nod your head, or you might even get right out on the dance floor to boogie! Some music is "fed" to us for different purposes: supermarket muzak keeps us peppy and upbeat so we'll be encouraged to buy things; church music puts us in a reverential, joyful, or praiseworthy state of mind; and TV commercial music often hooks us in order to focus our attention on the ads. In fact, the list of places we "normally" encounter music of some kind in our everyday life each week — or even each day! — could be very, very long. Why should it seem "unnatural," therefore, for many young actors to think of living in a musical world onstage?

So there it is: We sing and we respond to music at "special" moments all the time — why not onstage as well? Think for a moment of that time you just *had* to drag that guy onto the dance floor or just felt like *bellowing out* the song that was playing on your car radio as you drove along! Characters in musical theatre do the very same thing. They reach that point in scenes where the emotions are just too big for ordinary words; their songs and dances are *lyrical extensions* of their feelings, their wants, their objectives in the drama.

This is what Aaron Frankel and Michael Shurtleff meant when they said "more." What the character needs to express is big, not "larger than life" but "as large," expressing what is "up to life." The song is not a pause in "the play" for a pretty tune or a splashy dance routine or to give the star a "cameo" moment. It *is* the play. It's an extension of the dramatic action and it flows from it. It adds zing to that action as it swells and seduces and overpowers, as it changes to develop into new actions, or as it links one action to another — all the while driving the show across the apron to the farthest row in the balcony.

Problems with Musical Auditions

This magnification of experience is the essence of musical theatre, and as an actor you need to be up to the challenge. Let's take a look now at some of the unique features of musical theatre auditioning.

The first thing you need to keep in mind in tryouts is that your audition must be strongly outer-directed, off the stage, because the emotions are so big they must be shared! Never play the dialog in a scene, and certainly never play a song, just to the other character reading with you as you might in many realistic, non-musical plays; take it to the house as well. There is really no "fourth wall" in musical theatre. As Michael Shurtleff again reminds us: "Each twosome scene in effect becomes a threesome, with the audience the third member of the scene." [7] The character's need to communicate with his or her listeners (chapter 6) means here that you must push beyond the stage in order to connect with them. Often you'll have to play the scene or song directly to them.

Understanding this "outer-directed" quality of musicals is very important for an auditionee. All musical pieces look for those moments, situations, and encounters where they can turn out and embrace the public with urgency, surprise, and impact. Like Shakespeare's plays, the musical is a vibrantly public theatrical form, and it's today's musical that comes the closest to creating the kind of theatre experience that Shakespeare had in mind. [8] So don't be afraid of playing your song or scene out toward the auditors — sharing with the audience — more so than you would at an audition for a straight play. This is built into the dramatic situations of musical dramas in a way that you will not find in other kinds of scripts.

Second, *realize that the scene you're given to read isn't likely to reach a climax in the words alone; the dialog will often move toward the song or follow the song as the dramatic peak.* This is something that frequently confuses young actors because they're far more word-oriented than music-oriented when it comes to plays, so they don't look at songs as "dramatic." But they should! You need to accept this unique construction of the dramatic action in musical theatre, which often zeroes in upon a few bold aspects of life that the script can then explore in a lyrical, extended fashion (song and dance).

Third, *you must play the music as the subtext of all the scenes, many of which are underscored by instrumental accompaniment.* Even when characters aren't singing, the energy of the music in the numbers that precede and follow a monolog or a scene adds a certain concrete quality, tone, or energy level to that monolog or two-character scene. And often, as in many operas where the music never stops but plays under all the action in what's called a "leitmotif," dialog scenes in Broadway-style musicals frequently have musical underscoring as well.

Fourth, *events and character details in musicals (such as dialog) tend to be compressed, economical, and sketched-in, so you must work to fill them in.* Notice that I didn't say simplistic or superficial, but only that the details you're likely to find in the script will tend to be minimal in comparison with straight plays where more complicated psychology can be explored. If a picture is worth a thousand words, then how many more words can be compressed into an exciting *series* of pictures or images in dance and music? In musical theatre, less is more. Like soap operas, what you don't find in the script you must fill in by other means.

To some extent, therefore, a major problem for auditioners at musical theatre readings is to find ways of filling in the stage action. Shurtleff suggests that you concentrate even harder than in straight plays upon **creating a strong relationship** with your scene partner. Other coaches with whom I've spoken recommend **paying close attention to the pace** of your scene, because things "develop" faster in musicals as a result of the minimal dialog, events, and character details you have to work with. Still other coaches insist that students not try to "over-complicate" what is obviously a brief treatment onstage, but instead **focus on the broad effects** — in character, dialog, and action — the scene may contain.

You can certainly use any or all of these approaches in an audition; see which one is best for you:

- create a strong relationship,
- emphasize the fast-changing events, or
- amplify dialog, action, and relationships to exploit a scene's full potential.

These three pointers are especially valuable in a cold reading situation, but you should also keep them in mind when preparing musical scenes beforehand for general auditions or callbacks. Use the same procedure recommended in chapters 5 and 6 for working up material in straight plays, but remember the special problems of musicals as you proceed. To refresh your memory, the steps in preparation are:

1. select carefully and edit to retain only what you need,
2. paraphrase to be sure of the meaning and motivation,
3. identify goals, obstacles, and concrete actions as you event the script,

4. divide your script into beats in order to give it shape,
5. explore the vocal potential of the language, and
6. devise movement that reinforces the dramatic action.

Exploration #51: Playing Moment to Moment in Musical Scenes

Find a scene partner of the opposite sex and study the following scene between Polly and Tony from the musical The Boy Friend. The scene contains no extraneous material so there's no need for editing. The pronunciation and British dialect, however, are important for the playfulness of the style, so be sure to consult a dictionary or language coach. One piece of business, dropping the box, is essential to mime, so you already have one concrete action to play. The diction is contemporary, so you'll gain little from exploring the vocal sounds here. In other words, some of the steps in preparation can be reduced or eliminated altogether. Other steps, though, are crucial. For example, one way to open out the reading is to explore blocking patterns that frequently call for frontal positions. The action suggests this by the shyness of the characters. Thus, Polly and Tony may "blush and turn away" from each other at key points, sharing their nervousness with the audience and heightening the charming mood of two young people falling ridiculously in love at first sight. Notice also how the relationship can be established, how the spare dialog can be fleshed out with mushy and tender sentiment by playing the intentions and the obstacles moment by moment. At different times, Tony wishes "to bring" the package, "to praise" Polly, "to convince her" how much he'd like to go. Similarly Polly wants "to snare" this cute young man, "to conceal" her embarrassment, or "to date" him. The words may not give you much, but the scene can really fly if you play such beats and emotional colors strongly and clearly. The turns come clearly, and the pace must not suffer even though the moments need to be played fully one by one, as they arise.

From ***The Boy Friend*** by Sandy Wilson [9]

1 **TONY:** *(Coughing)* **Er — excusez-moi!**
2 **POLLY:** *(Turning)* **Oh! You startled me!**
3 **TONY: I'm sorry, miss. I'm afraid I came in the wrong way.**
4   **This is the Villa Caprice, isn't it?**
5 **POLLY: Yes.**
6 **TONY: I have a package here for Miss Polly Browne.**
7 **POLLY: Really? How funny!**

1 TONY: Funny? Why?
2 POLLY: Because I'm Polly Browne.
3 TONY: Well, it's a very pretty name.
4 POLLY: Oh, thank you.
5 TONY: And you live up to it.
6 POLLY: Oh!
7 TONY: I'm sorry, miss. I'm afraid I'm forgetting myself.
8   Here's your package. *(Tony hands Polly the package. Both hold*
9   *on to it. They are looking at each other. They both release it and*
10   *TONY picks it up and gives it to POLLY again.)*
11 POLLY: Oh, thank you.
12 TONY: If you don't mind my saying so, it's an awfully pretty
13   dress.
14 POLLY: Yes, it is, isn't it?
15 TONY: Yes, I'm sure that you — I mean it will be the prettiest
16   at the Ball.
17 POLLY: Oh, I don't expect so, really.
18 TONY: I do. In fact I know it. I —
19 POLLY: Yes?
20 TONY: Well, perhaps I'd better be going.
21 POLLY: Oh yes. Oh no. Oh yes, perhaps you had. *(He turns to*
22   *go.)* I say!
23 TONY: *(Turning back)* Yes?
24 POLLY: You're — you're English, aren't you?
25 TONY: Yes, as a matter of fact, I am.
26 POLLY: You don't seem like a messenger boy somehow.
27 TONY: Don't I? Well, to tell you the truth I don't usually do
28   this sort of thing, but just at the moment I'm afraid, I'm
29   rather on my beam ends.
30 POLLY: Oh, what a shame! And at Carnival Time too.
31 TONY: Yes, it is a pity, isn't it? I was hoping to be able to go
32   to the Ball tonight. I'll be watching.
33 POLLY: Will you?
34 TONY: *(Pause)* Of course.
35 POLLY: Why don't you come too?
36 TONY: Me? Come to the Ball?
37 POLLY: Yes. Why not? I've got an extra ticket and — Oh dear,
38   you must think me terribly forward.
39 TONY: No, I don't. I think you're terribly —
40 POLLY: Yes?

Exploration #51 (cont.)

After two or three rehearsals with your partner you should feel pretty much on top of it, but keep rehearsing it until you can perform it consistently the way you want it. Notice how disarming the scene is! You think you understand everything about it, no sweat, right? Well, you're wrong. Look, for example, at the unique choices you're making. Where does he fall in love at first sight (what *line* exactly)? Where does *she* fall in love? (We must see some concrete physical actions at those points, some dazzle!) Which are the moments of greatest embarrassment for the characters (which *lines*)? Where does each turn away? Where *exactly* does Polly get the impulse to invite him? And where does she *actually* speak it? And how do you build the series of reactions from the start of the scene so they reach a climax in the very last line (which is the first line of the love duet, "I Could Be Happy With You")? Have you understood the strict social conventions that govern the behavior of young men and women in snooty upper class boarding schools on the French Riviera in the 1920s? Have you listened to this duet from the album? Do so. Could you sing those lyrics believably? As in a fog, dreamlike, *completely* bonkers over the guy/girl, forgetting everything else in the world for him/her? And how hard is all of this *for you* to do? Can you play corny *for the entire scene with belief*? You *must*, because this is how the scene and the song work, this is the basis of the humor and the gripping charm of the moment. If you play the scene realistically, it falls flat and you'll never get the part. Now you can begin to see how "less is more" in musical theatre writing, and how the actor must bring all his or her imagination to bear upon the audition and play it fully if the scene is to come alive!

Exploration #52: Musical Theatre Scene Structure

Examine the following scene from Lerner and Loewe's Camelot. This is more complicated than the previous scene because it's longer, and also because of the greater emotional range and shifting goals that each character pursues. As you study the scene, look for the unique choices you can make in order to flesh out the charming, fast-developing relationship. For example, why is she so curious about him? Hasn't she just finished the song about maidenhood? What has happened to Arthur to make him so fearful of everything — including women? Is sex on the mind of either character here? What finally does motivate him to sing the praises of Camelot in the song that follows this scene? And does she really want to scrap the royal wedding that's been arranged? The answers to these questions are not contained in the play. Be sure to read or view it on video and listen to the music before attempting the scene in order to see which moments precede and follow this extract. The scene kicks off from her song and segues into Arthur's.

From *Camelot* by Lerner and Loewe [10]

1 ARTHUR: A thousand pardons, Milady. Wait! Don't run. *(She*
2   *stops in the corner of the stage and looks at him, cowering.)* **Please!**
3   I won't harm you.
4 GUENEVERE: You lie! You'll leap at me and throw me to to
5   the ground.
6 ARTHUR: *(Amazed, protesting)* I won't do any such thing. *(He*
7   *takes a step toward her. She takes a step backward. He stops.)*
8 GUENEVERE: Then you'll twist my arm and tie me to a tree.
9 ARTHUR: But I won't.
10 GUENEVERE: Then you'll sling me over your shoulder and
11   carry me off.
12 ARTHUR: No, no, no! I swear it! By the Sword Excalibur! I
13   swear I won't touch you.
14 GUENEVERE: *(Hurt)* Why not? *(Sudden rage:)* How dare you
15   insult me in this fashion. Do my looks repel you?
16 ARTHUR: No. You're beautiful.
17 GUENEVERE: Well, then? We're alone. I'm completely
18   defenseless. What kind of a cad are you? Apologize at once.
19 ARTHUR: *(At once)* I apologize. I'm not certain what I've
20   done, but from the depths of my heart, I apologize.
21 GUENEVERE: *(With sudden wisdom)* Ah! I think I know. You
22   heard my praying.
23 ARTHUR: I couldn't help it, Milady. You prayed rather
24   loudly.
25 GUENEVERE: And you know who I am.
26 ARTHUR: You're Guenevere.
27 GUENEVERE: Yes, of course. You're afraid because I may be
28   your queen. That accounts for your respectful, polite,
29   despicable behavior.
30 ARTHUR: Milady, I would never harm you for any reason.
31   And as for what to do with you, I'm at a loss. I know you
32   are to be queen, and I should escort you back to your
33   carriage. At the same time, you're a maiden in genuine
34   distress. It's chivalry versus country. I can't quite determine
35   which call to obey.
36 GUENEVERE: *(Looking off toward the foot of the hill)* You'd better
37   decide quickly. They'll soon reach the carriage and discover
38   I'm gone. Then all of Camelot will be searching for me. At
39   least that will be exciting. Unless of course everyone in
40   Camelot is like you, and they all go home to deliberate.

1 ARTHUR: *(Thrown off balance, enamoured, captivated, and captivated*
2   *by a great sense of inadequacy)* **Oh, why isn't Merlyn here! He**
3   **usually senses when I need him and appears. Why does he**
4   **fail me now?**
5 GUENEVERE: **Who?**
6 ARTHUR: **Merlyn. My teacher. He would know immediately**
7   **what to do. I'm not accomplished at thinking, so I have**
8   **Merlyn do it for me. He's the wisest man alive. He lives**
9   **backwards.**
10 GUENEVERE: **I beg your pardon?**
11 ARTHUR: **He lives backwards. He doesn't age. He youthens.**
12   **He can remember the future so he can tell you what you'll**
13   **be doing in it. Do you understand?** *(She comes toward him. He*
14   *never takes his eyes off her, as the wonder of her comes nearer.)*
15 GUENEVERE: *(Now at ease)* **Of course I don't understand. But**
16   **if you mean he's some sort of fortune-teller, I'd give a year**
17   **in Paradise to know mine. I can never return to my own**
18   **castle, And I absolutely refuse to go on to that one.**
19 ARTHUR: **You refuse to go on — ever?**
20 GUENEVERE: **Ever. My only choice is ... Don't stare. It's**
21   **rude. Who are you?**
22 ARTHUR: *(After a thought)* **Actually, they call me Wart.**
23 GUENEVERE: **Wart? What a ridiculous name. Are you sure**
24   **you heard them properly?**
25 ARTHUR: **It's a nickname. It was given to me when I was a**
26   **boy.**
27 GUENEVERE: **You're rather sweet, in spite of your name.**
28   **And I didn't think I'd like anyone in Camelot. Imagine**
29   **riding seven hours in a carriage on the verge of hysteria,**
30   **then seeing that horrible castle rising in the distance, and**
31   **running away; then having a man plop from a tree like an**
32   **overripe apple — you must admit for my first day away**
33   **from home it's quite a plateful. If only I were not alone.**
34   **Wart, why don't you ... Is it really Wart?**
35 ARTHUR: **Yes.**
36 GUENEVERE: **Wart, why don't you run away with me?**
37   *(Suddenly excited by the notion.)*
38 ARTHUR: **I? Run away with you?**
39 GUENEVERE: **Of course. As my protector. Naturally, I would**
40   **be brutalized by strangers. I expect that. But it would be**
41   **dreadful if there were no one to rescue me. Think of it! We**
42   **can travel the world. France, Scotland, Spain ...**

1 ARTHUR: What a dream you spin, and how easily I could be
2   caught up in it. But I can't, Milady. To serve as your
3   protector would satisfy the prayers of the most fanatic
4   cavalier alive. But I must decline.
5 GUENEVERE: *(Angry)* You force me to stay?
6 ARTHUR: Not at all.
7 GUENEVERE: But you know you're the only one I know in
8   Camelot. Whom else can I turn to?
9 ARTHUR: Milady, if you persist in escaping, I'll find
10   someone trustworthy and brave to accompany you.
11 GUENEVERE: Then do so immediately. There's not much
12   time.

Selecting the Song

Probably the most difficult feature of musical theatre auditioning is the singing. For an actor, song auditions are much more terrifying than monologs or scenes because they make you feel so "naked" onstage: nothing but your voice to work with, nowhere to hide, and if you aren't a good singer people will discover it right away. I know I always feel that way at a singing audition, as though it were alien territory. Speech, after all, is almost like conversation, but song isn't. The singing voice can't be faked.

Generally speaking, most actors are not well trained as singers, and vice versa, so auditors are often faced with a grim choice at auditions: cast a strong actor who may have to fake part of the vocal sections, or cast a fine singer who'll need some help bumbling through the dramatic sections. The dilemma arises frequently in university and community theatre productions, and in small summer companies as well.

As one might expect, directors with strong backgrounds in opera and lyric theatre frequently prefer accomplished singers. As one producer explained to me, musical "presence" is all-important onstage when it comes to moving an audience: "What I'm interested in seeing is do they have enough power to carry the strong musical moments ... do they have a strong enough presence when they're singing." [11] On the other hand, the type of show will often dictate the decision: "Everyone in the company had to sing, after a fashion," confessed Hal Prince of the New York production of *Company*.

> Everyone had to dance, after a fashion. But as they were
> to be real people, their footwork and voices were
> subordinated to their performances. Which is not to say

that some didn't sing well or move well. Some moved with agility, just as some of your living-room friends move with agility, but others were klutzes and we wanted that. [12]

Needless to say, it's best not to bank on your theatrical future as a klutz.

What I've found in gathering material for this book, however, is that *most directors will always tend to place a higher premium on the actor's ability to play the song, to move the audience dramatically — even if the actor's singing ability leaves something to be desired.* Why? Because show songs are written first and foremost to be pitched across the footlights in a way that pop songs are not. Show songs contain struggles and emotions that the character absolutely *needs* to share with the audience as well as with the other characters in the scene. If these songs are to work, they require strong and believable acting more than perfect pitch, pear-shaped tones, exquisite breath control, and many other qualities that good singers are trained to exhibit.

Given the choice then between a strong singer or a strong actor, stage directors and producers will usually opt for the former. As director/coach Jack Wann explains:

> Most of the people who are auditioning you — agents, casting directors, directors, choreographers, lyricists, librettists — are not as interested in the actual singing as in how you look, move, and fill the envisioned roles. The composer and musical director are the only two people who are vitally interested in true vocal expertise. You must be able to act and perform with style to be hired to sing in most musical comedy companies. [13]

When you audition for a role in a college or community theatre or entry-level summer production, concentrate most of all upon performing the song *dramatically* instead of giving a song recital.

To begin with, you need to *select your audition material very carefully in order to showcase your singing voice well.* Most general musical auditions require eight to sixteen bars of a song (not the whole piece); so in order to earn a callback you'll first need

- something well within your age, emotional, and dramatic range,
- something with challenging musical ability that promises you might do even more with different material,
- something appropriate for the role or show being cast (as with dramatic pieces, do not choose a song from the show under

consideration or you'll needlessly limit your casting choices with the auditors),

- something that is "complete" (beginning-middle-end, like your monologs) when edited to the requisite eight to sixteen bars, and
- something that you can fill with belief.

You should never choose a "signature-song" (one that has been made famous by a star celebrity in a hit show) no matter how much you love the piece: comparisons at auditions are *always* odious and unfortunate, and you'll never be able to deliver the song with the same pizazz that the auditors remember from the original performance. As one musical audition coach expresses it: "Never select a song to perform that is better than you are." [14]

In addition, *you should always bring the sheet music with you, arranged in your key and clearly marked for the accompanist* (whom you will *always* treat with the greatest respect). Ask beforehand whether an accompanist will be available, whether you should bring your own, or whether cassette accompaniment on your boombox is preferred or allowed. Always opt for the "accompanist option" if you can because live music gives you a powerful springboard for a dynamic, engaging audition performance.

Your repertoire of additional song material for callbacks requires just as much careful attention as your repertoire of additional monologs that casting directors may request during callbacks. In the callback, directors may actually want you to do a complete song or two or three, so you'll have to work these up. Your repertoire should contain at least one "legit" song or ballad (slow love song or lament) and one belt (guts-ball, upbeat number), and then any additional material that you personally like or that reveals your specialties. For example, some shows are written in folk-music style (*Woody Guthrie's American Song*), some in country-western style (*Pump Boys and Dinettes*), and so forth. If you're a trained singer to some degree and have experience with classical material of any kind, always keep that stuff fresh as well. You never know when someone will want to hear your voice work over a Schubert *lieder* or an Elizabethan love song or a Gilbert and Sullivan patter-piece. And of course, *always* work with a singing coach to prepare all this material, just as you work with a dramatic coach for your monologs and scenes.

Probably the most common mistake of young actors in singing auditions is their failure to choose the right musical vehicle for themselves. When selecting musical material, you should refresh yourself on the points made in chapter 5 because much of that advice also applies to the kinds of songs you need to present. For example, choose only songs that really do *mean* something to you: songs that you can fill with energy and conviction, that showcase who *you* are as a person, that *you* can live with for a long time. Forget about the technical virtuosity of the original piece, or the professional performance you saw with an actor who really impressed you, or that magical musical moment in the movie that really turned you on, or someone's super-musical arrangement — none of that technical stuff is going to matter at an audition. What's most important is that you can invest the song with *yourself*, that the music becomes a moving vehicle for what *you* are thinking and feeling at the moment you perform it. Use yourself, bank on what you've already got going for you.

A second common mistake made by young actors is to select a song that is not drawn from the musical theatre repertoire — students often pick pop songs instead because they're more familiar with this kind of music. Familiarity, however, should no longer be a problem for you if you've been doing your homework. In chapter 2 I explained how you can broaden your background in musical theatre by listening to recordings and viewing videotapes of musical shows. This activity should give you a lot of enjoyment and acquaint you with a lot of possibilities for audition songs. More importantly, however, is the reason *why* pop songs really are unsuitable for musical auditions: they lack punch, development, and energy.

When I'm casting a musical show — operetta, cabaret, children's theatre, Broadway score — I want to audition actors performing something that's written for the stage because a show song has very special features and places unique demands upon actors. I want to listen to a song that's designed to push across the apron a situation, a character relationship to a live theatre audience in order to entertain them and suck them into the action. That's what actors have to do in performance, and that's what I want to see in an audition.

A show song will move and develop into something because it's made to be dramatic, theatrically exciting, and just plain "big." To return to Aaron Frankel again:

A show song is a heightened action springing from a dramatic context, and as a result reveals character, develops situation, forwards plot. It ends somewhere else from where it started, it makes a difference. A pop song has no such specific pressure and function. It is an entity unto itself, which does not go anywhere ... A pop song furthers moods, not actions. [15]

To convince yourself of this, just watch some MTV for awhile. Those poor folks struggle through an entire song desperately trying to find something to *play* in the song while the cameras roll. They seize on lyrics that (infrequently) allow them to pantomime some physical action that might be described in the words, but for the most part they're simply left with "mugging" a boring and repetitive emotion for the life of the song — the visuals enhanced by one trick after another of the editor's, cinematographer's, or SFX or scene-dresser's art. They get angry, they get sexy, they get hurt, they look tough, they look needy, they dance hot — and that's about it. After a couple hours, music videos contain all the emotional color and surprise of a turnip.

A second distinctive feature of a show song is that it develops, changes, and turns direction vividly and frequently as the character "struggles" with his or her problem and shares this struggle with the audience. In a semi-cold reading, keep this in mind and play those turns — like you play the beats in monologs — with strong contrasts in your acting. Also look for the climax in a show song. It will always be there, though you'll frequently find twists, reversals, and surprises at the climax as well. The climax may be soft or big and splashy, it may be reached swiftly or slowly, but the "punch" or "payoff" is always there in a show song. So look for that and play it.

With these general points in mind, let's take a look now at specific methods for preparing your audition songs.

Rehearsing the Song

The three general steps in preparing show songs are roughly analogous to the separate stages of preparing dramatic monologs as explained in chapter 6: analyzing the lyric, clarifying the subtext and motivations, and staging the piece. The most valuable way of approaching your song when first rehearsing it is to treat it as a monolog — as something presented by a solitary character directly to the audience, using a dramatic convention that is highly revealing and emotionally compelling.

The major difference between songs and monologs is that a song will tend to be much more *personally* revealing because the human voice expressed in music carries the indelible stamp of the personality behind it. It is one thing for the vocal director to say that your pitch should be true, your breath support adequate, your phrasing precise, your tone and timbre pleasant, and so on, and quite another to cast someone because his or her voice belongs to a thrilling actor — an actor sensitive to the meaning of the lyrics, emotionally in touch with the subtext, and expressing absolute believability in the song and the situation.

Remember that you can never "hide behind" your character onstage, and this is especially true of singing auditions. Your performance will reveal *you* no matter what the lyric may be expressing. Your first attempts at auditioning are likely to be self-conscious, and you simply must get used to this; remember that this is true of amateurs and professionals alike. The trick is not to listen to yourself as you sing; instead concentrate on the sense behind the lyric, focus on belief in the dramatic situation that the lyric is attempting to express. As you practice and rehearse, this belief will come more easily.

Begin preparing by memorizing and then analyzing the lyrics. *As with spoken monologs, first do a denotative paraphrase of the lines, followed by a connotative paraphrase that identifies the underlying meaning and feelings.* Let's begin by looking at another selection from Sandy Wilson's *The Boy Friend*. In the example that follows, I've chosen what's called an "interlinear" (word-for-word, line-by-line) paraphrase, which is always preferable for songs. But notice that the interlinear model does not try to duplicate either the rhythm or the rhyme of the original. At this point, you should only be concerned with what the song is telling us. [16] Musical values must be set aside for the moment so you can clearly see just what the words are saying.

"Won't You Charleston With Me?" [17]

Won't you Charleston with me?
Would you like to dance The Charleston with me?

Won't you Charleston with me?
Would you like to dance The Charleston with me?
And while the band is playing that
And while the band is playing that

Old vodeodo
Familiar rhythmic pattern and dance style

Around we will go
We'll dance around the floor

Together we'll show them
Together we'll show everyone watching

How the Charleston is done.
How to really dance The Charleston.

We'll surprise everyone
They'll be surprised to see what fun it is

Just think what heaven it's going to be
Just imagine how wonderful it will be

If you will Charleston, Charleston with me.
For us to do The Charleston together.

I've purposely chosen a simple lyric because it reveals how much essential information an actor can gain from an apparently uncomplicated song. For example, the choice of words shows that the characters are fairly well educated and that they're sensitive to manners belonging to a certain social class. By comparison, the fragmented, violent sentences and sexually blunt language of many punk rock pop songs also reveal characters, though of an entirely different type. Also the kind of dance mentioned stamps the song as belonging to a definite historical period (the 1920s), and the "vo-de-oh-do" cliché suggests something about those characters' enjoyment of the dance itself (the rhythmic vocalizations and hand gestures of the Charleston that were the equivalent of our grunts, yells, pelvic bumps, and other movements in modern pop dance styles).

Now practice speaking your paraphrase aloud in a normal voice several times, delivering it in any physical manner or position you choose. You might find it helpful to repeat some of the movement improvisations for monologs contained in chapter 6 (*"Movement Rehearsals"*), as well as the *"Checklist for Staging"* exploration found at the end of that chapter.

After you've done this, the next step is to write a connotative paraphrase of the lyric, trying to capture:

1. the spirit or essence of the words themselves,
2. the feelings of the characters who are singing, and
3. your own particular associations ("substitutions") that help make the song meaningful to you.

Songs, just as any other artistic medium, can always be

explained on at least two levels: the surface and the subtext. You've nailed down the literal meanings of the words, now what do they *really* mean, imply, or suggest to you and to your vis-à-vis? What do you read into it? What will the audience get from it? The answers to these questions will take you much deeper, of course, into the song's purpose, the character's motivations and feelings, or the importance that this dramatic moment holds for the characters.

Just as with monologs, it is here in the connotative paraphrase that you'll uncover the lyric's genuine power, it's source of inspiration, that gut feeling for which the words and music are only a pale but necessary vehicle — perhaps even a "mask." Observe how one student created a connotative paraphrase of the Charleston song that genuinely captures the character's hopes, desires, and feelings (I think the frequent exclamation points are probably important):

Hey Sal! Come on, baby — let's rock! Grab my hand and leave the dinner table behind. Let's get right down and boogie! Whachousay? Push and pull and bump 'n grind and burn it out! Hey! Y'hear me talkin? You are sooooo fine — you turn me on with your foxy eyes and long legs and smiles and shifty moves! Shake that thang and get it on! Let's blow their minds out on the dance floor! Turns, kicks, flips, and you name it! I wanna feel that beat and move it and grab on! Come on, let's do it while the band's wailin!

Notice how this student has specified his vis-à-vis, the locale, and even some anatomical details concretely. There's also evidence of personal substitutions in the paraphrase. Above all, it certainly captures the feeling of excitement that the characters, Bobby and Maisie, must project in the song. Compare this paraphrase with the way the song is sung on the original cast album.

The connotative meanings of songs are crucial in your preparation because music doesn't work on its listeners as words do, in an intellectual way. Music works on the feelings and emotions, suggesting images that are beyond or beneath spoken words. Of course, the sound of poetry or prose without musical accompaniment can also be evocative and seductive, but these qualities are certainly enhanced by sustained use of the voice in songs with musical accompaniment. Actors, however, cannot let the music alone accomplish this for them; they must begin instead with the lyric and find the source of the song in the words.

The task now is to take this source-energy found in the connotation and turn it into a musical performance. ***First try to hold on to those*** *connotative values while you gradually return to the original lyric. Hold that connotative paraphrase in mind as you whisper the lyrics, and use a tape recorder of the tune in the background as you do so.* Perform the movement explorations in this way, *getting used to what you're saying and why,* gradually building it up before you ever start to sing it. Once you start singing the song, musical values will begin imposing themselves on you; you'll start to concentrate on vocal technique and tend to lose the motivation behind the lyrics.

When you've done this enough times so that you can not only speak but also sing the lyric at full volume, and so you can also move and gesture freely as you do this, then you can begin to work with a pianist.

This sequence of rehearsing a show song must be followed closely, because once the pianist begins to add the music, you must concentrate on using the music to enhance what you're doing. It's an extremely difficult process, more complicated than rehearsing a straight monolog, and you should expect to feel very awkward and self-conscious the first few times you attempt it. But it will gradually smooth itself out if you proceed step by step instead of rushing into singing it all at once. If you try to simply jump right into the song without this sort of preparation, I guarantee that the music will tend to carry you away when you least expect it, and you'll miss a lot of the meaning and emotional pizzazz that the song has to offer. You'll have a lot less "musical presence" when it comes to the audition.

Exploration #53: Musical Theatre Songs

Obtain an original cast recording of the musical *Company* and a copy of the sheet music for the song "Being Alive." Begin paraphrasing the lyrics using the methods outlined above for *The Boy Friend*. This is a very challenging song: complex, profound, and revealing. The lyrics to work with are as follows:

"Being Alive" [18]
Someone to hold you too close,
Someone to hurt you too deep,
Someone to sit in your chair,
To ruin your sleep ...

Someone to need you too much,
Someone to know you too well
Someone to pull you up short
And put you through hell ...

Someone you have to let in.
Someone whose feelings you spare,
Someone who, like it or not, will want you to share
A little a lot …

Someone to crowd you with love,
Someone to force you to care,
Someone to make you come through
Who'll always be there, as frightened as you
Of being alive,
Being alive, being alive, being alive …

Somebody hold me too close,
Somebody hurt me too deep,
Somebody sit in my chair
And ruin my sleep and make me aware
Of being alive, being alive.

Somebody need me too much,
Somebody know me too well,
Somebody pull me up short
And put me through hell and give me support
For being alive, make me alive
Make me alive,
Make me confused, mock me with praise,
Let me be used, vary my days.
But alone is alone, not alive.

Somebody crowd me with love,
Somebody force me to care,
Somebody let me come through,
I'll always be there as frightened as you,
To help us survive
Being alive, being alive, being alive.

You should make a cassette recording of these lyrics, speaking them in a near-monotone without trying to add any emotional expression to your delivery. Then when you've completed both the literal and connotative paraphrases, rehearse them according to the methods in chapter 6. The next step is to play the show album and listen to the professional rendition (singing — not musical) several times. Practice whispering or "lip-synching" the lyrics until the melody and phrasing are familiar. This should take about thirty minutes, after which you should return to your subtextual paraphrase and correct it. Be sure it contains all the meanings suggested by the singer's rendition as well as those associations you formed while listening.

Finally, rehearse the words of the song one or more times, speaking the lyrics and improvising movements and gestures spontaneously (don't set any blocking yet). When you can speak the lyric at full volume and still retain the connotative subtext much of the time, then you're ready to connect the lyric to the melody line.

This basic method for show songs should be followed religiously. Once you've done it properly you'll be able to rehearse other songs more quickly because you'll find your own personal approach that works best for you. No matter what approach you devise for yourself, however, you should never rush into the song in the initial stages. You'll always need to whisper or talk through the lyrics at first in order to let *them* suggest the way to sing and to play them. You should always avoid imposing your own personal style — vocally or physically in the staging — too early. Let the musical material work on you at first, let it suggest what needs to be done in order to communicate and express the relationship at hand.

You might also have your pianist help you out in this by "beginning small." He or she can play only the single notes of the melody line, or (as David Craig suggests) only the belltones (starting notes), in order to encourage you to build the song up gradually. You may need to correct the phrasing in a few places in order to bring the sheet music into line with the album, or vice versa. Or you may want to work out with the pianist the particular arrangement with which you feel comfortable. Working with a pianist in this way is essential because, if you don't bring your own pianist to each and every audition (and you certainly won't be able to), then you must give the rehearsal pianist a clean and clear copy in order to accompany you.

You should also have your pianist set down a pre-recorded track on an audiocassette, or burned into a CD, so you can practice with that at your convenience, and also to use for those auditions where pianos or accompanists are not available. In any case, keep in mind that *you don't have to use the published arrangement in your audition version, and you should never use a pre-recorded orchestral arrangement from an album* when you do the audition. An audition is not a finished performance. The auditors want to hear *you* sing; they'll worry about the accompaniment later.

As I pointed out earlier, this chapter is not an all-inclusive preparation for working up musical material; it's just a basic method of approach that should get you started. As you work more and more with a vocal coach (all professionals do this), you'll certainly modify this method to suit your own needs.

Staging Points for Singing Auditions

Here are a few suggestions from casting directors about how young actors can avoid common pitfalls when auditioning for musicals:

1. For highly competitive and serious auditioning (paying work, scholarships, etc.) *always* bring your own accompanist.
2. *Take care of your voice prior to the audition!* It's more sensitive and tender than you realize. If you come up hoarse or sick on your audition day, you're *really* sunk at the singing auditions (although you might be able to burble-through a monolog presentation). The auditors are nice and forgiving people, but they do have to hear you sing.
3. Always give the accompanist a clean final copy, clearly marked, and never ask an accompanist to rearrange or transpose or change things on the spot.
4. When using a boombox for accompaniment, be certain the tape is cued-up and the volume preset to a comfortable level so you don't have to fuss with the machine and distract yourself. *Load it with fresh batteries!*
5. Cue the pianist or boombox operator with only a single small gesture or nod of the head, then forget about it.
6. Never try to dance and sing simultaneously; casting directors will look at your dance abilities separately, with choreographers.
7. Never sing to the auditors. The only thing that is worse than someone acting directly to you is having an auditioner sing at you.
8. Your strongest point of visual focus is the middle of the orchestra section (main floor), or slightly over the auditors' heads if you're on the same level with them. Begin the song with this point of focus, end with it, and return to it at all key places in the song.
9. Change your visual focus from left to right of center only when the lyrics (not the music!) seem to call for it.
10. Keep movement and gestures minimal. As with monologs, any blocking and gestures should be motivated only by the sense of the lyrics.
11. Believe absolutely in what you're singing, fill each and every line completely before moving on to the next.

Review and Reflection

1. By the time you finish college, which six skills will you have to master in order to get cast in musical theatre?
- The ability to sight read music
- The ability to carry a tune, both rhythmically and tonally
- The ability to sing with a clear, strong voice within a reasonable range
- The ability to project feeling, meaning, and belief into the lyrics
- The ability to work in a disciplined fashion on dance routines and other forms of choreography
- The ability to work in a variety of dance styles

2. What are the four special features of musical theatre scenes that you must be aware of when auditioning?
- Your audition must be strongly outer-directed, off the stage, because the emotions are so big they must be shared.
- The scene you're given to read isn't likely to reach a climax in the words alone; the dialog will often move toward the song or follow the song as the dramatic peak.
- You must play the music as the subtext of all the scenes, many of which are underscored by instrumental accompaniment.
- Events and character details in musicals (such as dialog) tend to be compressed, economical, and sketched-in, so you must work to fill them in.

3. What are the five major criteria for choosing songs for musical auditions?
- Something well within your age, emotional, and dramatic range
- Something with challenging musical ability that promises you might do even more with different material
- Something appropriate for the role or show being cast (as with dramatic pieces, do not choose a song from the show under consideration or you'll needlessly limit your casting choices with the auditors)
- Something that is "complete" (beginning-middle-end, like your monologs) when edited to the requisite eight to sixteen bars
- Something that you can fill with belief

[1] The distinction between musical and non-musical genres in Western theatre makes for fascinating reading. For example, take a look at what happened during the seventeenth century in England and France. During this period of royal patronage of theatres, certain types of acting companies occupied certain theatres, and their "licenses" permitted them to perform only certain kinds of plays. Some specialized in musical presentation, others in tragedies, others in ballets, and so forth, and one company was prohibited by law from doing a genre of play that its rival company was licensed to present! In England, laws prior to the Restoration prohibited spoken drama ("plays"), but theatre owners were occasionally able to get around the law by sprinkling their plays with musical elements. Check out a good book on the history of musical theatre in order to learn a lot more, and put yourself in the picture when it comes to musical theatre!

[2] Joanna Merlin, op. cit., p. 141.

[3] Aaron Frankel, *Writing the Broadway Musical* (New York: Drama Book Specialists, 1977), p. 19.

[4] *Audition*, op. cit., p. 146. The only exception to this "triple threat" requirement is the possibility that the director will also cast performers who can only sing ("pit singers" who are located backstage or with the orchestra in order to help the acting chorus with certain numbers). As you know, even extras in musical shows are required to group-sing and dance as part of the chorus, in addition to acting.

[5] Robert Cohen, *Acting Professionally*, op. cit., p. 30.

[6] Mott interview, op. cit.

[7] *Audition*, loc. cit., p. 145.

[8] The great singing coach David Craig makes a strong Shakespearean connection when he remarks that show songs are really Shakespearean soliloquies, reminding us that "most actors would be almost as pleased to appear in a musical as they would a play of Shakespeare's." *On Singing Onstage* (New York: Macmillan, 1978), p. xxii.

[9] *The Boy Friend*, book, lyrics, and music by Sandy Wilson. Copyright © 1954–55 by Sandy Wilson. By special arrangement with Sandy Wilson.

[10] *Camelot* by Alan Jay Lerner. Copyright © 1961 by Alan Jay Lerner. Reprinted by permission of the Lerner Heirs. All rights reserved.

[11] Robert Peterson, interview with the author, New York, 6 May 1982.

[12] Hal Prince, *Contradictions: Notes on Twenty-Six Years in the Theatre* (New York: Dodd, Mead, 1974), p. 150.

[13] "The Auditions Game," *Dramatics*, March 1982, p. 46.

[14] Fred Silver, "Audition Doctor," *Backstage* (New York), 26 November 1982, p. 46.

[15] *Writing the Broadway Musical*, op. cit., pp. 81–82.

[16] In his singing workshops, David Craig recommends that students maintain as much objective distance from "the song" as possible when first approaching the piece and doing the literal paraphrase. He suggests avoiding the first-person pronoun completely and instead say "This is a story about…" or "She says that…" In Craig's terms, the student wants to produce "a piece of reportage. Be prepared to defend it if challenged, and know that the defense must rest in the stated lyric and not in what you have imagined or assumed it to say." *On Singing Onstage*, op. cit., p. 136.

[17] From *The Boy Friend*, op. cit., used by permission. Interlinear and connotative paraphrases taken from students in my workshop.

[18] *Being Alive* by Stephen Sondheim. Copyright © 1970 by Range Road Music, Inc., and Rilting Music, Inc. All rights administered by Herald Square Music, Inc. Used by permission. All rights reserved.

Chapter Ten

Supporting Materials
"The paper chase"

No matter what profession you choose to enter you're bound to reach the point where your output no longer sells you and you need more tools to advertise yourself. This probably happens far more in our industry than in other fields simply because actors are by nature "gypsies": constantly moving from one show to another, constantly auditioning for one client after another, constantly moving from one city to another in order to find work. The result is that we constantly have to leave behind us and send out ahead of us reminders of who we are and what we've done.

Actors are updating and using their resumes, photos, mailing lists, and other things a lot more frequently than the doctor or stock broker, who'll pretty much stick with one workplace for at least a year or more. In your case the materials I'm talking about are a resume for stage work, an 8-by-10 black-and-white headshot, an audition wardrobe, and computer files of these (except the wardrobe, obviously) so you can update them regularly and send them out quickly on the Internet when needed. Let's take an overview here of the basic stuff you'll need as a young actor, so you can begin to think about it early.

Developing Your Acting Resume

You've probably never thought about it before, but every time you've filled out an audition form for a show, you've actually been doing a resume. Right! The resume isn't just the formal, finished document you've carefully prepared and plan to submit with your scholarship application or give to the directors. Any time you list your experience on whatever kind of form that's required for you, any time you're talking to someone about what you've done as an actor, then you're doing your resume. You're translating your "cast-ability" into written or spoken form for someone you hope will give you a role.

Generally speaking, a collegiate actor ought to know how to present himself or herself effectively on a typical audition form for collegiate and community theatre tryouts. One should also be able to quickly and confidently highlight one's experience in the form of a "verbal" resume when asked by a director to "tell me a little about yourself" (see the final exploration exercise in chapter 3). And after four years in a university, a beginning actor ready for grad school or preparing to hit the streets should have a good promotional headshot and formal resume — for professional tryouts, school applications, and scholarship competitions.

You'll find that writing yourself up on paper is a valuable exercise in self-understanding. I mentioned in chapter 3 that one of the most important spinoffs of auditioning for different theatres is the sense of self-confidence and objectivity about your talents that comes from exposing yourself to strangers as a "castable commodity." While you're in school you can get a good head start on preparing yourself for hitting the job markets by developing good resume-writing (and interviewing) skills.

There is one fundamental point you must always keep in mind about your resume: It is the only thing that directors will have before and after you leave the stage. Everything about your resume follows from this — the paper you use, the format for laying out the information, the entries you choose to include, and the way everything is worded — *everything* should be geared to giving the directors a document that can sell you like an agent when you're not there to do it yourself. For professional work, the resume and photograph must be submitted in advance, and to a large extent they'll determine whether or not you'll get to audition. Once you've presented your audition, you'll want something very, very good to leave behind for purposes of callbacks and casting.

Let's begin with the broad picture. First of all, avoid your school's "career counseling center" or similar service, because they haven't a clue what an actor's resume must do or look like. If you're in high school, the counseling center will likely steer you away from acting altogether because "there's no jobs." And in college, these offices are mainly set up to mass-process business and professional students into the job world by finding interviews for them. At neither level are they able to lay out for a casting director an actor's background and experience on a resume in a way that's going to help you land a role. Instead, get to the library and the Web and study actors' resumes closely, using some of the professional sources I've listed in appendix B.

You must build your resume by listing your experience according to major categories. These are usually the designator, contact and personal information, acting experience, and training (in that order). The categories should be consistently laid out on the page along the left margin, and all the entries under each should be appropriate for that category. Although the format of an acting resume is never "cast in stone" in the sense of being the same for all actors, the categories are pretty much standard because directors need the same basic data about everyone. Unlike resumes for business, government, service agencies, and other fields, you enhance your image at an audition by adhering to this "professional format" for your resume; deviating from it runs the risk of appearing a "raw amateur."

The "designator" includes only your name and your occupation. Normally your name will appear at the top center of the resume in the largest font, with the designation "Stage Actor" beneath it. Does this sound stupid? I mean, won't they *know* you're giving them an acting resume? Well, not if the resume gets misplaced and mixed-up with piles of applicants for other shows or other assignments (which frequently happens). They're going to want to know quickly whose this one is and what you're there for. A bold and clear designator right at the top of the page enables the casting people to do this. It's also helpful for you, because in a few years after graduating you'll develop different resumes for each kind of job you apply for, such as stage actor, technician, assistant director, TV actor, stage manager, commercial actor, etc. When you join an acting union, your union affiliation must go here as well, right at the top.

"Contact information" includes information on how to reach you. It can appear directly beneath your name or at one side (personal data going on the other side of the page in order to balance the appearance). Normally it includes your answering service (you'll want an answering machine or service so your personal phone won't be ringing off the hook from every weirdo out there who gets your number), your e-mail address, your FAX number (if you have one you can use), and a mail drop (a post office box and *not* your home address, for the same reason of weirdos). This data *must* be current; you *must* be reachable on short notice, no matter where you are. When you find an agent, this will be a lot simpler; you'll just list your agency and all contacts will pass through them to you.

"Personal information" includes your age, height, weight, hair and eye color, and vocal range. By age, I mean the "age range" you're capable of playing, not your real age, and not your "in-your-dreams" age. Height, weight, hair and eye color, and vocal range are all straightforward facts, but if you can't sing a note then omit your vocal

range. This is all the "personal" information you should enter. Under no circumstances should you ever list your driver's license or social security numbers, religion, or racial/ethnic background. If this is needed for employment purposes, they'll request it separately.

The next section of your resume is "stage experience." This includes the show title, your role (no tech assignments, only roles), and where the show was produced. You should list your most important credits at the top, not your most recent, and you should never include the dates of when you performed which role. The reasons for this are to "place your best foot forward," and to avoid cluttering the section with distracting verbiage. No director cares who wrote the play, who directed it, what star actor was in the show, or anything of the sort. If the director does want to know, he or she will ask. For those of you in school, use the name of your theatre whenever possible instead of the school name, because it will sound more professional. Again, if directors wish to know more, they'll ask. If you also have commercial, radio, film, or other media credits, *don't* list them here; simply state "Camera Experience On Request." This particular resume, remember, is for *stage* acting.

The final section of your resume is your "background training." Underneath this heading you should include your school education, workshops, and other special training or awards you've had that apply to acting. List your high school graduation date, your university graduation date, the degree you earned, and your major field. If you didn't graduate from college, then list the acting classes you had in college along with the workshops and classes you've taken outside of school. By "special training" I mean only those things that pertain to acting. We don't care if you're an expert in philately or making guacamole, but we do care if you can tap dance, have done modeling, distinguished yourself in forensics and debate, or can play a musical instrument.

This section of your resume — often overlooked by beginning actors — can be very important when it comes to casting. For example, I've frequently preferred one actor over another based on the fact that he or she did a lot of acrobatics and gymnastics in school, and I need them for a physically demanding role. You'll also find a lot of directors want to see what theatre workshops you've taken — dance styles, monolog, camera acting, voice, combatives — because this suggests strong commitment on your part to acting and growing. And they also want to know the name of the person who led the workshop, because the theatre world (believe it or not) is very small and a lot of us know each other's work.

If you're a "raw beginner" without much stage experience, avoid inflating what experience you do have and never, ever lie about a credit. You *will* be found out. Simply list what you've done, however modest it may seem, and concentrate instead on getting your resume carefully set up and professional-looking. It's no crime to be perceived as studying for this profession. In fact, it can often set you apart from a lot of wannabes who are just hanging around "muscle beach" and street corners and not studying or working at all! As you persist in auditioning, the roles and entries will come. Be patient.

Don't forget that you can also list your live acting experience that is not part of a play, if you have such experience. I'm referring to things like promotional shows you may be cast in for commercial clients (like a shopping mall "season special" or a song-and-dance routine for your parents' local trade shows), benefits you may do (like a scene or two from plays presented as part of annual theatre fundraisers), or special dance and singing programs you may get involved in (such as working with your local civic ballet or opera society). Although these aren't as important as identifiable stage roles in "regular" plays, they can be listed because they indicate your versatility and your continued commitment to disciplined work of some kind. Naturally, as you gain more experience with regular stage credits, you can drop these other minor credits off the bottom of your list.

An optional category that may or may not go at the bottom of your resume (if you have room) is "references." These can be important for beginning actors who lack a lot of acting experience if an auditor feels he or she is taking a risk with you. In most cases, though, directors don't behave like business and professional people who will always "check references" on everyone being considered for employment. Directors haven't the time. Be certain you've informed those people that you're listing them on your resume as references, and secure their permission.

Your next step in preparing the resume is to streamline the format so it's easy to read. First, control the length; under no circumstances should an actor's resume ever exceed one page. If yours does, then lop off the least important credits. You have to remember that no one reads actors' resumes — they glance at them for two to three seconds. In the corporate world, people definitely will read your resume or your longer "vita," but not in the theatre. This means that whatever is important should go right up front on the page and should be clearly legible. There should be no excess verbiage, no cute artwork, no fancy typescript (font) — nothing to get in the way of a harried director seeking to "cut to the chase" of what you've done. "What roles has she played?" "Where has he acted?" "Where did she study?" "Can he sing or dance?" These are some of the questions that directors are going to ask, and they'll just toss your resume if they can't find it clearly stated.

On the other hand, streamlining the format *also* means laying out information so that it's visually pleasing when your audition does persuade the director to read more about you! Note that I didn't say that your resume should be "spiced-up" or "flashy" or "cunning and seductive" or "bizarre." You're not writing advertising copy here. I do mean that your category headings should be in larger, bolder type, neatly balanced as they run down the margin of the page. I mean that each entry of a particular show you did should be consistent with all the others: systematic, dependable, and clear.

In other words, *just glancing at your resume should reassure the director that he or she is dealing with a professional* and not with an airhead, a confused mental case, a wannabe graphic artist, a sloppy organizer, or something of the sort (and there are plenty of those kinds of people who give us their "resumes"). "A well set-up resume is extremely important, especially for paying work," one West Coast producer points out. "Spend a few bucks to get a good clean bunch of resumes printed. You know much about a person from the visual format of their vita." [1] So remember that a good resume won't get you a role or a job, but a bad one can send up red flags that'll certainly keep you from getting an audition in the first place or receiving further consideration.

Another important reason for avoiding exotic type fonts and artwork is that your *paper* resume will have its *virtual* counterpart. There are times when you'll want to send your resume and other documents over the Internet. If you've ever tried to transmit documents in this way, you know that certain types of formatting can frequently get bungled in the transmission: automatic indents, footnotes, italicizing, etc. By formatting your virtual resume in a simple manner you'll minimize the garbling that's bound to occur in transmission. I know that *your* computer is the finest machine ever built, but the machine *getting* your e-mail might not be. And besides, you may have to update those materials down the road with a word processor that can't handle your original settings. So keep it simple, visually pleasant, and clear.

When you print your resume, be sure to use heavy grade white onion-skin or parchment paper. Some actors do prefer paper in subtle colors (sand, buff, ivory, etc.), but be sure to avoid anything jazzy, because the paper stock is just *background* and not the "main event." The heavier-grade paper will stand up to a lot of shuffling and handling, particularly when things like photos get stapled to it. You should spend a couple bucks at the stationery store for some good quality paper like this, but only print off a few resumes at a time, because you'll constantly be updating the original (one great advantage of the PC!). What you want is a basic document that communicates professionalism and dependability — not something hand-corrected, flimsy to handle, or distractingly cute and jazzy.

Some actors prefer to have their resume printed on the back of their headshot, and this is certainly a more professional way of presenting the two documents to auditioners. It's handier for you and for others than fumbling with two separate pages, and miniprint services nowadays can easily run off two-sided photos for you. The disadvantage, of course, is that whenever you update either your photo or your resume, you'll have to run off new *two-sided* copies, which is more expensive. But that may be a small consideration for you, and I always recommend my students do this if they can afford it.

Developing Your Photo Materials

Getting photos done is probably the most stressful aspect of resume building for young actors. For one thing, it costs real money (as opposed to printing resumes on your personal computer). For another, it's hard to know just what kind of photo is going to best represent you. Photos can turn all of us into our own worst critics! We're never really completely satisfied with our pictures, none of our friends seem able to give us helpful comments about them, and there's always something "wrong" about them — the shadows, the expression on our mouth, the look in our eyes, the background — something! We're ready to stick our heads in the oven every time we get a set of proofs back from the photographer!

Well, you're never going to escape this uncertain feeling about your photos, so just get used to it. If nothing else, remind yourself that actors usually re-do their photos at least every eighteen months, so you'll be able to correct the problem if you follow their example! Bear in mind that it really does take years to get some good photos with which you're going to be satisfied, and that you can spend a small fortune getting pictures done again and again. And remember, too, that as long as you're "covering the basics" each time you get new photos, then you can't go too far wrong. After all, if your photos really are terrible, someone's surely going to let you know!

You will have to learn on your own about publicity photographs and guide your photographer to produce the kind you need. Do not under any circumstances allow the photographer to take charge of the photo session and give you the "standard package" or what he or she thinks is necessary. Any good photographer, in fact, will speak with you in detail about just what it is you want, so you have to make intelligent choices beforehand about your photo. [2] There are a dozen kinds of publicity shots that are widely used in the industry, and each has a different purpose (see appendix C). You'll look like a raw amateur and you'll certainly waste a lot of money submitting the wrong kind of shot for the audition.

Don't rush out and throw your money away on photographs until you know what you're doing! And don't try to do this at the last moment! It takes time to research the background here, and time to get yourself prepared for a photo session. You've got to know what's wanted by directors, what's expected of the photographer, and what's expected of you as you guide the photographer. This will put you in the ballpark about what you need and what to avoid. With this in mind, let's now turn to a list of the basics.

Your first step is to read up on what a publicity photo looks like and must accomplish. Check out some of the pointers about photos in Bob Funk's handbook, *The Audition Process*; Pat Dougan's guidelines, *Professional Acting in Television Commercials*; and Robert Cohen's text, *Acting Professionally*, all of which are listed in appendix A. Then visit some of the Internet sites also listed there and survey more current samples of headshots. Especially note the distinctions between headshot, corporate video shot, three-quarter shot, commercial shot, character shot, etc. *You want a legitimate theatre headshot.*

Next, you really do need to locate a photographer who specializes in actors' headshots and pay the money (normally a couple hundred dollars or more) for dependable professional work. Perhaps the biggest mistake that young actors make when it comes to getting their photo done is that they try to get it cheap — most likely they have a friend do their photo at the last minute in order to save money. This wastes everyone's time, believe me. A pro will know the kind of shot that you need for the market you're seeking to enter and how a theatrical "headshot" differs from a portrait or modeling shot. Nothing looks more amateur than an amateur publicity photo, and it can easily lose you the audition, the role, or both. Here's a piece of good advice from a pro:

Every marketing aspect of your acting business has to look completely professional. If you start out with a so-so picture and resume, it will take you years to recover from the damage. Although not all casting directors or agents remember everybody's bad picture and resume, if they remember yours, you are doomed. You'll spend the next several years trying to prove that you're not really an amateur. Obviously, spending time and money compensating for earlier bad judgments takes valuable time away from the task at hand, getting work. [3]

Next on the list of photo basics is that your photo must be an exact likeness of you. A theatrical headshot is not a modeling photo, a glamour shot of you, a movie still, or a work of photographic art. Your head contrasts with the background and fills the frame, your eyes focus directly into the lens, you're smiling and showing teeth, your skin texture is there, and we can see you clearly without shadows, hand poses, jewelry, or anything else. Your face is not in profile and your head is not bowed so you're looking up at me. The camera is at your eye level and not shooting radically down or up at you. And every time you change your look — dye your hair, get a special cut, etc. — you need to change your headshot.

You must remember that the directors want to see the person in the photograph walk into the room when you're called. They don't want to look at a photo and see a bald head instead of a brunette, a coy mood or attitude, a gorgeous costume, or anything else that gets in the way of that *person* in the shot — the real you. So avoid the tendency to "design" yourself overly much for photographs. The photo should communicate an unpretentious, honest "you" without any overlays.

The most important feature of your headshot is your eyes. They must seem "alive" and communicate expressively to the viewer. They must connect with the camera. Your eyes should invite us to call you in for the audition, consider you seriously as a confident professional, call you back, or hire you. They should assure us you're a pleasant and cooperative person to work with, a warm, energetic, and conscientious actor who'd be great to have in the cast. You should seem a friendly, intelligent, and creative actor or actress who can take direction and is eager to get onstage in a role.

In order to accomplish this, you need to "play an action" during the photo session when the shutter is clicking and you're looking into the lens. In your imagination construct a sort of script you can play, that might run as follows. "Yes! I have a lot of good experience, so let me show you!" "You can depend on me!" "I'm ready to work on this show!" "I'd like to get to meet you and talk about the role!" "Even if you don't cast me for this part, you certainly want to hear my audition!" And so forth. Some actors like to bring a boombox to the shoot and play some favorite music that helps them generate the mood or feeling they want in their pics. Whatever it takes, these kinds of things will keep your eyes expressive and your energy alive in all your photos.

Next you must carefully control the makeup, jewelry, and costume elements in your shot. Jewelry can be very distracting in a headshot, as well as jazzy clothes of any kind. Busty tank-tops, coat and tie, Dior gowns, etc., are all out. Clothing should enhance your look and not stand out. Women must be especially careful of their makeup, because they tend to want to "glamorize" themselves more than men. Luscious lips, seductive eyes, airbrushed complexions, bangly earrings and sparkly necklaces, perfectly tanned skin — all that is out. If you have freckles or a mole, the freckles and mole should show. Directors don't want to see Barbie or Ken walk into the audition room; the theatre has plenty of makeup and costume artists to transform the "basic you" into a hag or a dashing leading man.

Makeup deserves a special note here, for men as well as women. *If you have training in makeup and feel comfortable making yourself up for black-and-white, then go ahead and do it yourself. Otherwise, you need to ask your photographer to recommend a good makeup artist or stylist.* Yes, it will cost extra, but if you don't know what you're doing in this area, the results can be awful! Pros use stylists all the time; it's a necessary cost of doing business in this business. Black-and-white, after all, is not how we see you onstage nor in real life. What may work fine for you on the street or in the club, and what was excellent onstage under the colored gels and hot lights of that show may not read at all in the photo studio.

It's also necessary to remind young actors to *avoid wearing "fashion" jewelry in the shot.* The guys at the dance hall may go for those nose studs or eyebrow piercings, and women may get all excited about all those earrings a guy wears, but they're *definitely* out when it comes to your photo and your audition. And tongue studs may seem foxy and daring to men at the local bar, but they only keep you from speaking clearly and twist the auditors' nerve endings to distraction. These are definitely not the kind of effects you're seeking to produce in a photo, an audition, or an interview.

Also keep the rest of your body out of the shot. This means hands, arms, and chests. And no posing please! For example, I receive a lot of photos with the actor or actress resting the chin on folded hands, like a graduation portrait or something. Other actors occasionally frame themselves with part of their chest exposed by the blouse or shirt; that too is unnecessary. The problem is that this sort of thing takes attention away from your face, which is what we want to see. The same holds true for photos that are not really headshots but more like three-quarter commercial or movie shots where we can see a leaning body angle or some kind of clothing also calling for attention in the shot. Again, the face and the eyes should be where we're drawn to look.

At the end of the photo session be sure to come away with two 8-by-10 headshots. There is no need to pay your photographer to duplicate the number of photos you need, nor to pay extra for the negatives, for your name on the shot, or anything else. Commercial duplicating services can add your name to the bottom of your headshot much less expensively and run off the necessary hundred copies you'll need to start with. You'll keep one pic as the "master" and send the other out to be duplicated.

Related Supporting Materials: Show Photos, Reviews, Testimonials, Cover Letters, and Post Cards

In addition to the basic materials I've just described, beginning actors should also pay attention to accumulating several other kinds of backup materials that will be useful to them as their careers develop. These include show photos, press clippings, and testimonials of one kind or another.

By all means save those reviews and show pics! They make great reading when you're eating mac and cheese in Manhattan while struggling to get cast, or when you're old and gray telling the grandkids what it was like before you became a Tony-winner! On the serious side, however, you really never know when those photos of you in performance or those printed reviews will help land you a role. The community theatre director didn't get a chance to see you in *Peter Pan* last month? Flash her a copy of the review (with your name highlighted, of course). Your theatre professor didn't realize you did a comic walk-on for the local opera society's production of *Pirates of Penzance*? Slip him a copy of the review where you got mentioned (so when you apply for a scholarship next semester you'll have a little edge!). Mom wants to know if you've been hanging out in the bars and discos before she'll send you a check? Send her … well, you know what to send her!

No fooling, you have no idea how important these things become over time. *Start now to keep a scrapbook of your show photos and notices, and don't just throw them higgledy-piggledy into a shoebox somewhere.* Keep the originals in plastic sleeves, perhaps in a three-ring binder. You can use them informally as I just mentioned. Or you can show them to agencies as further proof of your talent after you graduate. You can attach press to scholarship applications. You might want to show things to a café or theatre owner sometime when you're ready to do your one-person show in order to demonstrate your talent. And of course, reviews are a handy reference file years later for looking up important people you once worked with.

Show photos serve another purpose. You should save these — and also modeling photos if you've done that — and try to get them digitized if you can, because they may come in very handy and save you money when you're just starting out and seeking commercial work. Commercial work (see appendix C) requires things like photo composite sheets (three to four looks of you as various characters), photo postcard mailers, and so forth. If you have some good black-and-white or color pics of yourself ready, then you don't have to scrounge for the costumes and props and pay money to a professional photographer for a shooting session. A lot of them may be just fine for starting you off until you can afford a real slick photo file on yourself.

You should also save those "testimonial letters" and comments that may come to you from time to time: award letters for scholarships, prize letters you receive from forensics competitions, thank-you recognition letters for participation in festivals, and so forth. When you're applying for scholarships, grad schools, or acting studios, it never hurts to include these along with your cover letter and application and the rest of your materials. They're another indication of how seriously you take your acting career.

Copies of your cover letters are also important to hold on to. For example, you'll send a cover letter with the rest of your materials to a theatre company requesting an audition, and you'll be writing a lot of essays to scholarships and grad school committees as part of the application process. Likely as not, you'll find yourself writing a number of these things as time goes on: explaining your personal reasons for seeking admission to a school, describing your career objectives, and so forth. By keeping copies you simplify the process the next time you come to write a similar letter.

A follow-up postcard to the auditions staff costs next to nothing, and it's always a good move. The typical follow-up arrives at the scholarship committee, the casting director, or the agency about a week or two following your audition. Normally, you'll want to thank the auditors for their time in watching your audition, and remind them that you're still very interested in the role, the job, or the scholarship. These things seem unnecessarily time-consuming and of little importance, but they're definitely something that will help to single you out from the crowd of other auditioners. Don't be fooled by the cliché, "don't call us, we'll call you." A phone call is a no-no, but a postcard is always acceptable.

In addition to becoming very handy resources, record-keeping in the form of resumes, press reviews, and the like is a way of "keeping your hand in the game" when you're not acting. It keeps you focused on advancing your career, fine-tuning your acting goals, and building up an important body of resource material that you'll need to draw upon from time to time. You'll find later on when you land an agent that the agency will keep a similar kind of file on you, one that contains records of contracts, resumes, press reviews, photos, and so forth. So you can help move yourself in that direction by getting started early in your career to develop a more complete personal file of material on your own.

The Audition Wardrobe

Before your audition day arrives, you need to give some thought to your appearance. I don't mean that you should "dress the part," however. Only professionals auditioning for character media roles (plumbers, doctors, cops, etc.) will do that sort of thing. I mean the look that you intend to communicate to the auditors before and during your monolog or scene. So avoid thinking of a "costume-costume," but do think of *some* costume. In fact, by the time you reach your senior year in college, you should have an audition costume set aside for just that purpose, ready to go at a moment's notice. You don't want to wake up on your audition day and reach in your closet for your black dress or slacks, only to find your roommate has borrowed them for a beer party the night before.

You want to be sure that your look helps you land the role or the scholarship by expressing something positive and professional about you. What does "positive and professional" mean? It means first of all that you take yourself seriously, that you have some self-respect. It means that you'll wear something neat, clean, and presentable that other people wouldn't find run-down or bizarre.

You could go into a decent restaurant, for example, or a symphony concert and not be asked to leave. Notice that I'm not talking anything formal here; an audition is not a job interview for the local insurance or sand and gravel company. But take a look at the people doing the casting and dress like them. If you want to spend time with those kind of people (and you do or you wouldn't be auditioning!), then your personal appearance should reflect that.

Whether we admit it or not, we all like to dress nicely. And certainly we'd all like to have the money to sport thousands of dollars of clothes and jewelry every day of our lives like movie stars, wouldn't we? Have all the world "ooohh!" and "aaaaah!" over us, and take our picture when we walk down the street? Well, of course, that ain't gonna happen in your lifetime, but what you *can* accomplish is being sure that your clothes give the image that you're an upbeat, open, and creative individual; someone that a stage director would probably like to work with in a small room for five or six weeks of rehearsal. *That's* what you want, right? To put it bluntly, your clothes should say that you've worked hard at acting, you know what it takes, and you're proud to have made it this far.

A second thing your clothes should communicate is a workman-like attitude. Wear something to the audition that — while being neat and professional — also allows you to move freely and expressively. For example, no actors in their right mind should ever go barefoot (I've seen it happen!) or wear spiked heels, Doc Martin boots, Hip Hops, platform sandals, and other fashion statements to an audition — you simply cannot walk in those things but one way, so you limit and typecast yourself unnecessarily. Similarly, outfits like granny dresses, "baggy-look" street sweats, tight miniskirts and other "character clothes" typecast you for one type of role, often restrict your movement, and prevent directors from seeing how your body looks and moves.

The "workman-like attitude" of an actor's wardrobe most often consists of a leotard top for women in combination with a full skirt or pants, and what are called "character shoes" — usually black or beige shoes with a small heel. For men, slacks and a sport or dress shirt, combined with black or brown "character shoes" is a good basic choice. Clean jeans in good condition are always acceptable as well. You can modify this basic outfit a bit with a sweater top, vest, jacket, or blouse; and women as well as men should also consider wearing unfooted dance tights underneath. Why dance tights? Because they'll help keep your body energy "up," and they might also be needed for any improvisational work, floor work, or dance and movement work that may be part of the audition.

Hair styles are also important. Women want to be sure to avoid any sort of "coiffure" or hairdo that, again, can typecast them; and both men and women should keep their hair out of their face. One of the most irritating auditions for directors to watch is an auditioner flicking locks of hair away from his or her face, hooking it behind an ear while they're performing. It's a terrible distraction. Hairstyles can vary greatly, from simple pageboy cuts to ponytails for both men and women. But remember, you always want to avoid limiting your appearance to one "type." And think about the answer you'll give to this question: "If you're cast, are you willing to shave your beard? Will it be all right to cut your hair very short?"

You must remember that you're there at an audition to present a monolog or scene. As one British director points out: "An audition is not a model's catwalk!!" [4]

This advice on costume, jewelry, and hairstyles is fairly general and applies largely to university, scholarship/grad school, and community theatre auditions. Auditioning for professional theatre work — especially with high-end casting people in New York and Los Angeles — creates some exceptions (see appendix C). But I always recommend to my students that they consider their personal appearance very carefully, even when auditioning in a university setting. Looking like a professional is very important for landing the role (as it is for landing most other things in life!). Perhaps no one has stated this more succinctly than southern California acting coach Robert Cohen:

> … *look* like a professional actor. That does not mean to look like a college actor. As a rule, college actors are poorer and dress in a more slovenly way than professional actors. This may be fine in college, but it doesn't cut the same figure off the campus. Let's face it: professional CDs [casting directors], producers, and directors make good incomes, have American Express cards, stay in good hotels, eat in good restaurants, and associate mainly with *employed* actors. They may be artists, but they are also adult businesspersons in a grown-up world. Regardless of what we might think of the artistic temperament, the lifestyle of most regional theatre directors (and for that matter New York and Hollywood casting directors) is fairly conservative and fairly middle class. Ripped jeans, bare feet, and stained T-shirts just don't have the same effect at AEA studios, in Hollywood or New York offices, or on

resident theater stages that they do in the state university experimental theatre. You, of course, have every right to be yourself and dress as you choose, and people will rarely *think* they are judging you on the basis of your clothing ... but to dress down for an audition (even if you simply cannot afford to "dress up") can create a level of alienation that your audition may not overcome. The image of disaffected youth is not one that you want to project in a professional audition. [5]

Whatever you wear, be sure that you feel comfortable in it. Don't wear it to the audition for the first time; rehearse in it and perform in it with your coach so you don't suddenly feel wooden and self-conscious at the tryouts. You might also add something memorable to your costume: a vest, a colored sash for the ladies, leg warmers over the tights — something. I don't mean something outrageous or garish, but something that can make you stand out a little bit from all the others. And be sure to always wear the same costume and hair style to the callbacks that you wore to the general audition.

So, okay! You've got a lot of busywork ahead of you here, building up all this stuff! Not all that creative, I know, compared with the excitement of preparing and presenting your audition for a show, but necessary all the same. Think of it this way: your supporting materials will come to be that proverbial 80 percent of the iceberg beneath the surface of your career. In the last analysis, as Shakespeare points out, our acting is really "such stuff as dreams are made of," and will quickly pass away when the final curtain rings down on this or that particular show. But the resume, the press, the photos — all of this will remain down the road as something concrete and *marketable* for you, if you play your cards right!

Review and Reflection
Reflection

1. What are the eight basic points on your checklist for building a good resume?
  - The resume is the only thing that directors will have before and after you leave the stage.
  - The designator section includes only your name and your occupation.

- The contact information includes information on how to reach you.
- Personal information includes your age, height, weight, hair and eye color, and vocal range.
- Stage experience includes the show title, your role (no tech assignments, only roles), and where the show was produced.
- Background training includes your school education, workshops, and other special training or awards you've had that apply to acting.
- Streamline the format so it's easy to read.
- Use heavy grade white onion-skin or parchment paper.

2. What are the eight basic guidelines for getting your photos done?

- Guide your photographer to produce the kind you need.
- Read up on what a publicity photo should look like and accomplish.
- Locate a photographer who specializes in actors' headshots.
- Be sure that that your photo is an exact likeness of you.
- The most important feature of your headshot is your eyes.
- Limit the makeup, jewelry, and costume elements in your shot.
- Keep the rest of your body out of the shot.
- Be sure to come away with two 8-by-10 headshots.

3. What are the four basic criteria for building a useful audition wardrobe?

- Be sure that your look expresses something positive and professional about you.
- Your costume should communicate a workman-like attitude.
- Looking like a professional is very important for landing the role.
- Whatever you wear, be sure that you feel comfortable in it.

---

[1] Kirk Frederick, Director, Cameo Productions, San Francisco, 29 December 1981.

[2] The basic "20 questions" to ask a potential photographer before you sign up with him or her — whether you're having photos done for stage or screen — are clearly stated in Pat Dougan's book on commercial acting, *Professional Acting in Television Commercials*, op. cit., p. 20. Do not hire a photographer without asking these questions!

[3] Pat Dougan, op. cit., p. 18.

[4] Frank Whately, Associate Writer and Director, National Youth Music Theatre of Great Britain, Internet conversation with the author, 25 February 2002.

[5] *Acting Professionally*, op cit., p. 128.

Chapter Eleven

Auditions and the Computer
"Get wired!"

Actors and Computers

It should come as no surprise if I point out that one way the world is glued together these days is with cyberpower, and showbiz is certainly no exception. What *is* surprising is how swiftly live theatre (like practically every other field of human endeavor) has seized upon computers, and especially computer-based electronic communications as the medium of choice for its day to day business, including a lot of its traditional business like research and archiving. Playwrights, producers, advertisers, actors, designers, critics, students, patrons — all are now married in some way to the cyberworld that characterizes so much of our everyday environment.

I suppose it *is* ironic, though, that practitioners of such an "unmediated" art like live theatre should have already become so dependent upon the computer for what they do. Often we hear theatre folks decry the pervasive and perverse influence of "screen culture" upon human relationships. At the same time, it's understandable that — in its place — electronic communications and powerful software applications enhance the work of performing artists. And most of these folks will probably tell you that this is just the beginning.

At present, however, you need to bear in mind that the virtual community of actors you're likely to find through the Internet is going to be only that small percentage of actors — especially "working" actors — who have access to computers. And that's not a whole lot of people. For one thing, the bulk of acting *jobs* are still only accessible to those willing to spend the shoe leather or gas money seeking them out, auditioning for them, and following up on them in person. And for another thing, you have to remember that not every actor has either the savvy or the bucks to go online. Here's a quote from an expert who's also a working Equity (union) member and writer in Chicago:

> The online community is weighted toward those actors who have either enough money to buy a computer, are

fortunate enough to be allowed to use computers at work for leisure purposes, or are lucky enough to have received a computer as a gift. So, as in all Internet communities, the actors you find on the Net will be a little more computer savvy and often more affluent than other actors. [1]

In any case, let's take a look here at how aspiring young actors like you can exploit the advantages of cyberpower for your auditions in ways that your predecessors (like me) were powerless to enjoy. *Though it's likely you'll begin acting in live theatre and concentrate on developing your performance talents for that medium, you can start early — right now, when you're in school — to become computer-savvy in order to give yourself an added edge.*

Some of the major advantages computer-friendly actors enjoy over their cyber-impaired counterparts include greater access to job listings, training opportunities, and background information on acting methods and audition techniques, in addition to the personal advantages of more efficient record-keeping, correspondence, tax accounting, updating personal PR materials, and a host of other premiums. And as we move farther into the twenty-first century, these advantages are continuing to expand.

Correspondence and Networking

There's a lot to be said for the old cliché, "It's all in whom you know." And *the Internet lets you stay in touch for hardly any cost at all.* Right now you've probably found e-mail a great medium of personal communication with your friends and family, and sometimes it's even a great way of making friends. (Remember the Tom Hanks movie, *You've Got Mail?*) But beware the weirdos, the world is full of them!

As you get older and your life as an actor becomes busier and busier, you're going to find it more difficult to make face-to-face contact with those close to you. Even as early as college, you're going to find yourself depending on e-mail to chat and share news and ask questions of family, old friends, teachers, new friends, boyfriends, girlfriends, acquaintances — just about anyone and everyone. And many of you will use course or faculty websites for your day-to-day school assignments and advising. In fact, writing an "old fashioned" letter to someone will become a special event for you.

Let's not get into the philosophical questions here of whether the availability of e-mail will *force* you into sustaining a larger network of correspondents, or whether you're *really* interacting with people when you interact with a computer. The point I'm making is that you're already "networking," and you're going to keep networking the older you get. What's going to change as you get older is that your e-mail correspondence is going to become more specialized, your correspondents will tend to be people who are special to you, personally and professionally. You won't have time to waste on the others; you'll be using the "delete" key more frequently as you get older. Don't feel guilty or bad about this: it's a good thing. As an actor you've got to learn to look out for number one, and using the "delete" key for unwanted or unimportant correspondence is one way to do that.

Acting can be a lonely business sometimes, believe me, particularly when you're making rounds and rounds of auditions and not acting much at all. You'll be wearing out the shoe leather, competing against every other actor for a small number of parts, wondering if you've missed an audition that someone else is going to get, surviving unemployment, and working jobs that pay so little that you just can't afford to socialize and share the fun with friends. A lot of acting, especially at the beginning stages of your career, just ain't much fun.

This is where the Internet will play a very important role in your life, enhancing your sense of belonging and making you feel a lot less isolated. For example, I've had many students tell me after graduation that the shock and stress of job-hunting in a new city becomes more bearable because they can inexpensively stay in contact with old friends. Their e-mail has become their "personal comfort zone." And you don't need me to remind you of the horror stories concerning would-be actors who have no support system and who buy into destructive "comfort zones" in order to numb those terrible feelings of isolation, loneliness, and helplessness.

Naturally, you don't want to get carried away by your correspondence. You've probably already realized by now how much e-mail can suck *enormous* quantities of your time! You could become a geek instead of an actor, right? That's what I meant by "being selective" about the people you keep in contact with. Use your e-mail to correspond with those you really *need* in your life. No one is going to pay you to become a professional letter writer, believe me — although a lot of people in "day jobs" spend most of their time doing just that: babbling on e-mail to anyone and everyone. But it ain't gonna pay the rent, right?

There's also a second dimension of correspondence that will become important to you following your graduation: sustaining professional contacts. Keep in touch with your teachers and directors. I can't tell you how frustrating it is to try and get hold of somebody who may have once done a show for me a year or two ago. Tracking down someone's phone number, for instance, or learning *right now* if someone is available for a role can be a monumental and agonizing effort. Don't forget that your teachers and directors get a lot of requests from people looking for talent, and they have a lot of irons in the fire. The more you work with community and professional theatre directors, the more important it becomes to stay in touch with them, too. So stay in contact with the good ones from time to time, and keep picking their brains for useful bits of information that might help you further your career.

Another way to sustain professional contacts with the Internet is to nurture and develop your new contacts. Once you get started after school, you're going to meet a lot of new people — actors, directors, agents, publicists, friends of friends, etc. Whenever possible, drop that person an e-mail afterward on some casual subject or other, just to see if you can "stay on their screen." You never know when that chance meeting at a party might be the vital link you need for an audition, or how someone you met might just zap you an important piece of information, right out of the blue. And as your social world of contacts expands — sometimes exponentially, it may seem! — your e-mail records and addresses help you to keep these people in focus and aid you in moving your career along.

Related to this subject of new contacts is the way in which you can use the World Wide Web to form new contacts through national and international websites. I think all you web surfers out there are going to be very surprised to discover that there are hundreds of young actors just like you who are starting to use the World Wide Web to contact each other and share ideas. Be sure to do exploration exercise #54 at the end of this chapter, where you'll find these actors in the U.S. and Europe chatting away excitedly, marketing themselves with personal web pages, and fielding questions about markets, directors, and casting agencies.

As you start to work conscientiously at this business of staying in communication with important people, you might find it valuable to transfer some of the information in your actor's journal into computer files. A lot of my students just starting out have told me they use computer address books *with accompanying files* in order to record auditions they've gone to, the people they've met there, the dates they went, what audition pieces they used, and so forth.

If you have MS Windows on your computer, then you likely

have Outlook or Outlook Express applications for record-keeping. This kind of software is valuable for business people and other professionals like yourself who need to organize and file contact information. Then a simple click on someone or agency's name can accurately refresh your memory the next time you're seen by those people. If possible, keep all those post-audition entries you make (see exploration exercise #46 in chapter 7) on your computer for this purpose. It makes for a very handy journal-record!

This brings me to my final point of your need to *create a professional address book for yourself.* A lot of people seem to get by (I don't know how they do it) with everyone's addresses sort of all jumbled into their computer address book higgledy-piggledy. You should use that factory-installed application on your computer to create categories of listings that will keep all these people, agencies, publications, organizations, and services manageable. For example, after reading this chapter, you may want to create links (an address book) with categories of "friends and family," "recent contacts," "professional contacts," "news," "casting resources," "play research," etc. It can make your cyberlife easy.

Industry News

All young actors certainly need to keep themselves informed by reading the "trades." A trade magazine or newspaper is a publication serving your field, and there are a host of them out there. Some of the major trades used as "Bibles" by actors are *Ross Reports, Variety, Backstage* and *Backstage West, Drama-Logue,* and *Show Business.* Many of these are also on the Web. You want to plug into these for general reading for a couple of reasons: you'll find time-sensitive information on work opportunities that might be important for you, and you'll broaden your understanding of the industry in which you're seeking to build a career.

Trades can give you performance listings and information on casting calls that are being scheduled. They can also give you the names of people who are doing all that stuff (are they listed in your contacts links?). They can inform you of workshops being offered and showcases for your talent. They can bring you news of old buddies who are now acting with some show somewhere. Of course, you can always buy trade magazines in any industry city, but you can also go broke doing it on a daily basis! So learn to access these publications on the Web for little or nothing. [2]

You'll find that working actors read the trades religiously. In New York, L.A., and London alone there are four or five publications that certainly deserve daily reading. People in L.A. really *live* by them in order to keep informed of what's going on in the audition scene. Even when an actor has an agent, he or she must often "rattle the agent's cage" in order to schedule an audition for a play or feature that the actor happened to notice in a trade journal. [3]

An added advantage of Web-based trades is that the home page often contains a lot of other exciting information you may need. For instance, a map (where exactly *is* that agency or theatre located?), phone and FAX numbers, ticket prices and discounts, and the complete schedule dates of a show or a theatre's season. In addition, on the home page of a Web trade, you'll often find some interesting links to click on.

Finally, you'll need to *keep your eye open for various listservs and get your name on them.* A "listserv" is a mailing list assembled by a person or organization that automatically e-mails to people on the list announcements and other features that are important. Businesses and nonprofits use this a lot to send notices or stock offerings, travel deals, consumer alerts, environmental action campaigns, etc., to people who've indicated an interest in those fields. People just add their names to a list that "serves" the addresses automatically (because it's voluntary, it's different from "spam" e-mail).

A lot of theatres nowadays are building such services for actors and the general public who want to keep abreast of what's happening at a theatre: casting calls, show info, and the like. A listserv will send this information to you automatically without your having to request it. And if you ever start to feel like there's too much garbage popping into your e-mail, you can always delete your name easily from the listserv.

Reading news in the trades can help you feel connected to the larger universe of theatre and entertainment. This is another big advantage of the Web: everyday you can read up on things in *Showbusiness, The L.A. Times,* or *The New York Times* entertainment pages just to see what splashes are going on out there. This keeps you from developing a terminal case of career tunnel-vision, obsessing with your immediate job scramble.

Kick back, take a break, and see what "the big boys" are doing in New York, in London, in Chicago, and elsewhere. For most of you, that's where you'd like to be, right? Living that life and pulling down that dough? Enjoy the breadth and depth or everything happening in the modern entertainment industry both at home and abroad. It'll inspire you with a lot of valuable and comforting perspective on your acting career and your choice of profession, believe me. Is someone actually doing a production of *that* play on Broadway? And is this or that superstar really planning to spend her summer doing George Bernard Shaw in New Hampshire? And how did so-and-so in this London revival of *Miss Julie* play the role that you once played?

Even more than idle curiosity and entertainment, the news features keep you in touch with where the "biz" is going these days (part of "biz-buzz"). For example, is the cruise ship industry expected to boom this year, so they'll be seeking a lot more actors? What agencies work that circuit? Where are they casting? Are a lot of actors starting to find work in Minneapolis or Toronto or Vancouver? With what? Is there some opportunity there for you, too? Do you have to be union? What of the new rage for interactive something-or-others? Are these being produced in Chicago or Dallas or somewhere, and is there a growing market for actors doing voice-overs ("narration-over-image," like the character voices on interactive video games)? Why not try a voice-over workshop sometime and see if you can find some more work out there?

If nothing else, the perspective on the industry that you'll gain from keeping abreast with industry news will help you to talk and act intelligently as you advance your career in the field. You'll be able to make much better judgments about the directions in which you want to steer yourself. You'll be able to speak comfortably with important people about subjects other than your own immediate acting job and your broken-down Subaru. You'll be able to share a lot more things in common with potential contacts who might be very valuable for you to know down the road.

Background Resources

Your research skills from high school and college should teach you how to *use the World Wide Web for valuable background features on acting and auditioning.* This means using your computer to visit actors' chat rooms, retrieve background information on a particular play, answer your questions about a specific theatre group, learn what publications are available, find biographical facts on actors, and similar acting/auditioning tasks.

For instance, if you've never tried it, you'd be surprised to *learn what casting agencies, unions, and professional training schools are recommending these days on their home pages.* (I've listed a few of these important website addresses in appendix B.) Certainly they use the Web for important information regarding their classes, special events, and fees. But agencies and schools also provide you with "cameo" testimonies of their students' auditioning successes, real-time interviews with agents and actors, "soft news" items about casting trends and emerging markets, samples of photographers' work, auditioning and interviewing tips, and even chat room services for their students and alumni. And the websites of the major entertainment unions give you up-to-date information on membership, fees, and procedures as well as articles on frequently asked questions and actors' union-related concerns.

You could spend weeks poring over the material thrown up on the Web by only one or two of these big agencies or schools in New York or L.A. Many actors are visiting these sites because there's a lot you can get there for free. Just reading over the concerns of other actors, or even "chatting" with them about their problems and gaining tips is an education in itself. Or consider another benefit: you could simplify your decision-making when it comes to professional photographs (what a nerve-wracking experience!) by spending time poring over the twenty to thirty professional showbiz photographers who advertise their services through an agency or school by throwing up their portfolios on the home page.

Nothing, of course, succeeds like success, and that's why you should *read about professional actors' careers on the Web.* These people are "the horse's mouth" and their testimony about their lives and work habits is invaluable. You can find interviews with and features on other young actors who've found that lucky break by slipping through the Webzine ("Web Magazine Edition") of monthly theatre and show business trades like *American Theatre, Backstage,* and *Drama-Logue.* There are also many biographical profiles on actors, directors, producers, and others in the mainstream press like the *Los Angeles Times, New York Times, London Times, Chicago Tribune,* and others.

Related to this (though I cautiously suggest it) is the "star industry" of motion pictures and television, which has recently spawned a veritable sea of public relations Web pages about who's doing what and what's coming down. Many of you, in fact, have probably already browsed the websites of some of your favorite films or TV shows and noticed the numerous links to "stars" connected with the film or series. With a single click you can find the whole life and career of a particular actor, often including a lot of personal information.

This is fun background reading, and *it can also tip you off about ways of presenting yourself, even at the beginning stage of your career.* How many of *you*, for example, have had to write your own bio for a show program? Well, reading over professional actors' bios could give you some new ideas. Upon what kind of jobs should *you* be concentrating? How does *she* deal with stage fright at auditions? And though it may seem pretentious to you now when you're just starting your career, the possibility of creating your own actor's home page has become appealing to hundreds of professional actors. And they're getting work out of it! Anyone who wishes — casting directors, friends, agents, family — can instantly find a wealth of constantly updated material about an aspiring actor.

In the past few years I've found actors' personal Web pages very useful with several individuals I've worked with. The information has helped me contact some people who may not have seen the casting notice; or I've been able to consider them a little more carefully during the casting period by reading more of their backgrounds; or else I've found quickly and easily the data I needed for my publicist on a show. Like an agency's "book" of talent (photos and basic information on all the actors handled by an agency that clients can look through and "shop" for), the personal Web page is fast becoming a low-cost and effective marketing tool for the young actor.

In addition to locating such career information, you must also *learn to use the World Wide Web as a source of play information*. One immediate application, for example, is to help you find the plot description of a play before the auditions occur. The scripts of a lot of classical plays, for example, can be accessed for free over the Web by means of very simple use of the search engine. With contemporary or even very recent plays, you can often find plot descriptions and other valuable details in reviews, also by means of a simple search. And similar research can then lead you into other plays by the same author. This is a very quick and easy way to beef up your understanding of a play in preparation for an audition, or even for working on a role once you've been cast.

You can also gain useful Web-based play information by learning to *locate hardcover texts and background criticism on a play or character*. Online purchasing of scripts and texts is commonplace, of course, but you could spend a fortune these days just building up your own personal library. On the other hand, just the *lists* of books on an author, a historical period, or a dramatic style that you'll find on publishers' websites can be handy in the library when you want to dig these things out at no cost.

In school, of course, you've probably learned to do a major library search for information on a topic, and then you've learned to sift through all of that for the useful items you think you'll need. When you do this on an author, play, or period, you'll again turn up an enormous amount of data to consider, but it might not always be in print or easy to get. That's why I always make sure my acting students are doing occasional online searches of publishing houses in order to see the current stuff that *is* available, and that they're learning to use theatre reviews for immediate and handy information on a show.

Job Information

If nothing else, the Internet has become a powerfully efficient tool for actors to instantly *send a lot of the materials I discussed in the previous chapter to casting agents, directors, talent agencies, and others.* A resume, some photos, a bio — all these things (easily updated!) can be quickly sent out to the show's PR person who may be preparing the program, or to the director who mentioned she'd like to see your last review. Sometimes when you're unavailable by phone (a major sin for a beginning actor!), that important person may just have to resort to an e-mail in order to inform you that your audition tomorrow has changed its locale, or that the director made a mistake and needs you to do a callback *tonight*.

On the other hand, you also want to *locate and read the websites of major listing organizations for casting opportunities*. You'll be surprised to learn how much information is available on the Web about auditions that are being scheduled, so begin even when you're in high school and college to seek out audition notices appearing on the Internet. For example, not all audition notices are listed in the trade magazines: low-pay and no-pay showcase work, late announcements, pickup auditions, community theatre auditions, and similar opportunities may not be carried in the published trades, but they're there on the Web. Additionally, websites such as *American Theater Web* contain background information on roles that are being cast: pay ranges, preferred ages and skills, and so forth. So the World Wide Web can also play a valuable role for you here.

The most obvious place to obtain announcements of upcoming auditions are the major agency notices, most of which are now on the Web. For example, the Actors' Equity office in Chicago lists union and open calls for shows, while Chicago's *Performink* magazine and Webzine get the word out on *every* sort of casting call that's being scheduled.

In addition, websites also provide cast "breakdowns" for auditioners (brief descriptions of the roles being cast). In New York these appear in *Show Business* and *Backstage*; in southern California you want to turn to *Backstage West* and *Drama-Logue*. And as I mentioned earlier, a lot of the acting training schools in industry cities — TVI Actors Studio, New Actors Workshop, HB Studio, American Academy of Dramatic Arts, and others — regularly update their home pages with information on workshops, special seminars, audition "clinics," and the like.

Behind the obvious need for immediate information on the who-what-when-where of upcoming auditions lies the need to *use the World Wide Web to understand the background of producers and producing organizations.* You can learn a lot about a theatre company or summer festival by visiting its home page and seeing how it's organized, the kinds of shows it does, the kinds of runs it normally schedules, and so forth. A number of the larger theatres also include background on the directors and the shows being done. This sort of information becomes extremely valuable for you at interviews when you'll have to talk with people from those theatres about the work they do. One thing they'll want to know from you is how you might fit into their company. So do your homework on producing organizations by using the Internet before they call you in for the interview.

And don't forget the things I mentioned earlier that are invaluable for advancing your professional career by use of computers:

- actors' chat rooms tip you off about common problems that others like you are encountering out there and how to solve them;
- photographers' portfolios tip you off about photo basics and trends for your materials that you'll bring to auditions;
- personal Web pages can help you market yourself at the beginning stages of your career;
- professional actors' resumes and background statements help you to design your own materials and keep them updated for every audition; and
- your "post-audition entries" can jog your memory about the last time you auditioned for a certain person or group, what you presented, how it went, etc.

Computer Savvy

I hope you can see from this chapter that in addition to "getting wired" by use of the Internet, *you want to be sure that you have some strong computer skills going for you*. It's important that you don't wait until you're older in order to start exploring how a personal computer can make your life easier. The earlier you get yourself organized on a Mac or PC, the more power you'll have at your fingertips.

I've already mentioned one way of doing this: separating your job information (audition dates, people, etc.) from the general commentary you're keeping in your acting journal (personal reflections). One thing you should seriously consider is learning to *keep a calendar schedule on your computer (a sort of "mini Franklin planner")*. Business people, of course, do this as a rule, using fancy personal gizmos like palm pilots and other multi-function communications devices that are entering the market every day. A lot of you may already have explored some of these possibilities by using your cell phones for Internet messages and short, personal memos/notes. Although putting your calendar on a computer means that you'll have to depend a lot on the machine, there are certainly a lot of advantages to be gained from being able to see your whole week or month at a glance when you flash your calendar up on the screen.

A second invaluable function of your PC is the ability to *record all your acting-related expenses in a spreadsheet or ledger record for financial accounting.* The IRS respects a computer record like Moses did the stone tablets — it shows you're really professional about keeping your financial records accurate and organized. As a student, this may not seem very important, but once you graduate you'll be looking for every possible loophole to cut your taxes.

Or perhaps it'll be your accountant who'll do the looking! That's right, an accountant. For a modest fee every April 15, an accountant can save you hundreds more dollars than the fee by deducting all your acting-related expenses. Then you'll get taxes back! Nice possibility, huh? When you're pinching pennies and eating dog food as a single actor just getting started, you're going to resent every dollar you have to send to the Fed on April 15.

Don't be scared about this just because you've never done it before; you don't need to go to any fancy accounting firm, because it's a very simple accounting procedure. **All you have to do is take a minute to make entries a few times each week and turn that record over to a junior accountant somewhere at tax time (and save all**

your receipts for five years). He or she will easily be able to deduct those expenses from the income you're getting from your day job, your commercials, or whatever. A typical software package like MS Money often comes with new computers, and it's tailor-made for just this purpose! So, learn some of this accounting lore while you're in school in order to make it work for you once you graduate.

What exactly can you deduct from your income (in order to show less income and pay less tax)? Actors need clothes to present themselves well in auditions and interviews. Actors have to buy trade magazines, pay for Internet access, purchase acting books, pay postage and bus fare (or mileage expenses if you use a car) in order to do what they do. Actors also pay for photographers and mini-printing, in addition to occasional lunches with people they hope will get them work. (Though in reality, most actors have cunning strategies for how to get someone else to pay the lunch tab!) Actors must also have cell phones and telephones and answering machines, personal computers (and supplies); and a substantial portion of their apartment space (rent and utilities deductions!) will be taken up with keeping their "acting stuff" organized.

In fact, there's a whole raft of acting-related deductions that might be helpful to you at tax time, assuming you're in a tax bracket from your day job where it'll pay to itemize rather than pay a straight (non-itemized) tax. And once you do start to earn money from acting, there are even more deductions that can kick in: agency fees, union dues, entertainment tickets, and the like. Some of this stuff is explained in books that I've listed in appendix B. If nothing else, you'll likely be surprised to learn how much you actually *do* spend on your career once your computer throws it up on the screen for you. This is your "cost of doing business," and a personal computer makes it all a whole lot easier to pull together.

In conclusion, if I had to point to one piece of advice contained in each and every how-to book on breaking into the acting business, it would be this: *remember that acting is a business and conduct yourself accordingly.* This doesn't just mean behaving in a professional manner whenever you're doing an interview or audition (although that's important, too); it also means treating your schedule, notes, and expenses in a businesslike manner because this is the profession you want to support you. Playing a role onstage or on screen is nice, but it's nicest of all when it also pays the bills. And by "getting wired," you can cover ground toward that goal much faster!

Exploration #54: Scope Out the Networks

Take an hour to visit either of these fun websites for actors: "The Thespian Net" at http://www.thespiannet.com, or "AWOL" (Acting Workshop On-Line) and its links at http://www.redbirdstudio.com/AWOL/acting2.html. Investigate how the actors you find there are using computer networking to stay in touch with each other. Be sure to explore some of the links at each site! Do the actors have specific questions they want answered? An audience to listen to their problems or share their successes? Are they seeking friends in industry locations, or "inside information" on various acting markets? Where are they networking from, where are they living, and does that really matter? Does it seem they're new actors just getting started, or actors who are already established to some degree? Click on the links there to other actors' websites both in the U.S. and overseas to see the range of possibilities that are currently being exploited on the World Wide Web. Does it look like some actors are actually finding work this way through the Internet? Why are they exerting such effort to jump into cyberspace in this way? What exactly is their "payoff"? Write a two- to three-page report on what you've discovered, including the important new links you've uncovered, and present it to your drama teacher or to the class.

Exploration #55: Scope Out the Stages

Use your search engine to generate a list of *regional theatres* in the United States. Click on the links to three or four of them that might be within driving distance of your home in order to access their home pages. Then note which of them contain messaging links to the staff at those theatres and send those people a simple e-mail inquiring about their casting policies. Do they hire non-union actors each season? When do they hold their auditions? Do they have any guidelines for auditioning? In your journal or in a report to your theatre class, explain which of those theatres responded to your inquiry and what you learned.

Exploration #56: Scope Out the Trades

Use your search engine to generate a list of major trade publications on acting. You might start with http://www.backstage.com and click on the left-margin links entitled "career chat" and "artist's toolbox." What do you find there? How much does it cost to subscribe to Backstage online in order to get a full array of features? Then access others. Which of the trades contain audition listings? Which contain features on "getting the job" or even "getting an audition"? What can you learn about the chances that non-union actors have of locating auditions? In your journal or in a report to your theatre class, explain which of those trades seemed to contain some useful information for young actors and what you learned.

Exploration #57: Scope Out the Pros

Get to a library computer where you can use for free the archives of major newspapers to locate back issues where play reviews are contained. (Normally, you can't access online archives from your own PC unless you pay a fee.) Be sure you're calling up the major nationals like the *L.A. Times, New York Times, Chicago Tribune,* and others. First, go to that newspaper's listings of current stage offerings in their region. List the titles and authors of some shows being done (wow, there's a lot of them, so pick only a half-dozen for starters), and then go to the newspaper's own search of its archives to locate features on that play or that author. Normally you'll find a review of the show, as well as features on the show, the writer, the stars, etc. Read through those features, looking for comments about the acting or the roles. How was a role played? What other plays by the same author might be able to throw some light on the current show? Was there a feature that explained how some of the casting was conducted? In your journal or in a report to your theatre class, explain how much of this research might be useful for young actors, especially when auditioning. On the other hand, how much of this information might be useful to a young actor already cast, who may be working on a show?

Exploration #58: Cyberphotos

Wondering about publicity headshots and how to start building your cyber-resume? Visit the following website: http://www.takeoneacting.com. How would you describe the purpose, range, and usefulness of this website? Click on the link entitled "headshot info." What do you find there that isn't contained in this book? Click on "resume info" and then go to http://www.actingresume.com. What does this service provide? Be sure to click on "get your act together" and explore this link thoroughly. There you'll find a section on "terminology" where you can test yourself — are there terms you should know about? You'll also find a section on "wardrobe" — do they recommend things that are not in this book? Write up a report and present it to your drama class.

Exploration #59: Scope Out the Union #1

Do you want to see what professional acting unions offer actors on the Internet? What you're going to face one day after you're out of school? Visit http://www.sag.org. Read any two of the current reports or press releases there, and choose one for an oral report to your class.

Exploration #60: Scope Out the Union #2

Curious about professional-level stage acting in the United States and what you might have to know once you leave school and enter "the biz"? Go to the Actors Equity Association website: http://www.actorsequity.org. Read through this website in order to get an overview of all the main issues affecting people today in the profession you might someday want to enter. Read through those sections called "About Equity," "Member Responsibility" (under "About Equity," scroll down to "Membership"), and "Casting Call." After you've read awhile, write up a report on what is expected of a union actor, what the union can do for an actor, what's the procedure for joining the union, or what a union actor earns. Present your report to your drama class.

Review and Reflection

1. **What are the five overall uses of computer skills for enhancing your audition abilities and castability as a young actor?**
   - Maintaining a correspondence network with friends, professional associates, and other actors.
   - Keeping current with the latest industry news.
   - Accessing audition and acting-related resources via the Internet.
   - Using e-mail and websites for accessing and sending vital audition information.
   - Organizing correspondence, contacts, files, and financial information in an accurate and efficient manner.
2. **What sort of Internet correspondence is valuable for young actors to develop and maintain when starting to launch their careers?**
   - Maintaining a support network among friends and family.
   - Expanding professional relationships they've formed.
   - Making new contacts through chat rooms and industry websites.
3. **What sort of industry news can young actors find valuable on the Internet that will help them with their careers?**
   - Trade journals can give performance listings and information on casting calls.
   - News and information in the trades can help you feel connected to the larger universe of theatre and entertainment.

4. **What background resources can I find on the Internet to help me with auditioning and launching my career?**
   - Use the World Wide Web for valuable background features on acting and auditioning.
   - Learn what casting agencies, unions, and professional training schools are recommending on their homepages.
   - Photographers' portfolios via the Internet tip you off about photo basics and trends for your materials that you need at auditions.
   - Read about professional actors' careers on the Web.
   - Learn about ways of presenting yourself even at the beginning stage of your career by visiting actors' websites.
   - Use the World Wide Web as a source of play information.
   - Locate hardcover texts and background criticism on a play or character.

5. **How can I use the Internet for immediate job-related purposes?**
   - Send your materials to casting agents, directors, talent agencies, and others.
   - Locate the websites of major listing organizations for casting opportunities, character breakdowns, and similar information.
   - Research the background of producers and producing organizations.
   - Consider the possibility of building a personal Web page to help you market yourself.

6. **What are some of the main advantages of becoming a computer savvy actor?**
   - You'll learn to do all the skills listed above.
   - You'll be able to organize your personal and professional contacts efficiently with computer address books.
   - You'll be able to quickly update your resume and other materials.
   - You'll be able to create job-related files on directors and performance groups for quick, handy reference.
   - You'll be able to keep accurate expense records for personal and tax purposes.

[1] Rob Kozlowski, *The Actor's Guide to the Internet* (New York: Heinemann, 1999), p. 8. If you're a young actor who's also a computer expert, then you should definitely buy this book. See also Ed Hooks' book listed in appendix B for more ideas on how to cash in on acting during the digital age of the twenty-first century.

[2] Many of the trades have at least part of their regular issues available free to anyone, although almost all of them require that you subscribe (online) for added material, and all of them contain some "premium" services they want you to buy. Some of the trades have a special "online edition" which is different in important respects from the hard-copy version you buy in a store.

[3] Brian Stokes Mitchell was a new actor in L.A. seeking work and an agent. He points out the benefits of keeping up with the biz by religiously following the trades — a practice that led to his landing a role in *Ragtime*: "So I was working up here and I was getting a subscription to *Drama-Logue*, because that's the paper that gives you all the scoop on everything. I would just read it religiously every week, and one week I opened it up, and I saw a listing for *Roots: The Next Generation*. I thought, 'maybe there's something here for me.' I had no agent, I had only been in Los Angeles a few months at that time. So I wrote a letter and sent it in with my picture and resume, and two weeks later the casting director Reuben Cannon calls me in to read for him. I got the part of John Dolan, and that was my start. So I consider *Drama-Logue* one of the spokes in the wheel of my career." Quoted in an interview with Elias Stimac, "Brian Stokes Mitchell: Backstage with the Star of *Ragtime*," originally published in *Drama-Logue* (Hollywood), taken from Brian Stokes Mitchell's website where he reprinted it: http://www.brianstokes.com.

Scenes and Monologs for Class Work

From *Minor Leagues* by Gustavo Ott [1]

1 GOOSY: Vanessa, what happened to me was a heart attack. A
2   pre-attack, really. I'm sentenced to die from it, but it never
3   happens. At least, never in any decisive way. I don't know,
4   maybe I'm very strong physically. But, my desire, my will
5   to go on living is … I'm a real wimp, you know? Last night,
6   while you were sleeping I couldn't do anything but sit here
7   and watch you. It's that, watching out for you like that, it
8   made me want to go on living. I've got to fix things. Put an
9   end to this fantasy about my son, so he can rest peacefully.
10   And that's … that's why I want to go so soon. I have the
11   feeling that I've thrown away so much time in my life
12   already doing what I've been doing … I mean that your
13   vacation and mine is over.
14 VANESSA: My … vacation?
15 GOOSY: The reason you kept me here for the whole week of
16   Christmas.
17 VANESSA: *(Looking at him, trapped)* You knew?
18 GOOSY: Everyone makes up stories about the things they
19   want. Like you made up a brother and called him Alfonso.
20 VANESSA: What — *(She turns away and begins playing with the*
21   *radio, rapidly tuning through stations that only play hard rock.)*
22   What … what are you trying to say?
23 GOOSY: It's obvious that there is no Alfonso. *(Pause.)*
24 VANESSA: How do you know?
25 GOOSY: Because when you're talking about an $80,000 deal
26   people want to see who they are dealing with, in person.
27   Because everyone spends the last day of the year with the
28   people they love. And you didn't. And if you didn't, it can
29   only mean one thing: there is no Alfonso. *(VANESSA panics.)*
30 VANESSA: You knew the whole time and you were laughing
31   at me.
32 GOOSY: No, no, no. I wouldn't laugh at you. In my country,
33   we might talk tough, but we panic at the idea of being
34   alone. When you fear something, you respect it. It's just
35   you, you're acting alone in this, aren't you?
36 VANESSA: I'm with my mother.
37 GOOSY: And where is she?

1 VANESSA: She's in a private hospital. With the nuns. She's
2   sick. She has injuries … lots of injuries. She almost died in
3   the accident. You're wrong about Alfonso. Alfonso does
4   exist. He does. But he's just not here, in this world.
5 GOOSY: What happened? *(Pause.)* **Vanessa?** *(Pause.)* **Tell me.**
6   *(Pause.)* I told you everything. *(Pause.)*
7 VANESSA: Two Christmases ago … *(Pause.)* It was a Saturday
8   and it was raining. We were on the highway. Going to one of
9   Alfonso's games. Actually, it was his … his first game. So, we
10   were listening to the radio. Good music, something
11   American. Then, I closed my eyes. There was this noise, this
12   really, really loud noise. I always close my eyes like that,
13   when strange things happen. The first thing that happened
14   was that … After the noise, it stopped raining. For a few
15   seconds it stopped raining and then it was nighttime. But
16   just for a few seconds. Then, there was a crash. And someone
17   screaming. I closed my eyes even though it was already
18   night. The rain was still stopped, like frozen in place. Or
19   falling very softly but in a different time. I don't know.
20   *(Pause.)* My mother says that I called for her. We were
21   spinning to one side, then to the other. We fell for a few
22   seconds. It was hours. It was so long. I was going to cry, but
23   I didn't. So I decided to keep very still. Not even to move a
24   little but … Then I opened my eyes. It had stopped raining.
25   When I woke up my brother was already dead.
26 GOOSY: Dear God … Vanessa, sweetheart …
27 VANESSA: We were in a hospital. Surrounded by doctors
28   and stretchers.
29 GOOSY: Your brother — Alfonso …
30 VANESSA: There was blood everywhere, all over him, but he
31   hadn't cut himself. I never understood that. Even telling you
32   about it, now, it seems strange. Where did it come from?
33 GOOSY: I'm sorry … I'm sorry, Vanessa …
34 VANESSA: It hurt inside — hurting was breathing. It's still in
35   me and there's been no place for happiness, not in two
36   Christmases of hurt. Then two weeks ago we met. You were
37   sad, you with your heart. And I had mine. And then it almost
38   happened. *(Short pause.)* I want to believe that it was me.
39 GOOSY: If you hadn't been with me, I'd be — *(VANESSA*
40   *blasts the radio.)* **Vanessa!** *(She turns off the radio.)*
41 VANESSA: *(Quietly)* Please, don't say it. Goosy, I want other
42   Christmases. I want to know things about your country, the

1   way I like. You can meet my mom. I want you to meet her.
2   You could have someone to call and we wouldn't have to lie
3   about anything, not even the stupid little things. You could
4   even stay. *(Short pause. She steps away from the radio towards*
5   *him.)* **Who'll take care of you there?**
6   GOOSY: It's true. *(Pause.)* Who else is there?
7   VANESSA: *(Very close)* You know that you don't have to be
8   alone all the time.
9   GOOSY: *(Quiet)* There's you.
10   VANESSA: *(Turns away, flips on the radio.)* After all, I saved you.
11   GOOSY: *(Turns away and pours champagne.)* It's true. *(He laughs*
12   *a little, it hurts.)*
13   VANESSA: *(Radio plays loud thumping music)* Why is it always
14   so loud? *(Suddenly they hear fireworks, clocks chiming, music and*
15   *distant laughter.)* Oh. *(With relief:)* Yeah, the year is over.
16   GOOSY: Good-bye. And good riddance. What did you wish for?
17   VANESSA: Just a second.
18   GOOSY: What?
19   VANESSA: That your heart never breaks.
20   GOOSY: Thanks a lot, Vanessa.
21   VANESSA: What about you? What'd you wish for?
22   GOOSY: To take you to the World Series.
23   VANESSA: *(Toasting)* Happy New Year! *(She kisses him.)*
24   GOOSY: Happy New Year, sweetheart. *(They both drink champagne.*
25   *VANESSA drinks hers in one gulp. GOOSY watches her. She fills her*
26   *glass again and drinks more slowly. They look at each other.)*

Voices from the Shore by Max Bush [2]

1   *(BETH, seventeen, is desperately trying to patch things up with her*
2   *boyfriend who has meant more to her over the years than "ordinary"*
3   *boyfriends ever could. Unfortunately, she's also very dependent upon*
4   *him, and that makes the following impassioned speech not only desperate*
5   *but also somehow threatening — she's very vulnerable at this moment.)*
6   When I first started liking you, there were a lot of opposing
7   forces — such as my past reputation. But still I wanted to see
8   you. So I started to try and dress better and clean up my act for
9   what seemed like the fifty billionth time, but somehow I knew
10   that this time it would work. Instead of "Gimme drugs!
11   Gimme drugs!" I'm saying "Gimme Joel! Gimme Joel!" And
12   then, when I went three weeks without being grounded for
13   life, again, my parents even liked you. *(Pause.)* And then you,
14   you made this dream with me, about college and getting

1 married and a family. I hadn't thought about that before — not
2 really, not for me. It's taken me about four years to go through
3 the garbage to finally find a person like you, and if we break
4 up now, I'm afraid I'll go back to what I was. But I can't do this
5 by myself; you have to talk to me. Because ... because Freebe's
6 calling, again, and I didn't know what was wrong with us, I
7 almost went out with him last night — you have to stop me,
8 Joel, or I'll just go. I will. I'll just go!

Written in Water by Bob Mayberry [3]

1 *(This Native American teen works on the pool deck at a Vegas resort*
2 *in the 1950s. The boy seems both fascinated and repelled by the whites*
3 *who waste their resources in the desert, just as he seems fascinated*
4 *by — and impatient with — his grandfather's disbelief of the boy's*
5 *descriptions of how the whites live in their fancy hotels. But he*
6 *cannot ignore the whites, any more than he can ignore the warnings*
7 *of his grandfather.)*
8   Grandfather says there was a river here once, but
9 grandfather says a lot of crazy things. He says when the
10 whites first came here, our people thought they were the lost
11 brothers told of in the old stories and dreams. The ancestors
12 rushed out to greet the wagons, arms wide open like birds ...
13 *(He demonstrates.)* ... but the whites shot them. Grandfather
14 says we didn't know what guns were then. I can't believe it.
15 Arms wide open? Why? To hug them? I would sneak up at
16 night and steal their pockets. Whites have all the money in
17 the world in their pockets. I find it every day. See that man
18 bringing the woman in the two-piece swimsuit a drink from
19 the bar? Money's in the back pocket of his swim trunks.
20 When he sits down on the lounge chair, the heavy coins will
21 fall out. I'll be picking up towels near there in a minute. It's
22 easy. White people are careless. They waste everything. But
23 you don't go running at them with your arms wide open!
24 Grandfather has a story — no one believes it — about the
25 river he says was here once. Here, in this desert? He says the
26 whites drank it. That's why all the water is gone. I tell him
27 he's wrong. I tell him how the whites sit around and stare at
28 the water with drinks in their hands. Don't lie, he says.
29 Whites are too busy making their bombs to sit around and
30 stare at water, he says. I tell him to come and see. Come with
31 me to my job, I say. Come to the deck where I gather towels
32 and see the water. Little crazy one, he calls me. Each night

1 after work I fill a tin can with water from the pool and carry
2 it home, to the colony where we live, just across Main Street
3 near the park. I carry the water to show Grandfather, and
4 because we have no water except what we carry. The well
5 went dry last year, when they first filled this pool with water.
6 I'd like to jump in, feel the cool water all over me, drink so
7 much I'd never be thirsty again. But they won't let me. No
8 Indians in the pool, they say. So I pick up towels and save the
9 coins they drop and watch the pink clouds from the bombs
10 they make float across the sky. It's kinda pretty. But
11 Grandfather still doesn't believe me about the water.

From *A Midsummer Night's Dream* by Shakespeare

1 *(PUCK, Oberon's fairy assistant, finds the lovers asleep in the woods*
2 *and sprinkles the love potion upon their eyes.)*
3   Through the forest have I gone,
4   But Athenian found I none,
5   On whose eyes I might approve
6   This flower's force in stirring love,
7   Night and silence. — Who is there?
8   Weeds of Athens he doth wear:
9   This is he, my master said,
10   Despised the Athenian maid;
11   And here the maiden, sleeping sound,
12   On the dank and dirty ground.
13   Pretty soul! She durst not lie
14   Near this lack-love, this kill-courtesy.
15   Churl, upon thy eyes I throw
16   All the power this charm doth owe.
17   When thou wak'st, let love forbid.
18   Sleep his seat on thy eyelid.
19   So awake when I am gone,
20   For I must now to Oberon.

[1] *Minor Leagues* by Gustavo Ott, translated by Heather McKay. Copyright © 1996 by Gustavo Ott, all rights reserved. Reprinted by permission. Information concerning rights should be addressed to the author: Gustavo Ott, 5093 White Pine Circle NE, St. Petersburgh, FL 33703. Website http://www.gustavoott.com.ar.

[2] *Voices from the Shore* by Max Bush, copyright © 2000 by Max Bush, all rights reserved. Reprinted by permission. Information concerning rights should be addressed to the author: Max Bush, 5372 132nd Avenue, Hamilton MI 49419.

[3] *Written in Water* by Bob Mayberry, copyright © 2000 by Bob Mayberry, all rights reserved. Reprinted by permission. Information concerning rights should be addressed to the author: Bob Mayberry, mayberryr@gvsu.edu.

Appendix B
Selected Auditioning Resources

Anthologies of Scenes, Monologs, and Songs

Beard, Jocelyn A., ed. *100 Great Monologues from the Renaissance Theatre* (Lyme, NH: Smith and Kraus, 1994).

_____. *The Best Women's Stage Monologues of 1996* (Lyme, NH: Smith and Kraus, 1997).

_____. *The Best Men's Stage Monologues of 1997* (Lyme, NH: Smith and Kraus, 1998).

_____. *The Best Men's Stage Monologues of 1998* (Lyme, NH: Smith and Kraus, 1999).

_____. *The Best Men's Stage Monologues of 1999* (Lyme, NH: Smith and Kraus, 2000).

_____. *The Best Stage Scenes of 1995* (Lyme, NH: Smith and Kraus, 1996).

_____. *The Best Women's Stage Monologues of 1997* (Lyme, NH: Smith and Kraus, 1998).

_____. *The Best Women's Stage Monologues of 1998* (Lyme, NH: Smith and Kraus, 1999).

Bolton, Martha, ed. *Journey to the Center of the Stage: Monologues with Mirth and Message* (Kansas City: Lillenas, 1990).

Donnelly, Kyle, ed. *Classical Monologues for Women: Monologues from 16th, 17th, and 18th Century Plays* (Westport, CT: Heinemann, 1992).

Dotterer, Dick, ed. *For Women: Pocket Monologues from Shakespeare* (Rancho Mirage, CA: Dramaline, 1998).

_____. *Shakespeare's Monologues for Women* (Rancho Mirage, CA: Dramaline, 1990).

_____. *Shakespeare's Monologues They Haven't Heard* (Rancho Mirage, CA: Dramaline, 1987).

Dunmore, Simon, ed. *More Alternative Shakespeare Auditions for Women* (New York: Routledge, 2000).

Earley, Michael, and Philippa Keil, eds. *Soliloquy! The Shakespeare Monologues: Women* (New York: Applause, 1989).

_____. *Soliloquy! The Shakespeare Monologues: Men* (New York: Applause, 1989).

_____. *The Classical Monologue: Women* (New York: Routledge, 1992).

_____. *The Contemporary Monologue: Women* (New York: Routledge, 1995).

_____. *The Modern Monologue: Women* (New York: Routledge, 1993).

_____. *Solo: The Best Monologues of the 80's, Women* (New York: Applause, 1990).

Ellis, Roger, ed. *Audition Monologs for Student Actors: Selections from Contemporary Plays, Volume I* (Colorado Springs: Meriwether, 1999).

_____. *Audition Monologs for Student Actors: Selections from Contemporary Plays, Volume II* (Colorado Springs: Meriwether, 2001).

_____. *Multicultural Theatre: Scenes and Monologs from New Hispanic, Asian, and African-American Plays* (Colorado Springs: Meriwether, 1996).

_____. *Multicultural Theatre II: Contemporary Hispanic, Asian, and African-American Plays* (Colorado Springs: Meriwether, 1998).

_____. *Scenes and Monologs from the Best New Plays: An Anthology of New Scenes from Contemporary American Plays* (Colorado Springs: Meriwether, 1992).

Gale, Steven H., ed. *Outstanding Stage Monologs and Scenes from the 90's: Professional Auditions for Student Actors* (Colorado Springs: Meriwether, 2000).

Henley, Beth. *Beth Henley: Monologues for Women* (Rancho Mirage, CA: Dramaline, 1992).

Hooks, Ed, ed. *The Ultimate Scene and Monologues Sourcebook: An Actor's Guide to Over 1000 Monologues and Scenes from More Than 300 Contemporary Plays* (New York: Watson-Guptill, 1994).

Landes, William-Alan, ed. *Performance One: Monologues for Women* (Studio City, CA: Players, 1991).

Levy, Maya, ed. *Acting Scenes and Monologs for Young Women: 60 Dramatic Characterizations* (Colorado Springs: Meriwether, 1999).

Marlow, Jean, ed. *Audition Speeches for Younger Actors 16+* (New York: Theatre Arts, 2002).

_____. *Audition Speeches for 6–16 Year Olds* (New York: Theatre Arts, 2002).

McKenna, Shawn, ed. *Contemporary Scenes for Young Women* (New York: Theatre Communications Group, 2000).

Newell, Douglas, ed. *Shakespeare for One: Women* (New York: Heinemann, 2002).

_____. *Shakespeare for One: Men* (New York: Heinemann, 2002).

Nicholas, Angela, ed. *99 Film Scenes for Actors* (New York: Morrow/Avon, 1999).

Osbeck, Kenneth W., ed. *52 Bible Characters Dramatized: Easy-To-Use Monologues for All Occasions* (Grand Rapids: Kregal, 1996).

Sackett, Pamela, ed. *Two Minutes to Shine*. 4 Vols. (New York: Samuel French, 1993).

Schulman, Michael, ed. *Great Scenes and Monologues for Actors* (New York: Saint Martin's, 1998).

Scott, R. James, and Bianca Cowan, eds. *Multiplicity: A Collection of Monologues for Student Performance* (Orem, UT: Encore, 1997).

Shengold, Nina, and Eric Lane, eds. *Moving Parts: Monologues from Contemporary Plays* (New York: Penguin, 1992).

Slaight, Craig, and Jack Sharrar, eds. *Great Monologues for Young Actors, Vol. II* (Lyme, NH: Smith and Kraus, 1997).

Svich, Caridad, and Maria Teresa Marrero, eds. *Out of the Fringe* (New York: Theatre Communications Group, 1999).

Temchin, Jack, ed. *One on One: The Best Men's Monologues for the Nineties* (New York: Applause, 1992).

_____. *One on One: The Best Women's Monologues for the Nineties* (New York: Applause, 1992).

Uno, Roberta, ed. *Monologues for Actors of Color: Women* (New York: Routledge, 1999).

Walters, Richard, ed. *The Singer's Musical Theatre Anthology* (Milwaukee: Hal Leonard, 1986 + 2000), 3 vols.

Intermediate and Advanced Books on Auditioning Skills

Black, David. *The Actor's Audition* (New York: Vintage, 1997). Oriented to stage auditioning, the author is a veteran producer. Covers monologs, cold readings, musical auditions, and interviews. Professional-level.

Craig, David. *On Singing Onstage* (New York: McGraw-Hill, 1988). The United States' foremost musical theatre coach delivers sound advice to actors at all levels of experience. This widely-used, classic text also contains interviews with actors and a brief history of the American musical theatre. See below for David Craig's approaches illustrated on video.

Dougan, Pat. *Professional Acting in Television Commercials* (Portsmouth: Heinemann, 1995). Probably the very best text either for students considering the possibility of acting in commercials or for young actors seriously embarking on training and preparing for work in commercials. Her comments on resumes, photographs, and supporting materials are especially valuable.

Funk, Bob. *The Audition Process: A Practical Guide for Actors*

(Portsmouth: Heinemann, 1996). A thumbnail text for university students covering all the mechanics of auditioning for grad schools, summer companies, URTA, Irene Ryan scholarships, and other competitions. Somewhat dated now.

Hooks, Ed. *Acting Strategies for the Cyber Age* (New York: Heinemann, 2002). A pioneering text for young actors in the digital twenty-first century, this book deals with setting yourself up with skills and strategies for promoting yourself. See also Kozlowski's text, below.

Kayes, Gillyanne and Jeremy Fisher. *Successful Singing Auditions* (New York: Theatre Arts, 2002.) This is a complete guide for the singer and singing actor. It contains an excellent description of genres—concept musical, classic book musical, etc.—in addition to a lot of nuts-and-bolts information on preparing and presenting the song audition.

Keller, Dori and Dawn Lerman. *Twelve Steps to Becoming an Actor in L.A.: The Method to Create a Life* (New York: Writers Club Press, 2002). Widely praised by actors because it will save you years of learning the ropes in the jungle of Tinseltown, with everything from where to get car insurance to how to get interviews and auditions. Its step-by-step, one-year approach to building a career is outstanding. See also Michael Saint Nicholas' book below if you're planning to head to L.A.

Kozlowski, Rob. *The Actor's Guide to the Internet* (New York: Heinemann, 1999). The absolute Bible of how to put your Mac or PC to work for you, with a lot of nuts and bolts about software, web pages, record-keeping, dance opportunities, and more.

Merlin, Joanna. *Auditioning: An Actor-Friendly Guide* (New York: Vintage, 2001). One of the latest and best-received books on the subject, comes highly recommended by extraordinary theatrical and motion picture figures. Written by a professional actress and casting director, it covers stage and screen auditions. It's not set up as a class text, though, and it's geared to professionals rather than students.

O'Neil, Brian. *Acting as a Business: Strategies for Success* (New York: Heinemann, 1999). A good, solid text on setting yourself up and launching a career. Covers all the nuts and bolts about cover letters, breaking into soaps, etc. And an excellent section on frequently asked questions in interview situations.

Peithman, Stephen and Neil Offen. *Stage Directions Guide to Auditions* (Portsmouth: Heinemann, 1999). This collection of articles from *Stage Directions* magazine offers practical basic information about auditioning procedures. The first part of the book is designed for actors and the second part for directors. There are informative sections, however, for young actors about auditioning for college scholarships, overcoming stage fright, and other problems.

Saint Nicholas, Michael. *An Actor's Guide — Your First Year in Hollywood* (New York: Allworth, 2000). Another one of those step-by-step roadmaps to surviving the southern California scene, but nicely written and an enjoyable read. What exactly to do and whom to contact.

Shurtleff, Michael. *Audition: Everything an Actor Needs to Know to Get the Part* (New York: Walker, 1980). The "classic" auditions text that lays out Michael's "twelve guideposts" that are widely taught across the United States. The book is not set up as a class text, though; it's directed at professional actors rather than young students-in-training. See the listing below for this book's approach as presented by Michael on videotape.

Silver, Fred. *Auditioning for the Musical Theatre* (New York: Penguin, 1988). A dated but serviceable book presenting sensible pointers on everything from what to wear to what to sing.

Media Training Aids for Class and Self-Study

Audition, with Michael Shurtleff, 4 vol. 30 min. each, Insight Media, 1995, videocassette. Available at (800) 233-9910 or http://www.insight-media.com. This four-tape series by the United States' most prestigious teacher of auditioning methods will never become dated, and it demonstrates all the guideposts contained in Michael's best-selling book, the "benchmark Bible" for professional actors seeking roles (see above).

Auditioning for the Actor, with William Anton, 45 min., Insight Media, 1989, videocassette. Available at (800) 233-9910 or http://www.insight-media.com. In addition to show-and-tell presentations by actors that are very instructive, Anton supplies a large number of valuable performance tips — especially often overlooked points like creating a favorable impression, choosing audition material, evaluating personal strengths, selecting clothing, and introducing oneself.

Audition Techniques, 70 min., Insight Media, 1988, videocassette and CD-ROM. Available at (800) 233-9910 or http://www.insight-media.com.

Casting Directors "Tell It Like It Is," 40 min., Insight Media, 1993, videocassette. Available at (800) 233-9910 or http://www.insight-media.com. This video, though now a decade old, gives students an excellent understanding of what Hollywood agents are looking for, and stresses the importance of theatre training when seeking media work. Though it features casting for film, voice-over, and TV, students will learn much from the candid opinions of these business-minded artists who make casting decisions and what they seek in actors just starting their careers.

Cold Readings: Getting the Job, 51 min., Educational Video Network, 1991, videocassette. Available at (800) 762-0060 or http://www.edvidnet.net. An excellent beginning-level class in how to approach callback readings for camera.

Cold Readings Made Easy, 47 min., Educational Video Network, 1991, videocassette. Available at (800) 762-0060 or http://www.edvidnet.net. An excellent foundation-level class in the basics of cold readings for camera.

The Craft of Acting: Auditioning, with Allan Miller, 43 min., Insight Media, 1993, videocassette. Available at (800) 233-9910 or http://www.insight-media.com. Alan Miller speaks to beginning actors from both sides of the casting table. He is an actor with over 200 films, TV shows, and plays to his credit, who has coached luminaries such as Barbara Streisand, Dustin Hoffman, and others.

On Singing Onstage, with David Craig, 6 vol., Applause Books, 2001, videocassette. Available at (800) 637-2852. This six-tape series comes with a free copy of the landmark book by David Craig, the American musical theatre's most prestigious and experienced coach who "teaches actors how to sing and singers how to act." If you want "a leg up" on your musical theatre auditions technique, David Craig — in book or video — is an absolute must.

So You Want to Be an Actor, with Jerry Stiller and Anne Meara, 75 min., Insight Media, 1993, videocassette. Available at (800) 233-9910 or http://www.insight-media.com. This tape focuses on actors beginning their careers. It discusses resumes and photos, agents, unions, and auditioning procedures for plays, soaps, and commercials; though it's now somewhat dated. It also features interviews with new as well as established actors such as Uta Hagen and Christopher Walken.

Starting Your Film Acting Career, with Mick McGovern from the TV series *Matlock,* 2 tape series, 60 min. each, Theatre Arts Video Library, videocassette. Available at (800) 456-8285 or http://www.theatreartsvideo.com. Tape 1 is entitled "The Essentials" and deals with just that: getting your paper/tape/photos together, locating the trades and listings, etc. Tape 2, "The Process," then takes students step by step through the sequence for finding work, using interviews with a director, agent, and actor/coach.

Online Internet Resources

Actingbiz (Online resources for actors, with articles on every aspect of the business) http://www.actingbiz.com

Acting Workshop Online (A site for beginners to learn about acting and actors) http://www.redbirdstudio.com/AWOL/acting2.html

Actors' Equity Association (The union representing professional actors and stage managers, as well as Broadway dancers, in the U.S. and Canada) http://www.actorsequity.org

American Theater Web (Casting information, chatrooms, local and regional announcements of all kinds — a general catch-all site that has some useful networking possibilities) http://www.americantheatreweb.com

Backstage (The online edition of this well-established weekly contains national and local casting information and feature articles. Subscribers have access to archive articles, select casting announcements, personal webpage services, and more.) http://www.backstage.com

The Casting Society of America (Interesting website with lots of "chat" among young actors trying to find their "break.") http://www.castingsociety.com.

The Inverse Theater (A fun New York-based website for actors offering lots of information on auditions as well as classes, acting tips, a free newsletter, chatrooms, and more. Who knows how long this site will stay supported?) http://www.inversetheater.com

Kennedy Center American College Theatre Festival (ACTF) (The world's oldest and largest annual amateur theatre festival, involving university students and faculty from across the United States) http://www.kennedy-center.org/education/actf

New York Theatre Experience (A fun, gossipy trade for the New York scene, particularly Off-Broadway. Reviews, discount tickets, chatroom, etc.) http://www.nytheatre.com

Non-Traditional Casting Project (This organization works to increase participation by artists of color, women, and artists with disabilities in theatre, film, and TV) http://www.ntcp.org

Performink Online (This is the webzine for the theatre or film professional in Chicago, the nation's third industry center. Also includes reviews of current shows and links to all Chicago theatre activities.) http://www.performink.com

Screen Actors Guild (The union representing professional actors who work in film and TV) Advice for beginning actors, news and features, plus union boilerplate — (salaries, working conditions, etc.) http://www.sag.org

Show Business Weekly (A lively, gossipy trade with many reviews and features for an overview of the biz) http://www.showbusinessweekly.com

Take One Acting (A handy website for the nuts and bolts of auditioning, marketing yourself as a beginning actor, and other related topics) http://www.takeoneacting.com

The Thespian Net (A kind of "full-service" Internet site for actors with information on books, workshops, links, companies, auditions — just about anything!) http://www.thespiannet.com

TVI Actors Studio (Major New York and L.A. training institute for actors, with helpful and in-depth website information on auditioning: actors and agents interviews, class descriptions, etc.) http://www.tvistudios.com

University/Resident Theatre Association (U/RTA) (Opportunities for university students in all fields to pursue professional theatre training at the finest graduate programs in the United States) http://www.URTA.com

Your Type (An actor-friendly website with many services to help you launch your career online, and elsewhere!) http://www.yourtype.com

Books Listing Summer Theatre Work Opportunities

The Summer Theatre Directory, edited by Jill Charles: P.O. Box 519, Dorset, VT 0521-0519; Ph: (802) 867-2223

Regional Theatre Directory, edited by Jill Charles: P.O. Box 519, Dorset, VT 0521-0519; Ph: (802) 867-2223

Theatre Directory, published by Theatre Communications Group, 355 Lexington Ave., New York, NY 10017; order online at http://www.tcg.org.

Major Unified Auditions Centers in the U.S.A.

Illinois Theatre Association, Theatre Building, 1225 W. Belmont Avenue, Chicago, IL 60657

Indiana Theatre Association, Butler University Theatre, 4600 Sunset Avenue, Indianapolis, IN 46208-3443

Institute of Outdoor Drama, CB3240, Nations Bank Plaza, University of North Carolina, Chapel Hill, NC 27599-3240; Ph: (919) 962-1328; website: http://www.unc.edu/outdoor

Mid-America Theatre Conference, 12528 South Alcan Circle, Olathe, KS 66062

Midwest Theatre Auditions, Conservatory of Theatre Arts, Webster University, 470 E. Lockwood, St. Louis, MO 63119-3194

National Dinner Theatre Association, Mr. David Pritchard, P.O. 734, Marshall, MI 49068

New England Theatre Conference, Northeastern University, Department of Theatre, 360 Huntington Avenue, Boston, MA 02115

New Jersey Theatre Group, P.O. Box 21, Florham Park, NJ 07932

Northwest Drama Conference, Theatre Arts Department, University of Idaho, Moscow, ID 83843

Ohio Theatre Alliance, 77 High Street, 2nd Floor, Columbus, OH 43215-6108

Southeastern Theatre Conference, P.O. Box 9868, Greensboro, NC 27429-0868; website: http://www.spyder.net/sec

Southwest Theatre Association, P.O. Box 10661, College Station, TX 77842

Straw Hat Auditions, 1771 Post Road East, Westport, CT 06880

Unified Professional Theatre Auditions, 51 South Cooper, Memphis, TN 38104

Appendix C
Supporting Materials for Media Acting

Many of my students over the years have done work while they've been in school for commercials, industrials, radio voice-overs, and feature films, and most often they've been paid. Some of these students have from the outset of their studies wanted to go into the commercial acting field rather than the live stage, while others have been mainly interested in stage theatre but felt it might be a good idea to take some commercial media classes as well.

My university is one of the few four-year schools in the nation that offers camera acting courses as part of the theatre program, and it may not be so easy for you to earn your chops with camera and microphone acting at the particular school where you're enrolled. In fact, you may have to go outside your school — perhaps even to a larger city — in order to obtain this kind of training. But I support my students' desires to learn camera and microphone skills for two reasons, and I feel all acting students should consider this when they enroll in an acting training program. First, most actors in the United States and England unquestionably earn the bulk of their money by doing camera and voice-over work in addition to live stage. Second, the skills one learns for camera will serve an actor well on the live stage, and vice versa.

When it comes to breaking into media work, however, there's a big difference between how you proceed for live stage roles and how you audition for commercial film, television, and radio. And while it's true that a well-trained stage actor is definitely a prize when producers go seeking camera and voice talent, stage actors face very stiff competition from scads of individuals who specialize only in some form of commercial work, and who may very well be the only kind of "serviceable actors" that many producers really need. The reason for this is because there are many niche markets in media acting, while the same is not true of live theatre.

For example, there are actors who may only do TV commercials their whole lives or soaps, or industrial films, or sitcoms, or radio spots. They can earn a good living doing so, and once they get their "technique" down, they become dependable, high-earning actors whom any agent will love to market (for the usual fee of 10 percent of what they're paid!). You have to remember that, as of this writing, a union actor will earn about $550 per day — including pension and health benefits — for one "day's" work shooting a TV commercial or acting in an industrial training film in the U.S. And if you can open your mouth and actually narrate an industrial, you'll be earning about $900.

There are no live theatres that can come even close to this "day rate" for actors. As an illustration, you'd be very lucky to be taking home $300 per week as a recently-graduated actor hired by a professional repertory company in a medium-sized U.S. city. And who can live on that? So if you can pull down $500–$900 a day just doing commercials and industrials, then narrate kidvid cartoons or play mommies-in-the-kitchen for household product commercials while you do stage work. You'll earn a decent living.

For the same reason (money), you'll find a lot of people fighting to break into this lucrative market, which isn't just concentrated in New York, Chicago, or L.A. Thanks to the growth of technology, these camera and voice presentations are made in many areas of the country by ad agencies and independent film and video houses, who regularly employ thousands of actors every year. (TV commercials are the largest employer of actors, followed closely by corporate film and video productions.) So, you're going to find a lot of competition out there for this kind of work, and it tends to be highly specialized in terms of what kind of actors are needed to do all those jobs.

The point I want to make is that you can get started while you're in school on a career that mixes stage work with commercial camera acting — or on a strictly commercial career, if you wish. Other students have done it before with great success, and the door is certainly open for you, too. But if you seriously think you may want to do this work after you graduate, then you're going to have to develop some specialized "tools" to market yourself, and it helps to get started early.

First, you're going to have to read up on this field so you know the range of possibilities available to you and what each of them requires in terms of skills and supporting materials. You don't want to go handing your stage theatre headshot, for example, to a director who is casting industrials; nor do you want to deliver a monolog from an August Wilson play to a client who's seeking talent for her bank commercial. That ain't gonna get you hired. So my first piece of advice to students is to read the books on camera acting listed in appendix B before you do anything.

In fact, one of the most wonderful developments in the media acting marketplace over the past five years is the close attention being paid to making the transition from college or university to professional acting onstage or screen. There are now at least a dozen super books on getting started in the "biz" that cover everything from finding apartments in L.A. or New York to auditioning for the cruise ship market! It's great! And more are coming out all the time. I've listed what I think are the best of these in appendix B. So study the markets while you're in school and have time to think about that stuff. Think about how you might fit in, and I guarantee it'll be much easier to find work when you get out. You have no idea how many recently graduated, utterly clueless actors get off the plane in Newark or Burbank and spin their wheels for years before returning to Wichita!

Second, you should look to volunteer your acting skills to fellow students or others seeking talent for radio or camera presentations in order to gain contacts and experience. Don't feel that you're going to get paid right off the bat, even for commercial work, because a lot of producers around the nation are "non-union" and pay very little. Also, don't dismiss the opportunity to act in student films at your school. They can help you start building a commercial resume and can provide you with some basic marketing tools — demonstration tapes — that you'll need in order to get started.

One of the first things you'll need to have as a commercial actor is a resume of your camera or microphone experience. A media acting resume differs from a stage acting resume in several respects. Your designator will change to "Television Actor," "Radio Talent," or "Commercial Actor," depending on what media you're auditioning for. And your "Stage Acting Experience" section will also change; you should not include stage roles on your media acting resumes. Simply indicate at the bottom of your camera or microphone credits, "Stage Acting Resume Available On Request." Once actors begin earning money from their acting, they find their "Media Acting Experience" starting to add up very quickly and they "break out" their film and feature work (movies) from their commercial work (advertisements, public service announcements, etc.), from industrial shows, as well as from their radio (voice) work. Each of these areas then becomes a separate resume.

The reasons for this are obvious: directors casting you in one medium aren't really interested in what you've done for other media — they want to know only what else you've done for the live stage, or for other industrial narration projects, or what TV commercials you've been in, etc. By lumping all these together on a single page you just muddy up the important things that any given director is looking for (even though it may look pretty impressive to you!). Just remember that the resume is for the benefit of the person casting you, so keep it as clear as possible.

When you list your media acting experience on your resume, however, you're going to change the form of the entry a little bit. The credit now should contain the role, but you may also have to identify the type of role because a lot of media characters don't have names. For example, roles like "shopper," "cop," "housewife," "ditz," "store clerk," "troubled teen," "daughter," and others are quite common on commercial resumes, so don't be ashamed to identify the part that way when the character didn't have a proper name.

Also, you're going to replace the name of the theatre where the show was done with the name of the client for whom the commercial or the special was made. As with the name of the theatre where you've done a stage role, the more prestigious the client for your commercial roles the better. And if your credits come from freebie work you've done in student film, video, or audio projects, then the credit reads "Student Production" instead of the client.

As a final tip about listing credits on your resume, I want you to be sure to understand that the sheer *length* of your acting credits is impressive in itself, even if the individual roles are not Oscar-winners. (And once again, don't inflate your credits; directors can spot "puff" right away.) The reason for this is that a large number of credits testify to a person's dependability, and this is a very bankable virtue. Particularly in the technical media where "time is money" — serious money — directors feel good about working with talent who have solid, professional work habits. They'll look at your audition for the *quality* of that talent, but they'll look at your resume for an indication of your *dependability*. So don't be shy about listing all your experience.

Let me give you a couple of examples. A half-dozen camera acting experiences, even as an extra or in unpaid student films, tells a director that a person knows what's coming down on a camera set and won't be tripping over cables, laughing and talking when "action" is called, or struggling for his or her lines when the crew is earning $14,000 per minute waiting to record the scene. Just as a person who's done a lot of stage shows — even in minor or chorus parts — is not likely to behave like a whining prima donna backstage or dye their hair orange in the middle of a performance run. Of course, the more important the role the better; but when you're starting out, don't omit listing a role just because it's small.

As I said, it's a good idea to begin early to set up your media acting resume, just as it is your stage acting resume. If nothing else, doing so can serve as a stimulus for you to add to this resume when the opportunity comes your way. And of course, *all* acting experience is important for you. Developing your voice for radio spots will definitely help your projection and articulation onstage, and timing or controlling every little gesture and movement for the camera lens will certainly enhance your physical characterization abilities. If nothing else, commercial work of various kinds will make you *so* grateful for those meaty stage roles that all actors really like to do! You might also find, as I do, that media acting jobs are fun to do because they're short; you can often fit them into your schedule easily because a lot of them are done in the daytime and can take as little as an hour or two to "wrap."

A second important marketing tool you'll need to break into this field is a demonstration reel. A "demo reel" means an audio or videotape, film reel, or DVD approximately three to four minutes in total length containing samples of the work you've done in different media. Each of the snippets is usually no more than ten to fifteen seconds in length, and they're designed mainly to show the *range* of your talent: several different characters or character voices, different products you've sold with different looks, different moods and styles of commercial writing you've handled, etc. DVDs are fast becoming the medium of choice nowadays for actors (although CDs and audiocassette tapes are still widely used for photo and voice demos), because they're small, easily produced, and playable by just about anyone in the business.

Even if you have absolutely no intention of doing any commercial work, you may change your mind later on and find that you need some footage or tape of yourself. I use videos at theatre tryouts, along with photographs, just to keep actors straight and to refresh my memory in large casting calls. Theatre companies — particularly in summer — who cast early throughout the year will often request them of you, and even scholarship auditions can require "tape" of the student's performance skills. One of my graduating seniors, in fact, couldn't travel across the country to audition for an acting conservatory, so they accepted her on the basis of her taped demo, resume, and letters of recommendation! So it's not so far-fetched a possibility as you might imagine.

For commercial purposes, however, a good demo — like a good photo — will help you earn an audition, while a poor or nonexistent one may keep you from getting seen at all. All actors hoping to work in commercial markets need demo reels of themselves, because agencies use them to parade their talent for clients who are often very choosy about who gets cast in their commercial. (No demo, no photo: no agent and no audition.) While you're in college, of course, no stage director will expect student actors to have demos or photos, but when you're seeking paid work in the media, they're a must.

Most producers will always give actors a copy of the finished product at no charge, as a courtesy. Because demo reels are very expensive for you to produce on your own on account of their lighting, camera, sound, and studio needs, ready-made footage or audiotape of you in actual performance can be extremely valuable for you to take away with you every time you appear on tape in someone's production.

When you collect those dubbed copies ("dubs") from student directors or others for whom you've worked, you can start to develop vital skills that you'll use all your life when you "go professional." Learn to identify those brief sections of tape where you can be seen or heard at your best, rejecting footage that doesn't show you well at all. Also learn how to work with a student editor to put your demo together by arranging the best moments back to back in order to give a good survey of your talent. Although digital editing has made this process much smoother ("seamless") than was formerly the case, there are some important artistic considerations to think about when you assemble your tape.

A demo normally starts with a self-introduction by the actor, following the printed "credits" identifying who the actor is and how to contact him or her (audio demos obviously only contain verbal contact information). The actor usually speaks directly to the camera or microphone as himself or herself (no characterization), so the auditors get a sense of the "real you." Then the series of extracts, back to back with no commentary, credits, or introductions will follow. The demo can then conclude with the actor again as himself or herself, saying "thanks for watching" or "thanks for listening," and giving the contact information once again in verbal and/or printed form.

It's a little more difficult — and certainly more expensive — to keep your demo current than your resume, because you need an editing suite in order to do it. But once you have a good body of work already laid down on your demo from school or elsewhere, you'll find the addition of new material or the deletion of old stuff fairly easy to accomplish. Commercial agencies in industry centers are set up to edit these things for actors just as they can redo resumes and photos. You simply bring them the existing demo and the new spots you want added, direct them where to edit the new footage into the old and how much new footage to use, and that's it. Deleting old stuff is even easier. It's expensive, but it's a requirement for media work and definitely a good thing to have on hand for a stage director who wants to see more of you.

As a final reminder about demos: be sure to buy a bunch of DVD or cassette tape mailers and pre-stamp them with postage, self-addressing some of them. That way you can easily send or give your demo to people with its prepaid return envelope. And each DVD or audiocassette should also have a label with your name and your contact information on the face of it and the same information on the spine and face of the jacket. Some actors, in fact, also place their photo on the cover. Want to learn more? Visit the website http://www.killerreel.com and see what online computer services can do for you (for a price).

Your photo materials are similarly specialized for commercial work. Just as you'll need demo tapes down the road of your radio commercials, your TV characters, your commercial characters, and your industrial film work, so too you'll need photographs of yourself in all these contexts. And you can start to build up these photo materials while you're still in school.

Your first step, once again, is to survey what's needed, as explained in the commercial acting books listed in appendix B. However, you can also "make the rounds" of talent agencies in your area and ask what sort of photo materials are needed for finding work in your particular market. After all, these are the agencies you're going to visit once you graduate, right? So get to know them! Unlike demo tapes, photographs are a little more "tailored" to geographical markets, and they go in and out of fashion over time. So, while learning the general features of photos from the acting books I recommend, you also need *current* information on what types of photos are "standard" in your area.

This is where your school experience can be very valuable. Your stage theatre headshot will always be a black and white "natural you," but your commercial photos will also be in color and will show you in different "looks" or as different characters. You'll use them mainly for postcard mailers or for "composites" (a single sheet of several photos showing you as different characters). So, if you get some good photos of yourself onstage in various roles — especially color shots — be sure to hold on to them, and digitize them if possible. They can save you lot of money when you're just starting out and you've got to come up with photos of yourself for an agent. After you've earned some money from commercial work, you can spend some of it on better photos and replace the earlier ones.

Finally, you're also going to need a special wardrobe for this kind of work. In the field of commercials and corporate videos, the closer you resemble the character at the time you audition, the better chance you stand of getting cast. But a word to the wise here: read those acting books in appendix B carefully and note what those authors have to say about "type." It's essential that you understand what type of characters you can play, what your look is, and that you market yourself well only for those kinds of characters. The question of costumes, hairstyles, and props, however, is a complicated one, and too lengthy to cover in these pages. You'd do best to read those camera acting books carefully and then plan on working with an agent when you're just starting out.

Appendix D
Auditioning for Colleges, College Scholarships, and Graduate Schools

When you're a high school senior or a college freshman and you need to apply to a four-year school for admission, for entrance into a university theatre program as a drama major, or for a drama scholarship, ordinarily you'll be required to provide the following for the theatre faculty:

- A cover letter applying to the program or for the scholarship
- A transcript of your high school courses
- A transcript of your college courses (if you're presently in college or transferring from another college)
- An audition
- An interview
- One or two reference letters from teachers or stage directors you've worked with

When you're applying to a postgraduate training program in acting, you may also be required to take the Graduate Record Exam (GRE) for admission to that university.

Different schools weight each of these instruments differently. Some will emphasize your overall grade point average; others only consider the grades you earned in theatre courses. Some will scrutinize your scores on the GRE in order to determine whether or not you're "graduate material" and likely to complete graduate school. Others, however, may be less concerned with your academic abilities and may rely instead upon your statements in your cover letter and the comments of former teachers and directors regarding your motivation, stage skills, and ability to work with others as members of an ensemble. All, however, will place great emphasis on how well you audition and conduct yourself in the interview.

The first thing to remember about applying to an undergraduate or graduate program is that the teachers evaluating you will be looking for your potential to learn, to succeed, and to function well in their program much more than they'll want to see a "finished product," a fully formed actor. In other words, you're not auditioning and interviewing for specific roles or parts here, you're presenting yourself as someone who can contribute to their program, both while you're enrolled in it and following your graduation.

As a potential candidate for an undergraduate program, they'll be evaluating your maturity as a potential college student, your willingness to learn and take direction, your ability to function well as a member of an ensemble, your motivation to study theatre in general and acting in particular, and your general acting abilities.

As a potential candidate for a graduate program (pre-professional acting training) the faculty will not only look at your "trainability" as an actor but also scrutinize you as a potentially valuable professional asset. Depending upon their needs, this can mean such things as what you feel you've learned so far, what you *understand* about different acting styles, what your audition *actually* reveals about your acting skills (your actual strengths and weaknesses as an actor, in their opinion), your suitability as a teaching assistant in their theatre classes, and the strength of your motivation to advance your career in the field.

Graduate schools may have other criteria that come into play as well. For example, certain schools accept only a very small number of students each year in order to give them the closest possible attention. Some graduate schools and conservatories may specialize in particular forms of professional training (mime and comedy schools, musical theatre schools, classic acting, etc.). In such cases, the faculty admission committees will also have to balance the above-mentioned criteria with some sort of "quota" considerations: How many men and how many women do they want for this incoming class? How many actors of color do they find desirable in their programs? Do they need a certain number of strong singers, a certain number of ingénues, character actors, and so forth?

What all of this means for your audition is that you want to choose an audition piece that falls solidly in the range of what you can act well and like to do. Avoid picking a monolog or scene simply because you think it shows the skills "they" are looking for. If you give them a good, accurate idea of where your strengths and interests are, you make it easier for them to judge whether or not their program can take you "the rest of the way." But if you've picked a mouthful of Greek tragedy, or some cosmic Shakespearean hero, or some classical Irish monolog in unintelligible dialect, then you make it much harder for them to see just what you do best and where they can help you along.

At both the undergraduate and graduate levels you must also bear in mind that the faculty members interviewing you and watching your audition are trying very hard to gain an understanding of who you are as a person. You must be certain that the audition pieces you present help them to do that; you must identify with and reveal yourself as much as possible in your dramatic material and avoid "masking" your unique personality and enthusiasms behind character traits or scene structure. This is extremely important to them and their program because they're committing themselves to working with you for a number of years! Believe me, no faculty member wants to be stuck for years in hell with a prima donna, a manic-depressive, a person who never makes deadlines, a whiner, a know-it-all, or … well, you know the kind of problem-actors I'm talking about.

At my university we usually set aside forty-five to sixty minutes with entering students or scholarship applicants in order to interview them. But this is woefully insufficient, mainly because there are at least three of us faculty on the screening committee. Before we know it, time's up and we must move right along to the audition. And once we get to that point, we don't want a wall or a mask to come down over the student; we want to see how this person is making unique choices and using himself or herself onstage.

Finally, with regard to auditioning, I want especially to stress the need for all of you — high school, university, or grad school competitors — to *pay very close attention to your vocal and verbal skills.* You should read chapter 6 very carefully and work over your material in the ways I've suggested in order to be sure that you can understand and effectively interpret every word of your audition piece and that your vocal delivery has been well rehearsed.

There's a general awareness and shared agreement (some might say a "conspiracy") among university and professional theatre faculty that today's students are far less trained in the area of voice than they should be. This is particularly important when auditioning for postgraduate professional schools. By the time a student finishes a four-year program, it's extremely difficult if not impossible to eliminate bad vocal habits and teach new ones. With high school students it's a slightly different matter, but even there we often see distinct differences between some high school seniors who seem to be sensitive to language and the way they speak, and others who are not.

When gathering material for this book, poor speaking ability and vocal habits was probably the single most common complaint voiced by many directors, teachers, and professional coaches about the young actors they've auditioned. It can disqualify you very soon from any serious consideration, and it becomes more critical the older you are. So be careful about your vocal delivery: articulation, projection, inflection, energy, phrasing, pacing — pay attention to what you're saying and understand the language of the text you're presenting!

Pay close attention to your application cover letter and those essay questions that are frequently found on application forms. Read the question carefully and answer it directly. This is not the place for "B.S." Faculty committees read these things closely, and you'll do yourself a favor by spending time thinking through your statements before you commit them to paper. Your comments should be honest, concrete, succinct, and clear. That means honest, concrete, succinct, and clear.

You'll normally be expected to cover three specific subjects. One is why you've chosen to apply for this particular program scholarship. Another is what you feel the school or the training can give you as an actor. And a third is how strongly you're committed to pursuing a career in theatre. If you wish, your cover letter can also highlight one or two of the most exciting things you've learned about acting so far. And if there are strange or unusual features in your background — such as overseas study, transferring between a number of schools before you apply, low grade point average, etc. — these should certainly be addressed in your cover letter.

Your reference letters should come from people who are knowledgeable about your theatre work and your potential for disciplined study and learning. Your high school drama teachers will normally be the best references, although you might also look for references from community theatre directors if you have that kind of experience. When applying for graduate programs, your university teacher-directors are ordinarily your best bets, although here again you may have community or professional directors or workshop leaders whom you can rely upon for a good reference.

You should remind your references, though, that your adaptability and teachability in a disciplined program is a vital criterion that university faculty want to know about. Your references should also speak to your likelihood of succeeding in a training program — your potential as an actor and your commitment to an acting career (for graduate training). Finally, remind your references to speak about specific strengths and weaknesses you may have. Of course, never forget to gain people's permission beforehand when you list them as references.

Finally, when it comes to the interview, you should prepare yourself beforehand to be relaxed and open, informed about the program to which you're applying, and articulate about your own experience and future goals. Read through the conclusion to chapter 8 again in order to refresh yourself about the kinds of things that need to happen in interview situations.

About the Author

Roger Ellis is an actor, acting coach, and director who has worked in theatre, feature film, and video presentations in California and the Midwest. He studied auditioning techniques in workshops with Michael Shurtleff, at the Herbert Berghof and Riverside Shakespeare studios in New York, and at Chicago's Audition Center. He has been an actor and director with the Dell'Arte Players, the California Shakespeare Festival, and with numerous professional stage and opera companies in Michigan. He has adjudicated plays and festivals and has presented acting and auditioning workshops for high school and university students, community and professional theatre practitioners in the U.S. and internationally. He is also noted for a series of twelve books he has edited of new plays, scenes, and monologs that are widely used in the U.S. and abroad by acting students in schools and conservatories. Roger Ellis is currently President of the Theatre Alliance of Michigan and a Professor of Theatre at Grand Valley State University.

Order Form

Meriwether Publishing Ltd.
PO Box 7710
Colorado Springs CO 80933-7710
Phone: 800-937-5297 Fax: 719-594-9916
Website: www.meriwether.com

Please send me the following books:

_____ **The Complete Audition Book for** $17.95
Young Actors #BK-B262
by Roger Ellis
A comprehensive guide to winning by enhancing acting skills

_____ **Audition Monologs for Student Actors** $15.95
#BK-B232
edited by Roger Ellis
Selections from contemporary plays

_____ **Audition Monologs for Student Actors II** $15.95
#BK-B249
edited by Roger Ellis
Selections from contemporary plays

_____ **The Theatre Audition Book #BK-B224** $16.95
by Gerald Lee Ratliff
Playing monologs from contemporary, modern,
period and classical plays

_____ **The Scenebook for Actors #BK-B177** $15.95
edited by Dr. Norman A. Bert
Collection of great monologs and dialogs for auditions

_____ **Scenes and Monologs from the Best** $15.95
New Plays #BK-B140
edited by Roger Ellis
An anthology of new American plays

_____ **Millenium Monologs #BK-B256** $15.95
edited by Gerald Lee Ratliff
95 contemporary characterizations for young actors

**These and other fine Meriwether Publishing books are available at
your local bookstore or direct from the publisher. Prices subject to
change without notice. Check our website or call for current prices.**

Name: _____ e-mail: _____

Organization name: _____

Address: _____

City: _____ State: _____

Zip: _____ Phone: _____

❑ **Check enclosed**

❑ **Visa / MasterCard / Discover #** _____

Signature: _____   Expiration
date: _____
(required for credit card orders)

Colorado residents: Please add 3% sales tax.
Shipping: Include $3.95 for the first book and 75¢ for each additional book ordered.

❑ *Please send me a copy of your complete catalog of books and plays.*